DATE DUE

APR 26 '96			
9-2402			

Humans may run fast, read less, type more quickly, simply because someone else is present. The presence of one person affects the behaviour of another: this is known as social facilitation. It is one of the oldest topics in social psychology, first studied in 1898, yet Bernard Guerin's is the first ever book-length study of the phenomenon. Dr Guerin reviews all work in the area from 1898 onwards, looking at both animal and human research, and develops his own theory, based on modern behaviour analysis. Through his study of social facilitation, he also reviews the state of social psychology today, its strengths, its weaknesses and its future.

This book will be appreciated for its wide-ranging and balanced review of previous work on social facilitation. The author's theoretical stance is also innovative and important, and will make the work required reading for all social psychologists.

European Monographs in Social Psychology
Social facilitation

European Monographs in Social Psychology

Executive Editors:
I. RICHARD EISER and KLAUS R. SCHERER
Sponsored by the European Association of Experimental Social Psychology

This series, first published by Academic Press (who will continue to distribute the numbered volumes), appeared under the joint imprint of Cambridge University Press and the Maison des Sciences de l'Homme in 1985 as an amalgamation of the Academic Press series and the European Studies in Social Psychology, published by Cambridge and the Maison in collaboration with the Laboratoire Européen de Psychologie Sociale of the Maison.

The original aims of the two series are still valid: to provide a forum for the best European research in different fields of social psychology and to foster the interchange of ideas between different developments and different traditions. The Executive Editors also expect that it will have an important rôle to play as a European forum for international work.

Other titles in this series:

Unemployment by Peter Kelvin and Joanna E. Jarrett

National characteristics by Dean Peabody

Experiencing emotion by Klaus R. Scherer, Harald G. Wallbott and Angela B. Summerfield

Levels of explanation in social psychology by Willem Doise

Understanding attitudes to the European Community: a social-psychological study in four member states by Miles Hewstone

Arguing and thinking: a rhetorical approach to social psychology by Michael Billig

Non-verbal communication in depression by Heiner Ellgring

Social representations of intelligence by Gabriel Mugny and Felice Carugati

Speech and reasoning in everyday life by Uli Windisch

Account episodes. The management or escalation of conflict by Peter Schönbach

The ecology of the self: relocation and self-concept change by Stefan Hormuth

Situation cognition and coherence in personality: an individual centred approach by Barbara Krahé

Talking politics: a psychological framing for views from youth in Britain by Kum-Kum Bhavnani

Social facilitation

Bernard Guerin
Lecturer, Department of Psychology,
University of Waikato, New Zealand

WITHDRAWN

CAMBRIDGE
UNIVERSITY PRESS

EDITIONS DE
LA MAISON DES SCIENCES DE L'HOMME
Paris

Published by the Press Syndicate of the University of Cambridge
The Pitt Building, Trumpington Street, Cambridge CB2 1RP
40 West 20th Street, New York, NY 10011-4211, USA
10 Stamford Road, Oakleigh, Victoria 3166, Australia
and Editions de la Maison des Sciences de l'Homme
54 Boulevard Raspail, 75270 Paris Cedex 06

First published 1993

Printed in Great Britain at the University Press, Cambridge

A catalogue record for this book is available from the British Library

Library of Congress cataloguing in publication data

Guérin, Bernard.
 Social facilitation / Bernard Guérin
  p. cm. – (European monographs in social psychology)
  Includes bibliographical references and index.
  ISBN 0–521–33358–X
  1. Social facilitation. 2. Social psychology. I. Title.
II. Series.
HM291.G77 1993
302′14—dc20

92–11487
CIP

ISBN 0 521 33358 X hardback
ISBN 2 7351 0471 0 hardback (France only)

VN

Contents

Acknowledgements

There are a number of people I would like to thank for help and support in writing this book. Foremost is Mike Innes, who read most of the book, was active in getting it started, provided a number of references which were hard to get, and otherwise helped at some cost to himself. I am also grateful to Yoshi Kashima, Dominic Abrams, and Hugh Foot, who discussed parts of this work with me. Generous access to Glenorchy McBride's personal library helped locate many rare references in the animal studies, and I thank him for this.

I wish to thank the Departments of Psychology at the University of Adelaide, the University of Queensland, James Cook University, and the University of Waikato, for facilities, employment and time.

I wish to acknowledge and thank the journals which allowed reproduction of their figures. They have been acknowledged in the figure captions.

Finally, I wish to thank all the family, friends and colleagues who have provided support over the years.

I Introduction

Social facilitation is said to occur when one animal increases or decreases its behaviour in the presence of another animal which does not otherwise interact with it. Typically, a chicken might be found to eat more when another chicken is present, even if this other chicken does not reinforce, communicate, exhibit eating behaviour, or compete for food. Likewise, social facilitation is said to occur when humans run faster, read less, type quicker, or do fewer arithmetic problems in the presence of another person, but only if the other person does not reinforce the behaviour, show how it is done, set a performance standard, or compete.

These changes in behaviour were first studied as a phenomenon in 1898, and have since become known as social facilitation, whether the changes in behaviour are an increase or a decrease. In research, a human subject will perform a task alone and in the presence of another person, and the two types of conditions are compared.

It can be seen that social facilitation is defined through exclusion: it is said to occur when no other explanation (competition, reinforcement, cueing, cooperation) is possible. This makes it difficult to say exactly what social facilitation is, except by demonstrating that a behaviour has increased or decreased in the presence of another animal and that other explanations are not possible.

Put in these terms, it might be wondered why anyone would bother studying such finicky and elusive effects. The fact is, however, that social facilitation is one of the oldest topics in social psychology, and lays claim to being the first topic studied in experimental social psychology. In 1898, Triplett conducted a study in which children performed a task either alone or else with another child doing the same task. This was probably the first experimental study in social psychology (see Chapter 2).

Historical precedence does not, of course, fully explain why social facilitation effects should be studied at all. There are several other reasons for this. The most important of these, I believe, is that it deals with the minimal conditions for social behaviour: the difference between doing something alone and doing the same thing with another person present who is not influencing you in any direct way. That is, social facilitation tries to study the difference between behaviour in non-social settings and behaviour in social settings.

It is true that even when alone, we can be influenced by what other people have said to us, or how they have treated us in the past. It is also true that in real life we rarely perform a task when alone and then again with someone else present, but social facilitation is more concerned with finding out the most basic responses when other people are present than with how often this might occur in real life.

These two points mean that the study of social facilitation becomes abstract and somewhat artificial at times, but the theoretical points that come out of it outweigh, I believe, the remoteness from direct applications. Until social psychologists can dig down and find the underlying mechanisms by which people come to influence each other, the larger applications and conceptualizations of 'real' social behaviour will merely cover up fundamental mechanisms which are not understood.

Goals of the book

There are three goals I have had in writing this book. The first is to review all the work done in social facilitation from 1898 to the present. This involves reviewing the many theories that have been put forward and showing how they relate to one another, as well as examining the many experimental studies. I have approached this task with a taxonomic method, of collecting the many theories and experimental studies, collating them into groups on the basis of explicitly stated characteristics, and then comparing the groupings of theories to the groupings of experimental results.

In carrying out this first goal, I have tried to group together theories which can explain exactly the same experimental results or observations. Many social psychologists have suggested reasons for the differences found between acting alone and acting in the presence of another person, but few have tried to collate all the different theories and compare them. It will be shown that many of the theories can explain the same results, so they are merely talking about social facilitation using different words. This means that we only have pragmatic grounds for deciding which is the best theory, since they have not been (and probably cannot be) shown to be better or worse by experimental methods. It is for this reason that the results of the many experiments are discussed separately from the theories.

I have also added one more perspective on social facilitation by presenting a new theory in Section 5.5. While the social facilitation theories of the 1960s used the Hull-Spence version of behaviourism, a theory based on modern behaviour analysis has not been outlined in detail before. Modern behaviour analysis is not closely related to the old forms of behaviourism, although few psychologists or psychology textbooks seem to know this. I hope this new perspective can be developed further in social psychology since it also provides an excellent basis for applied social psychology, as well as a good foundation to general psychology.

My second goal was to outline some of the history of social facilitation. Besides making fascinating reading in itself (I think), we can use it to follow the development of social psychology from its sociological, philosophical and educational backgrounds, through the beginnings of the experimental methods in the 1920s, to the modern period of social cognition and the experimental analysis of social behaviour. All the major changes which have occurred throughout the history of social psychology have been reflected in the study of social facilitation, since this spans the whole development of social psychology. For this reason I believe that social facilitation makes an excellent platform for teaching the history of social psychology. I would be gratified if this book could make a small contribution towards this, since we are approaching the centenary of its foundation by Triplett (1898).

The final goal of the book was to use social facilitation as a test case to examine social psychology as it is today: what are its strengths and weaknesses; what does it leave out; and does it have a future? Originally, social psychology promised to explain and predict all social behaviour: where is that promise today? What does it mean that many of the theories can explain the same phenomena using different words, and that we have no way of deciding between these theories? Is social psychology unique in this?

Most importantly, I hope that examining both the history and present-day status of social psychology can suggest ways of improving and redirecting its growth, so that it becomes more applicable and more explanatory. In this I hope to see a new social psychology which can directly come to terms with, and help to shape, the study of social behaviour in the next century.

Plan of the book

The plan of the book is quite straightforward, although I depart from the traditional approaches to social facilitation in many ways. The first section deals with the development of social facilitation research from the very earliest work of Triplett (1898) up to the major paper of the modern period, that of Zajonc (1965), which revitalized research and had a huge impact in producing new theories and experimental studies. With few exceptions (e.g., Blank, 1979), the story has been that the early research was poor in content. I wish to depart from tradition and suggest that almost all the phenomena and explanations for social facilitation were identified prior to about 1935. The experimental tests before this time were, however, ambiguous and do not tell us much about social facilitation.

The second section of the book examines the different theories which have been proposed for social facilitation effects, and groups them into three categories. Some of the conceptual links between the theories are developed during the presentation in those chapters, but more are given in Chapter 9, which examines the theories as a whole and suggests which phenomena can be found in the social facilitation effects.

I depart again from the traditional approach in an interesting way when looking at all the theories of social facilitation together. The traditional view has been that there is a phenomenon of social facilitation whereby an animal increases or decreases its behaviour in the presence of another animal, and that this phenomenon is related to some other areas of social psychology. My view, after examining all the theories and data, is that the only thing which can distinguish social facilitation is the setting itself. The responses of the organism are purely functions of the setting and past experiences in that setting. The responses are the same as those that occur in other related areas of social psychology, the only difference being that those other areas change the setting slightly, and therefore change the parameters. In this rather strange sense, *the phenomenon of social facilitation is in the setting rather than in the animal's responses.* This will hopefully become clear throughout Chapters 9, 10 and 11.

The third section of the book reviews the experimental studies of social facilitation, looking very carefully at the smallest details of procedure. Included in this is a review of the studies which have used nonhuman animals. This has not been fully reviewed before, and shows some effects (such as disinhibition) which are hardly ever suggested as explanations for human social facilitation effects. There has been little animal social facilitation research over the last ten years, and I hope that this review might stimulate further work. To help with this, criteria for definitions of the different phenomena found in the animal studies are given in section 7.12.

Chapter 8 then reviews all the experiments using human subjects, with the taxonomic method of defining criteria and classifying the studies. Also included in the third section are studies comparing behaviour alone and behaviour in front of a mirror, in front of a camera, and with a computer. These have not been reviewed together before.

The final section of the book discusses the relationships between social facilitation and other areas of social psychology. These include many studies which come close to being social facilitation studies but which look at slightly different variables and settings. A comparison between these effects and social facilitation effects is useful to both areas of research. The concluding chapter summarizes the position of modern social psychology, using social facilitation as the test case.

It is hoped that by the end of the book the reader will have a broader understanding of social facilitation research, the history of social psychology, and of the future of social psychology itself.

I   The history and development of social facilitation research

2 The early history of social facilitation

This chapter reviews the history of research into social facilitation, which has a long tradition extending back to 1898. Figure 1 shows a cumulative record of all the social facilitation studies from 1898 up to 1983. The major seminal papers on social facilitation were written in 1898 by Norman Triplett, in 1920 by Floyd Allport, and by Robert Zajonc in 1965. Figure 1 shows the increase in publications which occurred immediately after those papers.

There are a number of points which will be emphasized throughout this chapter about the historical development of social facilitation research. They will be made here first.

(1) The first point is that the definition of social facilitation keeps changing. In the very early work the term was not used at all. Allport (1924a) coined the term to refer to effects of the 'sight and sound' of another person doing the same activity (now called *co-acting* or *co-working*). Later the term was used for the effects of an *audience* as well. In the work with animals the term referred to many other processes including *imitation*.

One reason that 'social facilitation' kept changing its meaning was that the field of social psychology was developing rapidly during this period. Indeed, the first social facilitation experiment has often been called the first social psychological experiment. As social psychology changed so did the terminology and the topics of interest. In tracing these changes we will, in fact, trace the whole development of the discipline: from the early work based on German educationalists; through the introduction of experimental methods; to modern experimental social psychology.

(2) The second point stressed is that the major explanations of social facilitation that have been put forward in recent years are already to be found in the earlier literature – even if only in a most rudimentary form. Most of these early ideas were not followed up with data collection, and when they were, the experiments were usually inadequate by present day standards.

(3) The final point of emphasis will be to show that a number of phenomena were confounded in the early experimental work. The events that the early writers were trying to explain contained a number of phenomena which in recent times have been treated as separate processes. A major point of the whole book is that there is no single social facilitation

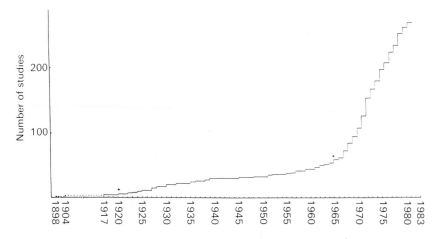

Figure 1. Cumulative graph of the social facilitation experimental studies from 1898 to 1983

phenomenon. It consists of a number of separate processes. This means that almost none of the early experimental work contains clearly interpretable results.

2.1 The early work of Triplett

Triplett's (1898) pioneering experiment has often been called the first social psychological experiment, although this has been queried (Haines and Vaughan, 1979). I will also break from tradition here and suggest that Triplett's experiment was really about competition rather than social facilitation (Vaughan and Guerin, 1992).

Triplett was interested in the observation by many cycling fans, including himself, that paced cycling results in faster times than unpaced cycling. Paced races have a much faster tandem or quod (four people on the one bike) riding at the same time as the cyclist in order to set a quick pace. Faster times seemed to occur when there was pacing as compared to both riders in competition against other riders and to riders racing alone – purely against time.

A second observation Triplett discussed was that the foreriders in paced races did not very often win in unpaced races. So strong was this belief amongst riders, that in unpaced competition races, the riders often held back because they knew the 'pace setter' would not be the one to win. Triplett mentions that for this reason these races are often called 'loafing' races. It is interesting to compare this with the 'social loafing' effect identified by Williams, Harkins and Latané (1979) (see Chapter 10.)

Using cycling records of the Racing Board of the League of American Wheelers, Triplett provided evidence that pacers led to quicker racing times. He also set out a number of explanations as to why paced cycling might be faster and he conducted some laboratory studies to investigate the phenomenon in greater depth. These will be outlined in turn.

Triplett's explanations

Of the reasons given by Triplett for paced cycling being faster, some are more plausible than others. The first reasons he gave were mechanical ones: the pacer in front provided shelter from the wind or provided a suction to pull the rider behind along and so help to conserve energy.

He also suggested some psychological reasons. Encouragement might have played a role since friends usually rode as the pacers and could thus encourage the other cyclists. The 'brain-worry' theory argued that the pace setters in an unpaced race did poorly because they worried more about whether they were going fast enough and when the others were going to commence their spurts. Triplett claimed that this worry exhausted both the brain and the muscles. It was also suggested that riders following a pacer could be hypnotized by the wheels in front, meaning that they rode in an automatic fashion, leaving more energy for a later controlled performance when they were in front.

In terms of more recent theories of social facilitation, Triplett suggested the possible effects of social consequences (encouragement), social comparison with the other riders, distraction, and automaticity. He believed that these all played a rôle in the phenomenon, but he was most interested in the effect of competition.

The theory of competition favoured by Triplett was a *dynamogenic* one. He listed three components to this. One was based on the contemporary thought of Féré (1887) that: 'the energy of a movement is in proportion to the idea of that movement' (Triplett, 1898, p. 531). Just the sight or sound of another rider is sufficient to increase the idea of riding movements and thus increase the energy of such movements.

In the psychology of Triplett's day it was thought that to perform a movement there had to be an 'idea' of that movement present; this idea 'suggested' the action to be performed. The stronger the idea – the stronger the movement. So the effect of a pacer in front was to suggest a higher speed which led to 'an inspiration to greater effort'. (p. 516)

Such theories were common at this time (see James, 1910), and although they no longer have credence in modern psychology, there are concepts around today which are very similar. One of the most influential theories of social facilitation, for example, is that the presence of others leads to an increase in 'arousal' or alertness which leads to a greater effort in responding. 'Arousal' is probably not too far removed from the 'ideas' of Féré. Another recent theory suggests that we compare our behaviour with 'standards' of behaviour. This mechanism is also not far removed from Féré's 'ideas'.

The second of the dynamogenic factors proposed by Triplett was that the other racers can lead to a release of nervous energy which the rider cannot release alone. Again, although 'nervous energy' is no longer a term used in psychology, it is close to the idea of arousal as a general level of activity of the nervous system.

The last of the dynamogenic factors was that the presence of another rider was a stimulus to arouse 'the competitive instinct'. This would today be referred to as a competition effect, the term 'instinct' no longer being used since it adds nothing by way of explanation. While the effects of competition on behaviour are now considered distinct from those of social facilitation, they may be equally important determinants of human behaviour. Furthermore, many experiments in social facilitation have probably found results due to competition rather than social facilitation.

Triplett's experiment

Triplett investigated these dynamogenic factors by using an apparatus consisting of two fishing reels which turned silk bands around a drum. To complete one trial, a flag sewn to the silk band had to travel four times around the wheel – the equivalent of sixteen metres. The time taken to do this was measured. Triplett presented the results for forty children who had six trials each. The trials alternated between working alone and working two at a time in competition. The results were broken down into those who performed slower in competition, those who performed faster in competition, and those little affected. Of the forty children, twenty were faster in competition, ten were slower, and ten were not affected.

While these results do not suggest an overall positive effect of competition, Triplett drew some conclusions from the data. He interpreted the faster twenty subjects as showing the effects of both 'the arousal of their competitive instincts and the idea of a faster movement' (Triplett, 1898, p. 526). For those who were slower in the trials, he presented observations that they were overstimulated, in 'going to pieces' during the race and in 'not being able to endure the nervous strain'. Accompanying this was 'laboured breathing, flushed faces and a stiffening or contraction of the muscles in the arm' (p. 523). Unfortunately, it was not recorded how often this occurred in the other groups. Another feature of the results was that the twenty who showed the strongest effects were also those who were initially slower. So the

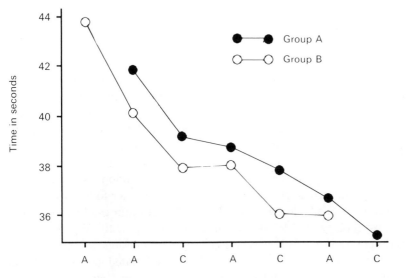

Figure 2. Time in seconds per trial for turning reels alone (A) or in competition (C) for groups A and B. (Data drawn from Triplett, 1898)

conditions may have affected these children more, or there may have been ceiling effects on the method used.

The mean results for Groups A and B are graphed in Figure 2. Overall, there was a tendency to do better on each trial, probably due to practice. When the differences between first, doing a trial alone followed by a trial together are compared with doing a trial together followed by a trial alone, then more of an effect can be seen. Looking only at Group B – as Group A had an extra trial Alone – the three mean differences between Alone (A) followed by Together (C) are 2.52, 1.14, and 1.51. The two mean differences between Together followed by Alone are 0.09 and 0.62. Clearly then, subjects did better going from an Alone condition to a competition condition. Given the emphasis on competing, which is evident in his descriptions of individual performances, it is likely that Triplett's results are due to effects of competition rather than the presence of a co-worker. In present day terms they are not evidence of social facilitation effects at all, since competition is considered to be a separate phenomenon.

The importance of Triplett

While Triplett did not control for all factors, his report is important for some of the distinctions he made in discussion. First, he distinguished between effects due to competition, rivalry and the desire to win, and effects due to just the sight and sound of another person performing the same behaviour. These latter effects are the proper subject matter of social facilitation in contemporary social psychology.

Second, he distinguished between co-acting or co-working situations and spectator or audience situations (p. 530) – those in which others are present as observers rather than performers. He commented on some of the results of spectator studies by Manouvrier (see Haines and Vaughan, 1979, note 22), and proposed that the increase in movement found with spectators present was due to 'wishing to impress'. With this, he raised the possibility that someone *passively* watching others perform a task might still affect their performance. He also foreshadowed a self-presentation explanation, in suggesting that people change their behaviour in order to impress others.

In the work of Triplett we can also see the beginnings of experimental social psychology which was to come to fruition with Allport (1920). Experimental social psychology proceeds by decomposing the phenomenon under study into a number of factors which are isolated and studied in an experimental setting which tries to control for all other factors. By studying reel turning, for example, Triplett controlled for all the mechanical factors of wind shelter and suction present with cycle racers, although his dynamogenic factors were mixed up in the experiment and not separated clearly. The last stage of the procedure of experimental social psychology is to piece together the results of all the different factors which have been studied separately and apply them back to the area of interest.

2.2 The German educationalists

In the years immediately following Triplett, little experimental work was done on social facilitation or competition. Most of the relevant material of the time came from Germany. In 1905, Burnham reviewed 'the effects on mental activity of the presence of a group of other persons' (Burnham, 1910, p. 761), which consisted mostly of work by German educationalists. This concerned the education of children: was it better for children to study in class groups or alone; at school or at home?

Schmidt (1904) had found on a number of tests that work at school was superior to work at home, with the exception of writing original essays in the mother tongue. Schmidt therefore proposed that original thinking was better in solitude. Although suggestive, these studies were not well controlled. There may have been any number of influences occurring in the homes, when the children worked there, which were not present at school. While Burnham (1905, 1910) discussed a number of these influences, the data reported are too messy for any firm conclusions.

Mayer (1904) studied children working in classrooms, when either alone or in a group. The superior work found in groups was explained as arising from ambition and competition. While these results were better controlled than those of Schmidt (1904), the teacher was present with all the children in all the conditions so they were never truly alone. To find out what exactly led to the superior performance in groups, a control condition in which the children were completely alone would have been needed. Triplett (1898) had already pointed out that a spectator could affect performance. This might be especially so if the spectator was a teacher.

In discussing this study, Burnham (1905) remarks that the children's behaviour is influenced by 'the consciousness of the pupils that their performance will be compared with those of other pupils' (p. 218). This suggests that social comparison, or the possibility of social comparison, can lead to better performance. This point was developed by later theorists as we shall see in Chapter 10.

Meumann (1904) found that children did less work when alone (although a teacher was again present), as measured by dynamometers, ergographs and tests of memory, than when others were present. His studies also led him to conclude that *distraction* from outside noises, whispering, movements and talk, had little detrimental effect. He even suggested that the distraction led the children to increase work to compensate. This is in opposition to some later views on distraction, which suggest only negative effects of distraction, but not all (Jones and Gerard, 1967; Sanders, Baron and Moore, 1978).

Burnham's conclusions from the pre-1910 work were as follows. Generally, superior performance had been found when working in groups as compared with working alone, except when original thought was required. Distraction by others had little effect except perhaps to further motivate concentration to overcome the distractions. The main explanation for the facilitation found with co-working was competition or rivalry: subjects tried to do as well, or better, than the other person. The reason for doing better with observers present was to impress them.

While many of these views rested on thought and common sense, there was no good evidence for them since the experiments were poorly designed and could support no firm conclusions about the specific factors which might be involved. Teachers had been present in 'alone' conditions and very few extraneous factors had been controlled. Conceptually, the area had been dissected into a number of social phenomena or factors, the first step towards an experimental social psychology. What remained was to experimentally isolate these and test their influence separately. This occurred in the work of Allport (1920) and Dashiell (1930), and signals the beginnings of a true experimental social psychology.

Before discussing the literature of the 1920s, however, two more points about Burnham's review of 1910 deserve mention. The first was the use of the term 'mere presence' (p. 766), to suggest that there may be effects from just the presence of a co-worker – even apart from competition. This was the first use of this term. The notion of 'mere presence' effects received greater treatment from Zajonc (1965) (see Chapter 3 and subsequent chapters).

The second point about Burnham (1910) was that he presented some data from studies of *non-human* animals, to show 'emotional' influences from the presence of others. This use of comparative psychology was overlooked for many years until Zajonc (1965) also used non-human animal evidence to support his theory of social facilitation.

2.3 The experimental studies of the 1920s

It appears that between 1910 to 1920 no work related to social facilitation was done. One study compared the distraction effects of anger, fear, looking at photographs of nudes, repulsion, and embarrassment from a large audience, on performing multiplications in the head (Moore, 1917). Further work on this seems to have been held up by the First World War.

While not truly a social facilitation study, the study by Moore (1917) is interesting for the trauma that was dealt out to innocent subjects. A subject was told falsely that they were under suspicion for cheating in an exam (to induce anger), they were put in a dark room for their fear of snakes and 'a five foot length of rubber tubing was drawn slowly around his neck' (Moore, 1917, p. 392). The assistant then put his ice-chilled hand suddenly on the subject's forehead. They were made to smell asafoetida, look at pictures of human entrails, hold a human brain over a jar of formalin, and put their hands into a formalin jar filled with sheep's brains! These and other feats were done while carrying out multiplications. It is unlikely that a modern-day research ethics committee would approve such an experiment!

Allport (1920)

In 1920, Allport reported a series of experiments on co-working which attempted to improve previous methods. He studied 'the mental process of the individual when alone with his reactions . . . and when a member of a "co-working or co-feeling" group' (Allport, 1920, p. 159). Under investigation were the effects on a non-social task from the presence of others. Allport conceptually separated direct interaction with others and competition from co-working effects, and viewed the former as phenomena which should be studied separately.

Allport improved on the earlier experimental designs by attempting to control for some of the factors not relevant to his inquiry. Most importantly, he tried to stop subjects competing (then called rivalry) and tried to stop comparisons being made between subjects. He also used fixed time limits for the tasks to help reduce competition effects. These experiments were therefore among the first in social psychology to attempt to separate factors and experimentally control them. 'In this way rivalry, which is a distinct social problem and which should be studied separately, was reduced to its natural minimum' (Allport, 1920, p. 160). This was to be an important step for experimental social psychology. While social phenomena had been separated conceptually in the past, Allport was the first to try and clearly control for them in experiments.

Allport's experiments

Allport's first experiments dealt with word associations. He distinguished between the quality and quantity of performance. *Social increments* and *social decrements* referred to the quantity of work done, while *social supervaluants* and *social subvaluants* referred to the quality of work done. In Experiment 2 (the study with the clearest design) fourteen of the fifteen subjects gave more associations in the group than when alone. The average difference was not large (63.6 Together and 60.3 Alone), but was nevertheless significant although Allport did not analyse it statistically (t = 3.85, d.f. = 14, p. < 0.01).

Allport also found that this effect was stronger in the first minute of producing associations and weakest in the third minute. This is shown graphically in Figure 3. Allport therefore suggested that the social influence was strongest when the associations came more easily, and that 'under difficult conditions therefore being alone tends to favour concentration' (p. 167). This was one suggestion that Zajonc (1965) later took up in his major review.

For the quality of associations, the clearest result was found with the number of personal associations. Twelve out of the fifteen subjects gave more personal associations when alone. Allport proposed that an individual in a group is taken 'out of himself' (p. 167) and that attention is directed to outside objects. Small differences were also found for words suggested by the environment, words suggested by the stimulus word, and free-rising ideas. It is interesting that while later theories of deindividuation suggest the same lowered self-awareness in groups, one theory of social facilitation suggests that the presence of others *increases* self-awareness (Carver and Scheier, 1981a). Clearly different types of self-awareness are being talked about.

Allport interpreted the results of his Experiment 2 as a reflection of 'speed of writing' (p. 170). Subjects could produce more associations than they could write. For this reason the experiment was replicated but with subjects writing down every fourth association. With this change the results were similar but less pronounced. Only eight out of fifteen subjects showed more associations

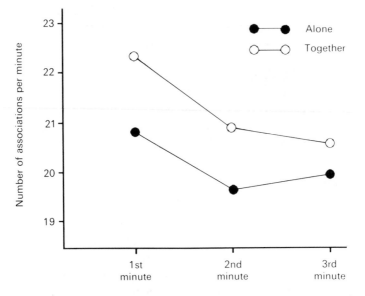

Figure 3. Average number of associations working alone or together for each of 3 minutes. (Data drawn from Allport, 1920)

in groups than alone. This was also found in a further experiment which used less subjects but which doubled the number of tests.

A further point to note about these experiments is the finding of higher self-reports of rivalry for those who did better in groups. Allport's Experiment 4 reports a correlation of 0.89 between performance and self-reported rivalry. So despite Allport's verbal instructions not to compete, the results are probably due to competition effects and not just the presence of co-workers.

In a final experiment Allport tested group and solitary performance of 'the more intellectual functions involved in reasoning' (p. 175). Subjects were required to write as many refutations of an argument as possible in five minutes. The quality of the ideas used in the refutations were judged from 1 to 3, a score of 3 for the more clear and forceful ideas. While the results showed no difference in the average number of ideas produced in the Alone and Co-working situations (8 and 8.8 respectively), all but one subject had a higher average in the group situation. Further, six of the nine subjects had superior ideas alone, and six of the nine had inferior ideas in the group situation.

Allport's conclusions

In his conclusions, Allport claimed that the group situation is favourable to greater speed of free association but that this may be a reflection of motor requirements which were a limiting factor. This effect is greater in slower individuals and at the start of the task. There are more personal associations given when alone, offset by more environmentally stimulated associations in the group.

Allport had identified a number of social factors thought to influence the association process. Facilitating factors were the perception or idea of movement in others, and the intrinsic rivalry of the group. His experiments seem to have shown only the latter, though. Impeding factors were distraction, over-rivalry, and emotions.

Allport's work in 1920 was important for a number of reasons. First, he vastly improved the methods and experimental designs of previous work, although his work was not without problems. He re-emphasized the distinction between quantity and quality of performance, and also examined social facilitation effects in the new context of word associations. He further improved the methodology by trying to control for the effects of practice and rivalry. Last, he took the study of co-working out of the educational context and viewed it as a wider social phenomenon, the effects people have on us even when they are directly interacting with us.

Allport (1924)

The conceptual and experimental work of Allport was extended in his later book (Allport, 1924a). In this he distinguished face-to-face groups from co-working groups (p. 261). In the former there is direct social interaction; in the latter the individuals co-work without interaction. He did not distinguish this, however, from the effects of *passive observers*, as had Triplett (1898).

Allport (1924a) recognized two social factors in co-working performance. The first he termed *social facilitation*: 'which consists of an increase in response merely from the sight or sound of others making the same movement' (p. 262). This was the first use of this term. The second factor was rivalry. So for Allport, social facilitation was the effect of the stimulus of a co-worker *performing the same action*. Whether or not he purposely excluded the effects of a passive audience is unknown. This was being studied at the same time by Gates (1924).

In his book of 1924, after briefly reviewing the studies of Triplett, Schmidt, and Meumann, Allport described further experiments conducted by himself. In these, subjects worked either in groups or alone. Verbal instructions emphasized that rivalry be kept to a minimum. The tasks used were a Vowel Cancellation Task, a Reversible Perspective Test of attention, and a multiplication test. In terms of quantity it was found that twice as many subjects did more work in groups than did subjects in the alone situation, although the differences were small. The quality was unaffected by the conditions.

Allport suggested that social facilitation works to release or augment some form of movement. Subjects who had produced social subvaluants, less work in groups, also reported distraction in questioning afterwards. So this was related to Triplett's notion that the *idea* of a movement from the presence of others can release that movement. The effect of distraction, however, was the opposite to that suggested by Meumann (1904). Distraction impaired performance, and did not motivate better performance.

A further experiment concerned the judgement of odours, either alone or in groups. It was found that the unpleasant odours were judged less unpleasant when in a group and that the pleasant odours were judged less pleasant when in a group. Allport generalized that there was a moderation of judgements when in a group.

The same result was found for judgements of weights. In groups, the heavy weights were judged as lighter and the light weights were judged as heavier. Again, the extremes were avoided in group judgements. Allport explained this as a conformity influence of groups. After presenting these results, Allport again considered the effects of social facilitation when rivalry is taken out of the setting. He viewed them as either arising from the ideomotor response or from over-compensation for the greater distraction in groups, as Meumann had suggested.

While Allport's experiments were an improvement on previous work, they were not without large problems. Williamson (1926) was the first to take this up. He suggested that Allport had not controlled rivalry enough when looking at social facilitation effects. As mentioned above, one of Allport's experiments in 1920 had actually presented data supporting this. Even in the Alone condition, the subjects could compete with standards set by themselves, the experimenter, or by the task itself.

A second criticism was that Allport had assumed that subjects' performances were only determined by his instructions whereas the situation, or the subjects themselves, could instruct or act otherwise. Williamson also pointed out that no details of Allport's subjects or their selection were given, limiting the generalization of the results.

In re-examining Allport's results, Williamson looked at the averages rather than the frequencies used by Allport. Only two of the four experiments showed a higher average frequency in the group situation and these both had large variances. He also pointed out that Allport's Table 2 presented results which did not control for the number of trials performed. When the average number of associations per trial were substituted, little real difference remained between the Alone and Group conditions.

Similar re-analysis occurs for Experiments 3, 4 and 6. If anything, the results favour more associations when alone. Williamson did not present criticisms of Allport (1924a) because no individual results had been given. It seems, then, that the data of Allport (1920) did not support his conclusions, although Williamson's paper has been totally ignored in later accounts of Allport's work. Despite lack of support, however, there was no evidence against either.

Allport's conceptual distinctions were still important, however. It had been shown that there was a phenomenon to be studied and that experimental methods could be applied. This generated an increase in experimental studies during the 1920s, as was seen in Figure 1 earlier. Most of these had Allport's work as their impetus.

Gates (1924)

Gates (1924) took a slightly different approach to the phenomena being studied. She compared the performance of a person alone with the same person in front of either a small or a large audience. She was interested in 'the reaction caused by the mere presence of the observers not of anything they might do in the way of friendly or unfriendly behaviour' (p. 334). Despite this, and despite earlier warnings, Gates failed to have proper controls when testing this hypothesis – the experimenter was present in all conditions. Thus performance was compared between audience sizes of one, four to six and large.

It should be noted in the quotation above, taken from Gates, that she contrasts 'mere presence' with 'friendly or unfriendly' actions of the audience. This reiterates the *encouragement* theory of Triplett (1898), that social consequences from others present may affect behaviour. Gates had, in fact, reported an experiment along these lines the year before (Gates and Rissland, 1923).

In an editorial note on her study, Allport (1924b) commented on Gates' finding that those with poorest ability initially improved more with an audience, and that those who were good alone were little better with an audience. This had been found previously by Allport (1920, 1924a), Mayer (1904), and Moede (1914), although these last two studies were not concerned with social facilitation as now defined.

In his editorial note Allport also suggested that a number of factors might have been present, and further commented: 'it might be worthwhile to repeat Dr. Gates' method using solitary individuals, in one set of trials working wholly unobserved, and in another set of trials working before an audience' (Allport, 1924b, p. 344). This raises a serious problem which has plagued social facilitation research up to the present time. The 'Alone' condition often has the experimenter present and the subjects cannot really be considered alone. If the experimental dissection of these phenomena is to be carried out faithfully, then this has to be observed.

Other studies of the 1920s

A further test of audience effects was made by Travis (1925). He had twenty-two young men practise a pursuit-rotor task with no audience, until there were no further rises over two days (controlling for practice effects). They then performed five trials, again alone, followed by ten trials with an audience of four to eight people.

It was found that eighteen out of the twenty-two men performed better with the audience. Although Travis found the actual difference to be non-significant, it was later pointed out that a proper test of the results, using a related-samples test, did show a significant difference, albeit a small one (Cottrell, 1972). The conclusions from the experiment must be tempered, however, because the experimenter had been present during the Alone trails.

Six more experiments in this area were published between 1926 and 1929. Sengupta and Sinha (1926) found an improvement with group presence on the vowel cancellation task used by Allport (1920). This was after subjects had practised until there was little variation from day to day.

Weston and English (1926) gave subjects IQ tests either alone or in groups. They controlled for order effects, which Allport had not done, and also tried to control rivalry. The experimenter was excluded from the Alone condition as well. With these changes an improvement was found for the group condition. It was admitted that a problem might have been a lack of control of test form; Form 1 was used by all those alone and Form 2 by those in the group situation. Farnsworth (1928) criticized them for this point and also for not controlling IQ levels. When subjects were matched for IQ no difference was found between the Alone and Group conditions (Farnsworth, 1928).

Travis (1928) obtained the opposite result to Allport (1920) for word associations when stutterers were the subjects. Eighty percent of the stutterers gave more associations when alone than when with the group. Anderson (1929) looked further at IQs and found that while in the normal IQ range there was improvement in the group on a number of tasks, those of higher IQ showed some disturbance in the group situation. Anderson (1929) also found greater variability in the group situation, as had Allport (1920).

A different approach was taken by Ekdahl (1929) who was interested specifically in the effects of an *experimenter* on word associations. He had subjects who were alone speak their associations into an Ediphone. He found that subjects were quicker to give associations when alone but only when the experimenter had been present for the first half of the session. When the Experimenter Absent condition preceded the Experimenter Present condition there was no difference. In other words, only when learning to do the task were effects found.

Ekdahl also asked subjects for their introspections. With the experimenter present, subjects reported being more distracted, less free, more hesitant to give associations, more embarrassed, more confused, more alert and more self-conscious. So a number of social and non-social factors appear with just the presence of the experimenter. Similar results were found with Ekdahl's second experiment using a mature group and again in a third experiment which also showed quicker associations when alone compared to having the experimenter present.

2.4 Conceptual and experimental advances up to 1964

Up to 1930 the advances had mostly been of a conceptual nature. The effects of the presence of others had been divided into several distinct phenomena. The research was no longer concerned with direct effects of social consequences or competition. The effect of others could be different when co-working, working in groups, or working in front of an audience. Clear experimental separation of these factors was lacking, though, and social consequences and competition often were mixed in the experimental conditions anyway.

The work of Dashiell (1930)

In 1930, Dashiell made several of these distinctions quite explicit. He suggested that there were effects from: 1) just the presence of quiet spectators; 2) from others who present 'overt vocal attitudes' (p. 190), making encouraging or discouraging comments; 3) from co-working without competition; and 4) from explicit rivalry and competition. Dashiell set out to test these four factors within the same paradigm using three types of tasks. He manipulated conditions so subjects were working alone, observed, co-working, or with rivalry.

It was found that the differences between the groups were small but there was a general tendency for greater speed in the Observed group and a lesser effect in the Rivalry condition. Speed was lowest in both the Alone and Co-working groups, with little difference between them. There was a slight tendency for accuracy to be higher in the Alone and Co-working conditions and lowest in the Observed conditions. Dashiell pointed out that the lack of difference between the Alone and Co-working groups went against the earlier findings of Allport and others. He interpreted his finding as showing that the 'competitive attitude' is all important in such circumstances.

Dashiell next made the distinction between two types of Alone conditions.

In one, the subjects were alone but in different rooms. Signals were controlled from a central room so that subjects were signalled simultaneously (AS). In the other situation, subjects were run independently (AD). A co-working (together) group was also run (T). Dashiell predicted that the AS group would adopt a competitive attitude.

The result, although again with problems, suggested that the T condition was the fastest and least accurate, the AD was the slowest and most accurate, and that AS held a middle position. So the AS did not behave like a true Alone condition and *mere synchrony* of performance was enough to induce competition. This explained why no difference had been found in Dashiell's first experiment between the Alone and Co-working groups.

This finding also indicates the *potency* of competition effects with humans. With just the knowledge that someone else is performing somewhere else simultaneously, speed is increased and accuracy suffers. This implies that if experimental methods are to dissect the effects of the presence of others then very careful manipulations must be used if competition and social comparisons effects are to be avoided.

The early 1930s

In 1931, Murphy and Murphy reviewed most of the extant literature and reached a similar conclusion to Dashiell: 'Despite the dynamogenic factor, it would certainly appear that the main factor at work in such results is the same old desire to make a good showing' (1931, p. 462). Like Triplett, this mentions the effects of trying to make an impression on the persons present. Five more studies were published in the following three years. Despite the plea of Dashiell for 'more and more *analytic* research' (1930, p. 198) these studies were not well controlled.

Burri (1931) tested the influence of an audience on recall with competition effects reduced. All subjects learned a list of words in the presence of the experimenter. Two of three groups were told that they would be asked to recall the words the next day in front of an audience. One audience was attentive and evaluative while the other was inattentive. The third group recalled with only the experimenter present.

The results showed that there was better recall with only the experimenter present and that there was no difference between the two types of audiences. This was despite the fact that subjects who had anticipated recalling in front of an audience had taken 30 per cent more trials to learn the list of words on the first day. This showed that merely the *expectancy* of performing in front of an audience had a direct influence on performance.

It is hard to interpret these data clearly, however. The experimenter present in the 'No Audience' condition must be considered an evaluating audience, as Dashiell (1930) and Ekdahl (1929) had both shown. It might have been that the experimenter's presence focussed the subjects on the accuracy of the performance, which was being measured, whereas in the audience conditions subjects may have concentrated on presentation features or else have been distracted. Little can be gleaned from the data.

Farnsworth and Behner (1931) looked more closely at Allport's notion of 'the attitude of social conformity' (1924a, p. 278). They repeated his experiment of judging weights alone and in groups, and found similar results. The heavier weights were judged lighter when in a group than when alone, and the lighter weights were judged heavier in the groups. When tested for statistical significance, which Allport had not done, only a few of the comparisons showed significant differences.

Perl (1933) reported evidence that visual or verbal jokes presented to a group were judged to be more funny than the same jokes presented privately. The evidence for this was not well controlled but may suggest a further example of conformity influence rather than any social facilitation.

Pessin (1933) compared the effects of social and mechanical stimulation on learning and recall. Each subject learned three lists of nonsense syllables – each list under a different condition. The order of conditions was varied. In the Control condition the subjects worked alone without extraneous stimulation. In the Mechanical condition the subjects had to contend with a buzzer and flashing lights. In the Social condition a passive observer was introduced. This consisted of Pessin himself watching through a small window.

Results showed that subjects needed more repetitions of the list and made more errors in the Social condition compared to the Control condition. More errors still were made in the Mechanical condition. There was also some weaker evidence in a follow up that subjects in the Social and Mechanical conditions retained more afterwards. This was probably due to those subjects having greater exposure to the lists.

Pessin and Husband (1933) tested two social conditions against a control using a fingermaze task. Large variability in the data, however, precludes any sure interpretation, but another feature of this publication deserves mention. The authors pointed out that Allport's definition of social facilitation only dealt with an increase in the on-going activity due to others co-working. It was the stimulus of the movements which increased work. It was pointed out by Pessin and Husband (1933) that there is no reason from Allport's conception to expect performance changes in the presence of a passive spectator, since in this case there are no stimulus movements.

To explain passive audience effects, then, new factors were needed. One reason put forward by these two authors was that subjects might exert more energy when in front of an audience. Ichheiser (1930) had reported greater 'eagerness and readiness' to do the task when in front of an audience.

Pessin and Husband (1933) also suggested (as others had before) that *distraction* might play a rôle in such effects. This explained some of the null results with passive audiences since the subjects all knew the members of the audience and could ignore them. 'Much more serious distraction was observed when the spectator was a room-mate or a close constant friend of the opposite sex. In these cases the subject worried so much about appearing stupid when he made errors that his main attention was distracted away from the close concentration necessary for the most efficient learning' (p. 153).

This again suggests effects due to self-presentation. It also raises the role of social relationships in such effects for the first time. Effects might be different for strangers and friends.

The reviews of 1935

In 1935, the social facilitation work was reviewed by both Dashiell and Hollingworth. After discussing early co-working studies, Hollingworth reached a similar conclusion to that of Pessin and Husband (1933): that the effects of Allport (1924a) do not apply to an audience situation. With an audience, claimed Hollingworth, there is no rivalry and no ideomotor stimulation. He did agree with Allport that 'working in the presence of others . . . establishes certain fundamental attitudes' (Allport, 1924a, p. 285). In particular, effects can come from the attitude of the audience, whether they register approval or disapproval. So like Triplett (1898) and Gates (1924) had suggested, social approval and social consequences may play a rôle in the effects which have been found.

Hollingworth reviewed the audience studies and concluded that most had design faults. What effects had been demonstrated also seemed to be small ones. In his book, Hollingworth also drew attention to the work of Ruger (1910), who had suggested that one interfering effect of audiences was due to self-attention:

> The self is felt to be on trial. 'What sort of self shall I and others consider myself to be?' is the question which occupies attention, and this is usually accompanied by a state of worry, of emotional attention, which still further distracts from the problem in hand.   (Hollingworth 1935, p. 205)

This states clearly the self-presentation perspective, that having to present an image to others distracts from the task. The effects of an audience are not just on the task at hand. The whole behaviour of the subject and the whole social situation is implicated. Increased self-awareness is also implied by Ruger.

The same year saw another substantive review published by Dashiell (1935). He now differentiated seven types of relationships between an individual and others. These were: a passive audience; co-workers with no competition; contestants; evaluators making comments on the work; co-operators; information controllers; and prestigious or large audiences.

Dashiell pointed out that few significant results had been found using analyses of means and standard errors so he relied instead on trends in individual results. He argued that 'a social influence ... is as validly measured by the number of people affected as by the relative intensity with which they are affected' (p. 1107). He also thought that this took account of individual differences in susceptibility. Pessin and Husband (1933) were criticized for having the experimenter present in all three conditions although no comment was made on other studies which had done likewise (and I have pointed out that this is most of them). Dashiell's conclusion for the effects of a passive audience was that 'the mere presence of others tends to speed up the individual's work but to make it less accurate' (1935, p. 1106).

His conclusions were based, as has been seen, on frequency data which were not tested for possible chance effects by non-parametric analyses. Performing binomial tests on the figures of Allport (1924a), as presented by Dashiell (1935, p. 1108), it is found that only two of the sixteen results differ from chance level. In fact, Dashiell strongly pressed his case against the analysis of means using Allport's data of the number of associations alone or together (p. 1107). He showed that mean values reveal no difference between these two conditions but that six of the eight subjects had produced more associations in the co-working situation. This, however, has a binomial probability of only 0.145. By present day standards, even this frequency difference must be judged as due to chance.

So despite Dashiell's optimistic review, the work up to 1935 had failed to show consistent results. Properly controlled experimentation had not been tried. The design problems which had been commented upon in the literature at this stage were: the experimenter's presence in Alone conditions; confounding and not controlling for other effects which had been shown to exert an influence – such as competition; insufficient data analysis; and little comparability between the conditions in different studies.

It must be kept in mind, of course, that statistics and experimental design were still young (Fisher, 1925, 1935). What is found in this literature is the first applications of experimental methods to social psychology. The steps of experimental social psychology at this stage consisted of conceptually distinguishing phenomena, and attempting to control for them in setting up experiments, but the proper analysis of any differences found was in its infancy.

Changes of direction during the war period

In their textbook discussion of social facilitation (wholly confined to a footnote!), LaPiere and Farnsworth (1936) raised again a problem with the early work. This was that it was doubtful that the controls of rivalry and competition used were effective. They suggested that it may be impossible ever to be rid of these effects: 'In fact, it is possible that social facilitation is nothing more than mild rivalry' (p. 377). With this doubt, and those expressed by Dashiell (1935), it is unlikely that any clear effects of just the passive presence of another person had been shown up to this time. Conceptually, the area had been refined, but efficient methods of testing these distinctions had not followed.

The next few years produced a number of reported studies, but only a few after the American involvement in the Second World War. Some of these claimed to be social facilitation but actually dealt with cooperation effects, which Dashiell (1935) had excluded. For this reason they will not be reviewed in detail. The areas seems to have changed direction, since the stricter control of experimental situations had led to a conglomerate of different effects. It was realized that many effects occur due to the presence of other people, and these were avidly explored in the following years.

All the studies of this period are listed in Table 2 of Chapter 8. Only a few of the better ones will be mentioned here.

In the two conditions of their study relevant to social facilitation, Taylor, Thompson and Spassoff (1937) found less work done in groups (Condition A) than alone (Condition H). The number of subjects used was small, but performing a two-tail test on these groups shows it to be reliable at the 0.01 level, ($t = 2.95$). Abel (1938) found better maze performance in pairs than alone using retarded subjects. Mukerji (1940) also found better performance in groups than alone but with trained children. Despite having no controls for order effects, the better results were found in the first test taken by the children (in groups).

Hanawalt and Ruttiger (1944) had subjects read the 'Ghost story' of Bartlett (1932), and then repeat the story from memory to another experimenter or to an audience. There was more elaboration given to the audience, although there was no true Alone condition for comparison. This perhaps suggests that attention is given to presentation rather than just performance with an audience, as was suggested earlier in this chapter for the results of Burri (1931).

Wapner and Alper (1952) varied the type of audience in a test of choice times. In the Unseen Audience condition subjects thought that they were being watched from behind a one-way mirror; in the Seen Audience condition subjects could see an audience through a back-illuminated one-way mirror; and in the No Audience condition only the experimenter was present. Again, no true Alone condition was used. The manipulations with one-way mirrors has since been frequently used for different purposes. It was used here to reduce distraction effects from an audience.

No difference was found by Wapner and Alper (1952) between the No Audience and the Seen Audience conditions but subjects were slowest on choosing in the Unseen Audience condition. It was not even suggested that the experimenter may have acted as an audience in the No Audience condition.

Finally, Seidman, Bensen, Miller and Meeland (1957) found that subjects tolerated more self-administered shock when a partner shared the shock than when alone. This occurred even though the experimenter was present in both conditions. From the instructions given it is likely that some form of rivalry, face-saving, or self-presentation produced the results. No true Alone condition was run to test whether the presence of the experimenter had an added effect.

Into the modern period

Gurnee (1962; Experiment 2) tested subjects on maze performance either in co-working groups with no interaction or else alone. He found no difference between these two conditions. Few details of procedure were given in the report but it seems that the experimenter was present after six trials at least, to collect the results from the Alone subjects. So there was probably no real Alone comparison.

Bergum and Lehr conducted three experiments on the effects of the presence of others on vigilance performance. In the first two experiments (1962), subjects worked alone or in pairs. A slight improvement in vigilance was found for pairs but the second experiment showed that this was proportional to the amount of conversation. As there was interaction between the subjects in pairs this tells us nothing about the effects of the passive presence of others.

In their later study (Bergum and Lehr, 1963), subjects either worked alone or had periodic visits from an officer. The latter conditions improved vigilance. Again, this tells us little about effects of a passive other, as the officers could converse with the subjects. In any case, the officers were hardly neutral stimuli for the soldiers taking part in the study.

Ader and Tatum (1963) found that more subjects who were alone learned to escape from a free-operant shock avoidance situation than subjects in pairs. Colquhoun and Corcoran (1964) found a very weak improvement in vowel cancellation for subjects alone when compared to subjects in pairs. The subjects alone, however, had the experimenter watching so a proper test of presence effects was not made.

2.4 Conclusion

What does the first sixty-six years of social facilitation research reveal? Conceptually, the results can be divided into audience and co-worker effects, though most of the tests suffer from methodological flaws which preclude a clear interpretation. What evidence there is suggests that co-workers lead to a greater quantity of behaviour but with less accuracy. It had been suggested that this is due to over-compensation for the increased distraction (Meumann, 1904), to the effects of rivalry and competition, even if implicit (LaPiere & Farnsworth, 1936), or to an ideomotor facilitation from just the sight and sound of the co-worker's activity (Triplett, 1898).

There are almost no clear results for the effects of a passive other person or audience. Proposed effects include distraction (Meumann, 1904), trying to look good or trying to make a good impression (Ruger, 1910; Seidman, Bensen, Miller and Meeland, 1957), tension and arousal (Ekdahl, 1929), evaluation and authority (Bergum and Lehr, 1963), and the presence of the experimenter (Ekdahl, 1929).

Although the effects of the passive presence of another person have come to be called social facilitation effects, this no longer corresponds to the meaning given by Allport (1924a). With a passive audience there can be no dynamogenic idea of movements in sight and sound. This was essential to Allport's definition. The effects are now divided into several categories, most clearly delineated by Dashiell (1935). Few new distinctions were added after this time.

The work starting with Zajonc (1965) concentrated on testing *explanatory theories* about why these different effects occurred, rather than exploring how social situations can be analysed into the various structural types. This leads us into the modern period of experimental social psychology. Instead of list-theories, which merely list the factors which influence a phenomenon, modern theories try to explain the effects in terms of some other psychological basis or foundation.

Several phenomena in the early literature became separate areas of social psychology and little reference, except in passing, was made to social facilitation research. The 1940s and 1950s saw a big increase in conformity research (Sherif, 1935), which researched how other people present can shape behaviour through interaction; this research mostly ignored passive conformity effects. Judgements of weights and opinions by groups and individuals also moved to study either the effects of different sized groups and group interaction (Lorge, Fox, Davitz and Brenner, 1958) or conformity in judgements (Asch, 1952). Competition and cooperation also moved to new themes (Deutsch, 1949).

Perhaps more importantly, social psychology moved sharply at this point in time to study the interaction between people, spurred on by great advances in learning and reinforcement theory, and in the use of observation of groups in laboratories (Bales, Strodtbeck, Mills and Roseborough, 1951). This all but excluded research on the more passive social facilitation effects until the mid-1960s.

3   The drive model of Zajonc (1965)

3.1 An outline of Zajonc (1965)

As we saw in the last chapter, social facilitation research was either ignored or not carried out enthusiastically in the years after the Second World War. In 1965, Zajonc produced an influential account of the social facilitation literature. In this he made at least nine points, which, because of the importance of his article in renewing interest in the field, will be discussed in detail. Before doing this, the changes in experimental psychology which had occurred need to be outlined.

The development of experimental psychology

It needs to be kept in mind that between the last of the social facilitation studies and 1965, the whole research orientation of psychology, as well as theoretical orientation, had changed. Conceptually Hullian behaviourism had dominated psychology for many years, with its hypothetico-deductive model of research, its mechanistic approach, and its emphasis on observable behaviour.

Hullian behaviourism was a reaction to the looseness and conceptual uncertainty of earlier psychologies. Too many of the psychologies of the first third of this century dealt only with what people said about themselves: the verbalizations (introspections) about their thoughts, behaviour, feelings and emotions. While it is clear that how people talk about their own psychology is important (Farr and Moscovici, 1984), it was no longer clear by the mid-century that such verbalizations should be the basis for how psychology talks about thoughts, behaviour, feelings and emotions. After all, physicists no longer took seriously how people talked about tables and chairs: they considered the constituent molecules and atoms instead.

With this background, Hull (1943) and others made a number of changes to the theories of psychology, and also how theorizing took place. First, they tried to avoid using common language ways of speaking about psychology, so as not to be misled by socially maintained fictions (Farr and Moscovici, 1984). Second, they tried to avoid (for the present at least) topics of psychology which seemed to exist only in talk, in the same way that ether existed only in the writings of physicists earlier in the century. For example, feelings of anger or honour mostly existed in the socially maintained talk about these topics, with the exception of related biological substrata which might be demonstrated, such as changes in the nervous system activity during 'anger'.

In practice, what this amounted too was that *unobservable* phenomena were excluded from psychological theorizing, because they were the topics which had to exist purely in talking about psychology. Some were deemed not to exist at all, such as 'psychic energy', while others were deemed too difficult to measure in other ways, such as thought and imaging.

The changes brought about by Hullian behaviourism also came from its hypothetico-deductive model of science. While it is easy to scorn this approach with present-day hindsight, it was in fact an exciting approach in its day. Isaac Newton had made much progress in physics by stating axioms which were taken as givens, and then deriving propositions from the axioms which could be tested. This led to theorems being postulated which could be tested from further deductions. In its purest form the axioms and theorems were in mathematical form.

The excitement of Hullian behaviourism was to try and do the same within psychology. At the time, some basic axiomatic reflexes of the nervous system, which had been demonstrated by Sherrington (1906), looked as if they could form a sensible basis for an axiomatic system for psychology. In addition, Pavlov had outlined some simple principles showing that the basic axiomatic reflexes could be conditioned to produce other more varied behaviours, and instrumental learning principles were showing the same effects in another way (Skinner, 1938). These developments were also coupled with advances in understanding the brain-stem and the reticular activation system of the brain, which obviously formed a basis for motivational systems. This gave a foundation for including drive and emotion into psychology beyond mere talk. So with all of these new foundations for psychology appearing at the time, a hypothetico-deductive model of psychology looked a real possibility.

I have emphasized the background to Hullian behaviourism because with smart hindsight, psychologists today often ridicule what Hull attempted. The Hullian psychologists were not fools, however, and taken in context, what they attempted was a major advance for psychology. To the theorists of the time, the plan was an exciting and real possibility. One wonders whether most present day psychological theories will look as good in 50 years time!

In 1960, the 'cognitive revolution' was announced (Miller, Galanter and Pribram, 1960). Theoriests wanted to keep the mechanistic approach to psychology, but wanted to be able to talk about events which could not be directly observed. Hullian behaviourism had looked at what stimuli affect the organism and how the organism responds to these. The causality is obviously a mechanistic one, but one which avoids talking about hypothetical mechanisms when they cannot be observed.

It was probably the social/scientific pressure to explicate the mechanisms between stimulus and response which finally convinced psychologists that they needed to talk about intervening mechanisms, even if they made them up. Put another way, the psychologists' social representations (Farr and Moscovici, 1984) that science had to have mechanisms was so strong that they socially supported (as scientists) the creation of hypothetical mechanisms. The key cognitive book by Miller, Galanter and Pribram (1960) is as much about permission-giving to psychological theorists as it is about detailing new entities. In the same way, physicists had socially maintained a fiction of the ether merely to provide an intervening mechanism.

Cognitive psychology, then, provided models of the way in which people represent the world in their head, to replace the observation of stimulus-response links. Cognitive psychology remains a mechanistic world-view which is still a stimulus-response psychology (see Spence, 1960): the mechanisms between stimulus and response are merely hypothesized to occur in the head of the organism rather than in the environment.

What is interesting from the standpoint of social facilitation is that as late as 1965, Zajonc used a Hullian framework to explain social facilitation, rather than a cognitive one. The reason was probably that cognitive psychologists had not quite finalized how to deal with drive mechanisms and dominance hierarchies in their new models. The cybernetic TOTE mechanisms (Miller, Galanter and Pribram, 1960) had replaced drive on a molecular level, but drive had been a useful concept at a molar level as well. The details of these hypothetical mechanisms took longer to eventuate (Schank and Abelson, 1977).

Whatever the reasons, Zajonc produced in 1965 his influential article which re-conceptualized social facilitation in terms of Hullian behaviourism. And since then, one of the few places in psychology texts where Hullian behaviourism is discussed is in the sections on social facilitation. As we shall see in later chapters of this book, cognitive social psychologists soon produced a number of more cognitive theories to account for the social facilitation results.

The arguments of Zajonc

The nine points made by Zajonc (1965) are now summarized:

(1) Zajonc first made a summary of the previous work in the area. Claiming that the area was 'nearly completely abandoned' (p. 269), he summarized six

human studies for audience effects, and eight animal and three human studies for co-working effects (also now called *co-acting*).

(2) From the audience studies Zajonc suggested 'just one, rather subtle, consistency' (1965, p. 270). This was that:

> The emission of well-learned responses is facilitated by the presence of spectators, while the acquisition of new responses is impaired. To put the statement in conventional psychological language, performance is facilitated and learning is impaired by the presence of spectators. (p. 270)

(3) It was next argued by Zajonc that for a well-learned task the correct responses are the dominant or strong responses whereas for learning tasks the dominant or strong responses are the incorrect ones. This meant that Zajonc's previous hypothesis could be restated as follows: '(an) audience enhances the emission of dominant responses' (p. 270). That is, for complex or learning tasks, audiences will inhibit performance; for simple or well-learned tasks, audiences will facilitate performance.

(4) To *explain* the increase in dominant responses, Zajonc used the Hull-Spence drive model (Hull, 1943). This states that reaction potential (sEr), the potential for a particular response to occur, is a multiplicative function of both habit strength (sHr) and drive. In this case Zajonc was concerned with Hullian generalized drive (D), rather than specific drives, such as for food or water. In the Hullian formula:

$$_s E_r = {_s}H_r \times D$$

This means that with an increase in generalized drive, those responses with a high habit strength, the dominant or well-learned ones, will become even more likely to be emitted than the less dominant ones. The response potential is not predictable from habit strength or general drive level alone. This means that if it could be shown that the presence of another person increases drive level then this would explain the increased emission of dominant responses.

To see that this is so, consider the following hypothetical values. Suppose that a complex or poorly learned response has a habit strength of two, meaning that they are weak responses. This might be the habit strength of learning the association between the words 'Goose' and 'Radio' which might have been shown once by the experimenter. On the other hand, the habit strength of the association between 'Goose' and 'Duck' will be high (say, eight) because of repeated presentations of these words through our lives.

If we are now shown the word 'Goose' and asked by the experimenter for the associated word, the word 'Duck' is six point values higher in potentiation (sEr) than 'Radio', if we assume a drive level of one. This means that we will make some mistakes in answering this question until we learn the

Goose/Radio association so well that its habit strength (sHr) also gets up to a value of about eight.

Now notice what happens if the drive level of the organism is increased from a (hypothetical) value of one to a value of, say, ten. The reaction potential (sEr) of Goose/Radio now stands at twenty, while Goose/Duck becomes eighty. The well-learned response is now sixty point values ahead of the less well-learned response, so there is even more likelihood of saying 'Goose/Radio' wrongly. This is because, while the drive is a multiplicative function of reaction potential, the reaction potentials are subtracted when comparing levels.

Hull (1943) has found some evidence for these propositions using forms of arousal such as caffeine, and by artificially training responses of different habit strengths. The work had been continued by Spence and his colleagues (Spence, 1956; Spence, Farber and McFann, 1956; Spence, Taylor and Ketchel, 1956; Taylor and Rechtschlaffen, 1959; Taylor and Spence, 1952).

(5) The next step in Zajonc's argument, an *implicit* step, was to equate the Hull-Spence notion of generalized Drive with *general arousal* level. It was assumed that the effect of increased arousal on performance was the same as an increase in the theoretical construct Drive (Spence, 1956).

(6) Evidence was then provided that the presence of others increases general arousal level. This evidence rested almost exclusively on the increase of hydrocortisone levels in plasma under crowded or stressed conditions with non-human animals. Studies had found higher levels of hydrocortisone in animals caged together than in solitary animals. This is linked to adrenocorticol functions which are linked to changes in arousal. Zajonc admitted, however, that this evidence was 'indirect and scanty' (p. 274).

(7) Zajonc further argued for a separation of different effects of the presence of others. He distinguished those effects which are *directed* by the behaviour of others present from any *non-directive* effects. Directive influences included imitation, cooperation, competition, reinforcement and distraction. He claimed that there can be effects apart from these due to just the 'sheer passive presence', or the 'mere presence', of others. He also made a case that almost all the co-action studies had confounded the directive effects with the non-directive effects.

(8) It was next suggested that the mere presence of another person is sufficient to increase drive or arousal and so enhance the emission of dominant responses. This means that simple tasks would be performed better and complex tasks performed worse. While not denying the importance of all the directive effects, non-directive influences are sufficient for social facilitation effects, Zajonc claimed.

(9) The final claim made was that although there were problems with the mere presence formulation, it was a parsimonious view of the literature. The

effects are reduced to a single process: the increased emission of dominant responses through increased arousal in the presence of others. Both the facilitation and the inhibition of performance come from this one process. Much of the appeal for Zajonc's model has come from this simplicity of its total formulation.

No major changes were made to these arguments in Zajonc's book which followed (1966); some experimental work which had been published since the review article was added. In 1972 he added more, both in a small publication on animal social behaviour (Zajonc, 1972a) and in a conference address (Zajonc, 1972b; partly reprinted as Zajonc, 1980).

In the small booklet of 1972 he claimed that generalized arousal was not like fear arousal, so an increase in arousal for most animals would lead to an increase in eating, a common dominant response. He likened arousal to alertness or preparedness to respond: 'states commonly associated with a heightened arousal' (p. 7). He further suggested that only for a normally isolated animal put in the presence of a conspecific should one strictly talk of heightened arousal. For normally social animals one should talk of a lowering of arousal when put alone.

In both of the 1972 publications Zajonc also suggested a basis for the increase in arousal due to the presence of others. This was that conspecifics are inherently less predictable than physical objects and their behaviour less certain. A chair which is present will stay where it is and need not be addressed, nor engaged in social interaction. With a person present there is always the possibility that they will interact in some way, and require some response. So in the presence of conspecifics, animals will be alert for the unexpected – in a state of response preparedness. *This* was the basis of arousal or drive increase.

3.2 Critical discussion of Zajonc (1965)

To examine the Zajonc (1965) paper, each of the main points outlined above will be dealt with in turn.

The drive construct and the dominance hierarchy of responses

The first two points claimed that the social facilitation area had been nearly abandoned and that one consistency was the facilitation of dominant responses and the inhibition of non-dominant responses. While it is true that very few studies were done from about 1940 to 1964, especially good ones, it is also true that there was more to the literature of the early studies than the one suggested consistency. As we saw in Chapter 2, a large number of factors had been put forward as important, such as impression giving, evaluation and authority, and compensation for distraction. As we also saw in Chapter 2, however, there was little direct evidence for these. What evidence there was, including that used by Zajonc, was poorly controlled.

Zajonc's third point has been widely accepted, that for well-learned tasks the correct responses are dominant while for learning tasks the incorrect responses are dominant. Indeed it seems a straightforward step, but some doubts about its place in his whole argument will be raised here.

The first problem is that this step changes the discussion into one about correct and incorrect responses while some of the more subtle behaviour changes suggested in the earlier work are not easily characterized in this fashion. Trying to make a good impression on an audience cannot easily be classed as a correct or incorrect response. So this point has led to an emphasis on measures of task performance which allow correct and incorrect responses. This means that although this formulation may accurately describe a number of phenomena, a number of other phenomena are ignored or excluded in making this step. This is not a criticism of Zajonc's view, just of its scope and its consequences.

Even with the use of task performance, Blank (1979) comments that Zajonc's formulation blurs the early differences found between the quality and quantity of performance in the presence of others, especially within the same task (Jones and Gerard, 1967; Kelley and Thibaut, 1954). The blurring enters at precisely this same point in Zajonc's argument. Performance becomes reduced to either facilitation or inhibition. It does not allow for both the facilitation of quantity and the inhibition of quality at the same time.

It has already been mentioned that Zajonc's use of the Hull-Spence model of generalized drive is a curious feature of his 1965 article. This is partly because the model was on the wane in most other areas in psychology, but also, as Zajonc himself later commented (1980, p. 38), because of the uncritical acceptance this part of his theory received.

Generalized Drive was originally a theoretical construct defined so as to mediate between stimuli and responses (Hull, 1943). Its early success was due both to its integration of an area previously fractured by instinct theorists (McDougall, 1923) and to its suggested possible physiological basis. Its later demise was due to its inability to explain a number of findings, especially ones relevant to cognitive mediations of motivational states (Bolles, 1975; Hinde, 1970; Petri, 1981; but see Smith, 1984).

The demise was also due to the vagueness of its conception, both as a theoretical device and as an indicator of physiological change (Dethier, 1966; Hinde, 1960). Even to explain the results found in his own time, Spence needed further constructs of incentive motivation (K), stimulus intensity dynamism (V), and conditioned and reactive inhibition (sIr, Ir). Zajonc (1965) used only the most simple form of Hull's work for his social facilitation model. Some attempts have been made since 1965 to add in other constructs. (See Chapter 4).

A final problem with Zajonc's use of Drive Theory concerns the dominance hierarchies of responses. The point has been made by a number of writers that while correct and incorrect responses may be defined by laboratory tasks, it is not clear how to specify response hierarchies independently of the tasks without post-hoc determination (Carron, 1971; Duflos et al., 1969; Glaser, 1982; Landers, 1980; Martens, 1974).

> . . . predictions cannot clearly be derived from the Hull-Spence position without a complete specification of the habit-family hierarchies elicited by the stimuli . . . and without a model of conflicts resolution which discloses the probability of each response, given a number of competing responses.
>
> (Weiner & Schneider, 1971, p. 258)

So even in a two-response task, there may be responses irrelevant to the task responses which may be dominant. These might interfere with task performance in a regular way if enhanced by increased drive. For example, if subjects were bored then body shifts and small scratching movements might be dominant responses. If these increased with increased drive then they could interfere with some tasks.

The arousal construct

As a theoretical construct, Drive could only be useful if measured or manipulated. To this end generalized drive has been equated with general arousal or general anxiety. Zajonc (1965) used this to provide some support for his position, although problems have arisen with this since 1965.

First, the two ways of grounding drive theory in arousal and anxiety both showed problems. One, the use of physiological methods, will be discussed below. The other was the use of the Manifest Anxiety Scale (Taylor, 1953). This scale has come in for a lot of criticism, and hardly serves to *ground* a theory (Cofer and Appley, 1964; Hill, 1957; Jessor and Hammond, 1957; Martens, 1971; Weiner, 1966).

A second problem is that the term 'arousal' turns out to be as vague as 'drive' and can refer to a number of different processes. In his discussion of arousal, Andrew (1974) isolated six different usages of this term: (1) arousal can be thought of as responsiveness, the likelihood that a response will be given to a stimulus at a particular time. (2) it can also mean the 'behavioural intensity' with which a response is made. Both these usages derive from Hebb (1949, 1955). (3) arousal is also used as a continuum along which different responses are made, aggressive and defensive responses at higher levels and appetitive responses or sleep at lower arousal levels (Moruzzi, 1969). (4)

arousal has also been used to refer to a common mediating mechanism underlying a pattern of related responses. For higher drive states such responses might include cardiac acceleration, increased muscle tension and the orienting response (Lynn, 1966). (5) arousal is often related directly to the level of sensory seeking, high sensory input being a higher drive state. (6) arousal has been equated with the activity of specific brain structures, especially the ascending activation system of the mesencephalon and thalamus.

Each of these usages of arousal have problems but these will not be raised here (see Andrew, 1974; Claridge, 1981; Martens, 1974). The point to be made is that until more is known about the exact nature of the arousal process it can neither be clearly measured nor used as a theoretical basis. The physiological evidence presented by Zajonc (1965) regarding hydrocortisone levels is based on the behavioural intensity usage of arousal. How this relates to the other usages and measures of arousal is unknown. More recent studies have used a wider range of physiological indicators (Cacioppo, Rourke, Marshall-Goodell, Tassinary and Baron, 1990; Moore and Baron, 1983). How these all fit together is also uncertain at present, but it should be profitable to continue developing such measures.

The last problem with arousal to be discussed concerns the relation between arousal and performance. Hull had predicted a monotonic relation between Drive and performance for a given habit strength. That is, as drive levels increase the reaction potential increases monotonically. Zajonc (1965) assumed likewise when linking this to arousal. Other work, however, has suggested an inverted-U relation between arousal and performance (Broadhurst, 1957; Welford, 1976), and Zajonc himself later (1980, p. 53) referred to this in explaining some contradictory results.

There are some problems with the inverted-U relation as well. In particular, two thorough reviews have found that there is little real support for the inverted-U function despite its widespread use as a post-hoc explanation (Martens, 1974; Neiss, 1988; but also see Anderson, 1990). Problems with the original experimental support have also been noted (Brown, 1965). As will be seen when reviewing theories in Chapter 4, a number of social facilitation theories are based upon the inverted-U relation despite it being problematic. Zajonc also connected arousal to the ceiling effects of drive although the paper he refers to (Broen and Storms, 1961) only discussed complex tasks and not the simple tasks he was trying to explain (Glaser, 1982).

Given the problems of the Drive and arousal constructs, and of their measurement, what is left of the evidence that the presence of others induces an increase in general arousal level? The evidence produced by Zajonc (1965) was admitted to be doubtful for a number of reasons. All but one of the studies concerned crowded conditions, where there was anything but the 'mere presence' of a passive other. In the one study cited by Zajonc as indicating the 'mere presence of other animals in the same room' (p. 273), the three monkeys were, in fact, in visual, auditory and tactile contact (Mason and Brady, 1964). The elevated hydrocortisone levels that were found could have been due to many sorts of social interaction effects. This was precisely the reason why Zajonc had earlier denied that some other social facilitation studies had shown mere presence effects.

Since 1965, many more physiological measures have been used, such as EEG, palmar sweat, galvanomic skin responses, heart rate and the electromyograph. As noted above, the evidence suggests that all these arousal measures do not correlate well with one another (Cacioppo, Rourke, Marshall-Goodell, Tassinary and Baron, 1990; Lacey, 1967; Martens, 1974; Martin, 1961; Moore and Baron, 1983; Poulson, 1970). This could be for a number of reasons. There might not be a general arousal factor, it might have several parts, or only parts of the one factor might become manifest under certain conditions. The point being made here is that until more is known with certainty about the physiology involved, a solid theoretical foundation for arousal has not been provided.

The criticism has also been raised a number of times that arousal measures are likely to be reactive (Gale and Baker, 1981). It is probably arousing to be brought to a room and hooked up to physiological devices. So the baseline condition, in this case the Alone condition, is probably arousing in some sense even before any experimental manipulations have begun. The problem is then one of interactive effects or ceiling effects.

A further reactive effect arises in the Alone conditions of social facilitation experiments. If the physiological measure is taken after the task is finished then it will not be measuring the same physiological reaction as occurred during the task. If the experimenter is present to take the measure during the task then this no longer constitutes an Alone condition. Even if the subject is asked to make self-measures during the task, such as palmar sweat fingerprints, novelty effects might change arousal levels and also lead to distractive effects.

In any event, most physiological measures have only been 'rough indicators' (Martens, 1974, p. 166) which means that mere presence effects might be too subtle to be registered anyway. One cannot even plot relative levels of induced arousal to make a test between the monotonic and inverted-U relationships of arousal and performance (Martens, 1974).

It seems, then, that there are serious problems with physiological evidence such that it cannot provide a sure basis for a social facilitation theory. It should be said, however, that the physiological technology appears to be improving and may someday be predictive (Cacioppo and Petty, 1983). At present, a recent review suggested that the rôle of physiological measures in social facilitation research should only be exploratory (Moore and Baron, 1983).

One final problem will be raised about Zajonc's conception of arousal increases in the presence of others. This concerns his use of the term *arousal* in two later publications (Zajonc, 1972a, 1980). In his 1965 publication Zajonc wrote of arousal in the ordinary conversational sense. In the presence of others we are alert to them so we can be prepared for contingencies. When we are alone we can relax this state of readiness.

In the later publications he wrote that by arousal he meant 'relative changes in arousal level brought about by moving from a state of isolation to compresence' (1972a, p. 8). He suggested that for animals which are typically with others, and only occasionally alone:

> . . . it would be more appropriate to speak of a lowering of arousal level that comes about when the individual is placed in isolation. For others that spend most of their time in isolation, we can speak of a heightened arousal that is associated with the presence of others.   (p. 8)

While this latter sentence is the usual interpretation of Zajonc's model, the first sentence suggests a different meaning of arousal. Highly social animals placed in isolation become more aroused in the usual sense of the word, showing increased distress calls, readiness to respond, and fear (Gaioni and Ross, 1982; Rajecki et al., 1975; Suarez and Gallup, 1981, 1982; Taylor, 1981). While less feeding (a dominant response) might be found in such a situation, this is compensated for by an increase in vigilance-related behaviours (Lazarus, 1979). These latter behaviours also seem consistent with Zajonc's notion of 'alertness and preparedness' (1972b, p. 8). So from this point of view, the animals can be said to be more aroused when placed in isolation.

What seems to be the problem here is a play on two meanings of the word 'arousal'. Zajonc wants to say that there is an arousal increase in the presence of others or an arousal decrease when alone, depending upon resting state level. The distress caused by isolating a normally social animal, however, is also indicative of an arousal *increase* in another sense of the word (closer to 'anxiety'). A similar distress can also been seen when putting a normally solitary animal (for example, a cat) with unfamiliar conspecifics.

It can be argued that these distress or fear effects are not mere presence effects and that because they are stronger, the lowering of arousal which also occurs might never be measured. It can also be suggested that mere presence effects are, in fact, some form of fear or threat reaction. This would occur when alone for normally social animals and when others are present for normally solitary animals. A model of mere presence effects based on this notion has been developed by Guerin and Innes (1982), and will be discussed in Chapter 4. This will also be pursued when reviewing the results of the many animal social facilitation studies in Chapter 7.

The construct of mere presence

The seventh step in Zajonc's argument, as outlined above, was that non-directive effects of the presence of others can be separated from directive effects such as giving cues, imitation, social reinforcement, and competition. This assumption is important because it is actually used to define mere presence effects: that which is left when the directive effects have been removed.

In practice, Zajonc himself admitted that mere presence effects can only be approximated (1980, p. 43). Most of our behaviours can be evaluated by others and the presence of others is usually distracting in some way: so these effects at least are hard to remove. Further, most co-action studies confound the effects of evaluation, competition, and sometimes imitation, with any mere presence. We can also recall from Chapter 2 that Dashiell (1930) found that when subjects in different rooms merely knew that they were performing in synchrony with others, they became competitive. Zajonc suggested that such effects are additive, and that although mere presence effects may be swamped, they are still present.

While it has been pointed out that the mere presence formulation leaves out a number of social facilitation phenomena found in the early work, what of the eighth claim that mere presence is a sufficient condition for social facilitation effects? While a review of the experimental literature will be left until Chapters 7 and 8, one comment will be made here. Markus (1981) considers that this question has been answered, that:

> some aspects of the social nature of individuals may indeed be instinctive or hard-wired and that this social nature or attitude may be stimulated by the presence of another member of the species . . . We are no longer interested in demonstrating just that an organism's dominant response can be enhanced by the presence of a species mate. It can. We are now left with the question of how. (p. 261)

To the extent that doubt has been placed on the meaning and measurement of dominant responses, and on the physiological measures that have been used, it cannot be said that the question is answered. As will also be shown in Chapter 8, there is little good evidence to exclusively support any of the theories of social facilitation.

3.3 Conclusions about Zajonc (1965)

In the light of the above discussion, Zajonc's final claim for the simplicity and parsimony of his drive model is correct, but only in so far as a number of terms are left vague and a number of phenomena are not considered. As Blank (1979) remarks, since Zajonc had to include evaluation apprehension to explain all the social facilitation findings (Zajonc, 1980), his explanation is no longer a simple one-process model. A large part of its appeal probably came from its simplicity and its 'great elegance' (Weiss and Miller, 1971).

The problems that have been raised with Zajonc's model are mostly problems with the evidence that was available at the time and with the use of the drive and arousal theories. As has been shown in great detail in earlier parts of this chapter, and also in Chapter 2, none of the evidence at the time was clearly interpretable. Similarly, the current arousal theory of the time had not been clearly examined and most of the problems were not raised until a later date. Even so, Zajonc's model provided a good account of what literature was available and it clearly led to a remarkable resurgence of work in the area (see Figure 1 in the last chapter). When some of the underpinnings of more recent social facilitation theories are examined closely, they too have many weak points.

Zajonc's model can perhaps be seen now as an elegant model of mere presence effects but not of social facilitation effects in general. There are a number of social facilitation phenomena (Desportes, 1969). While Zajonc's model retains its elegance, it does not deal with all of these social facilitation phenomena. But as a sufficient condition for social facilitation effects, it still has great importance.

3.4 Social psychology after 1965

In the years following Zajonc (1965) there was a surge in experimental and theoretical papers, as Figure 1 shows. Up to 1982 there were at least fifteen theories to explain social facilitation phenomena. Apart from a minor change in theorizing (Bruning, Capage, Kozuh, Young and Young, 1968), which will be mentioned later, a totally new approach had to wait until Wicklund and Duval (1971). After this, the next major theoretical change was not until Sanders, Baron and Moore (1978), but all of these were still based on arousal or drive mechanisms. Then, between 1978 and 1982, at least eight other explanations of social facilitation effects were published. Table 1 gives a list of the major social facilitation theories which will be discussed in the next section of this book.

The changes in theorizing which occurred, like those we saw in Chapter 2, reflected the changes in American psychology more generally. The drive and

Table 1. *The theories of social facilitation*

Drive theories of social facilitation
4.2   Zajonc's mere presence theory
4.3   Evaluation apprehension
4.4   Monitorability and alertness
Social conformity theories
5.1   Evaluation apprehension
5.2   Objective self-awareness
5.3   Control systems model
5.4   Self-presentation theories
5.5   Behaviour analysis
5.6   Behaviour inhibition
5.7   Miscellaneous social valuation theories
Cognitive process theories
6.1   Physical distraction
6.2   Cognitive distraction
6.3   Distraction-conflict
6.4   Attentional process model
6.5   Arousal effects upon attention
6.6   Attention model of Manstead and Semin (1980)
6.7   Cognitive information processing theory of Blank (1979)

learned apprehension models became less popular, not because they were proved false, but because of the wider theoretical changes that were taking place. The influence of S-R behaviourism had declined after Spence's death, and along with this, the use of drive theory also declined except in so far as it was equated with arousal.

These changes were concurrent with the rise of theories of cognition and information processing. The major assumption of cognitive theories is that people do not act upon or perceive the world directly, but have a representation of the world (inside their heads) which they use to interpret the world. This cognitivist position was initially the proposed answer to S-R behaviourism's failure to account for human behaviour purely in terms of the relations between observable stimuli and responses. It allowed all the unobservable (and any unknown) processes to be modelled as if they were inside the head.

Before long, the cognitive assumptions were applied to social behaviour. Social facilitation then seemed to become a testing ground for all the new information processing and social cognitive theories and models. As each was proposed, from 1971 onwards, a test was made using a social facilitation setting.

While cognitive processes were originally proposed for cases which seemed to have no obvious observable S-R relations with which to fashion an explanation, they were soon applied to most of human behaviour. This had two effects. First, it meant that environmental and learning influences were no longer looked for; a new process occurring in the head could be modelled to explain new findings without even looking for any obvious environmental influences.

The second effect was to turn psychological experiments into tests between competing models of cognitive processes, none of which could be pinned firmly down to observable behaviour or physiological processes. This meant a large influx of indeterminacy into social psychological theories (see Quine, 1960). That is, there were no longer any observable events which could decide between 'competing' cognitive models of unobservable events. Further, because the processes were unobservable, new processes could be posited to explain any discrepant results.

The importance of these two points will become clear as we review the theories of social facilitation in the next three chapters. While the theories seem to have different and testable assumptions, all the major theories end up explaining all the results – they are underdetermined. The point is also being made here that this is not limited only to theories of social facilitation; the same applies to most social psychological theories.

What will also become clear is that the falsification method of experimental research, which replaced the hypothetico-deductive model, still dominates psychology, and this had a large rôle in producing the negative side-effects. The method assumes that there is a clearly defined phenomenon about which to theorize. For social facilitation researchers this meant that the increase in simple responses and the decrease in complex responses was taken as given – it merely had to be talked about in a better manner.

The effect of this was that all the different behaviours which occur in social facilitation conditions were ignored in pursuit of falsifying theories which assumed that the increase in simple responses and decrease in complex responses were the only important behaviours. There were two side-effects of this. One was that the variety of behaviours which occur in the presence of another person were not observed in detail, a criticism that the ethologists Lorenz and Tinbergen had been making for many years about psychology in general.

The second side-effect was the one mentioned above, that the theories became underdetermined because they did not have links with behaviours other than the increase in easy responses and decrease in complex responses. So it turns out to be of no surprise that most of these theories are interchangeable if you merely change the words being used, as we will see in the next chapters.

While the cognitive revolution was being staged (Miller, Galanter and Pribram, 1960), the behaviour analysis started by B.F. Skinner (1938, 1953) was continuing. As we will see in Chapter 5, this has very little in common with the S-R behaviourism put forward by Hull and Spence (see Lee, 1988), despite most researchers still assuming they are nearly identical. It has a functional not mechanical basis, it is not positivist, it is not a stimulus-response psychology (it is a contextual, selectionist, or R-S psychology), and it does not follow either the hypothetico-deductive model nor the falsification models of science. Its scientific model is based more on the reversible control methods of Claude Bernard and Mach (Bernard, 1865/1957; Marr, 1985; Morris, 1988; Sidman, 1960; Thompson, 1984).

The experimental work in behaviour analysis continued unaffected by the demise of S-R behaviourism, but analyses of the more complex behaviours, including social behaviour, had to wait until the groundwork was fashioned. For social facilitation, this was eventually started by Ader and Tatum (1963) and Hake and Laws (1967). The behaviour analysis approach takes a fundamentally different position to both cognitive and S-R behaviourist theories. While not well developed even now in explaining social behaviour, the general outline will be developed in Chapter 5, and some new ideas pursued there.

II Theories of social facilitation

4   Drive theories of social facilitation

4.1 Types of social facilitation theories

Rather than review chronologically all the theories proposed after Zajonc (1965), they will be discussed in terms of their content. The theories can be usefully grouped into three types: arousal, social conformity and cognitive process theories (cf. Geen, 1989; Guerin and Innes, 1984). They will be discussed in terms of these categories in the following chapters. Table 1, shown in the last chapter, lists all the theories of social facilitation in these terms. The overlap between some theories is shown as well. This categorization highlights the similarities between many of the theories into some better order. The present categorization will go some way towards that end, and Chapter 9 will continue this in more detail.

Some of the similarities between the different approaches can be traced back to the influence of Zajonc (1965). One side-effect of Zajonc's formulation was that most of the opposing theories put forward were still based on the drive hypothesis and treated social facilitation as a single phenomenon. There was disagreement over what exactly *caused* the increase in drive in the presence of others, but the drive mechanism went unchallenged. In fact, the first real non-drive explanation did not come until 1978 (Carver and Scheier, 1978).

As mentioned earlier, a further side-effect of the Zajonc (1965) paper was that the majority of experiments used the same paradigm and looked only for the same type of behaviour change – the facilitation of simple responses and the inhibition of complex responses. The responses measured were also almost exclusively those of laboratory tasks, especially those which could be classified as correct and incorrect.

The basic design for the majority of the experiments consisted of subjects performing a *simple* or a *complex* task, in either an *Alone* condition or in a *Presence* condition. A significant interaction between these two independent variables was taken as evidence for social facilitation effects. For this reason, almost all the theories have been directed at explaining this particular interaction. Other types of behaviour changes in the presence of others have not been examined very often. It will be suggested later, however, that some of the theories probably refer to different phenomena and would be better measured in other ways.

As mentioned previously, the theories of social facilitation will be divided into three conceptual types despite a small amount of overlap between them. The first type involve the notions of *drive* or *arousal*. Most of these derive from Zajonc's model but posit new mediators of the arousal mechanism. Some have also been included in the third category because it is an attentional effect which produces the arousal increase in the presence of another person, or an arousal increase causes a change in attention.

The second type of theory involves the production or reduction of socially learned behaviours which conform to social standards of behaviour. The 'social conformity' behaviour usually increases in the presence of another person, but the opposite can occur. For example, we might wait until someone has gone out of the room before scratching our nose. That is, the theories in this section all make use of some concept of standard behaviours which subjects increase or decrease in the presence of other people, rather than some non-social mechanism which pushes the behaviour. These theories of social facilitation attempt to explain how just the passive presence of another person can produce effects – even when the standards of behaviour are not directly communicated. So all these theories suggest that standards of behaviour are current in social groups, and even when the standards are not directly made salient, they still have an effect when in the presence of another person.

The third group of explanations are all concerned with *cognitive* processes pushing a behaviour change in some way. These have the greatest overlap with the other theories but will be discussed separately. As will be shown in Chapter 6, there is little to decide between the particular social conformity and cognitive theories which have been put forward; they can each explain the same experimental results but using different words.

The three types of explanations will be discussed in turn. Evidence for each will not be given unless directly relevant to elucidating a particular point. Actual results of the experimental studies of social facilitation will be presented in detail in Chapters 7 and 8.

There are two reasons for leaving all the experimental evidence to later chapters. One reason is that many of the experiments have design faults which make their interpretation doubtful. Many experiments share these design problems, so they are better discussed as a whole, rather than critically evaluating each study one at a time. Chapter 8 will examine all studies for design problems, and separate the reliable studies from the others.

Another reason for putting off the review of experimental studies is that most of the experiments support a number of different theories of social facilitation. Presenting them at this stage as supportive of only one view will be seen to be misleading when they are viewed as a whole in Chapter 8. This will again show the indeterminacy of current social psychological theories.

4.2 Zajonc's mere presence theory

The mere presence theory of Zajonc (1965, 1980) has already been dealt with at length in Chapter 3. The alternative theories which followed his proposal continued to base themselves on drive and arousal while arguing that the mere presence of others was not sufficient to increase arousal. Instead, they proposed other conditions for this to occur. They still assumed, however, that the arousal was increased in the presence of others and that this increase facilitated dominant responses and inhibited non-dominant responses. As mentioned earlier, all were directed at explaining the statistical interaction between Alone/Presence conditions and Simple/Complex tasks.

The one extension which pursued Zajonc's drive approach as given was that of Weiss and Miller (1971). It was mentioned in Chapter 3 that Zajonc (1965) used only the most simple form of Hullian drive theory. Weiss and Miller drew out the implications for a drive model of social facilitation when using more complex drive interpretations. For example, if the effect of a person present is a learned drive effect, then extinction of the drive should be possible. That is, if the audience was continually present then the social facilitation effect should decrease over time, if no aversive consequences followed. The other predictions will not be detailed here.

Only one test of these implications has been attempted, it seems. Sanchez and Clark (1981) tried to show that audiences are aversive, which was predicted from the Weiss and Miller (1971) drive interpretation. Sanchez and Clark (1981) tested whether subjects would choose to work in front of an audience or not. While they found the latter, the test only measured the subjects' stated preferences, not any actual behaviour, so it is only a weak test of Weiss and Miller's hypothesis.

4.3 Evaluation apprehension theories

Cottrell (1968) and Henchy and Glass (1968)

The first opposing theoretical formulation which followed Zajonc (1965) was that of Cottrell (1968, 1972), who suggested that the basis of the social facilitation interaction effect was an increase in *learned* drive rather than generalized drive.

It was proposed that people learn throughout their lives that, depending upon how they behave, other people can give positive or negative outcomes.

that is, other people can praise a performance or they can give a negative evaluation. It was the learned *anticipation* of this, Cottrell suggested, which was arousing. So it was the increase in learned drive which led to the social facilitation effects, rather than Zajonc's proposed generalized drive.

The clear experimental implication of this is that only when members of an audience can *evaluate* a person's behaviour, and are 'potential dispensers of praise or reproof' (Cottrell, 1968, p. 105), will social facilitation effects be found. In line with this Cottrell, Wack, Sekerak and Rittle (1968) reported a difference between an Alone and a Presence condition, but no difference between the Alone condition and an audience which was blindfolded and therefore could not evaluate.

The task used by Cottrell et al. (1968) was a pseudorecognition task previously shown by Zajonc and Sales (1966) to be sensitive to social facilitation effects. With this task subjects were given lists of nonsense words to learn by pronouncing them. These were learned at different habit strengths (sHr) by having the words pronounced with different frequencies. Some words were pronounced once only, some twice, some 5 times, some 10 times, and some 25 times.

Hullian theory predicts that the better learned words are more likely to be emitted, since their reaction potential (sEr) is higher. It also means that with an increase in arousal the less well-learned words should be emitted relatively less often and the dominant, well-learned words should become even more frequently pronounced. It was predicted by Cottrell et al. (1968) that only when the audience could evaluate would this change in function be apparent. When the audience wore a blindfold, and arguably could not evaluate, there would be no change.

The question, of course, was how to get subjects to just pronounce words, so the relative levels of each trained word could be measured. This was accomplished with the pseudorecognition task, in which stimuli are quickly flashed on the screen so that it looks as if a word has been shown, but too quickly to exactly tell what it was. Subjects are asked to guess the words if they cannot recognize them, so the learned words are then sometimes given as answers. The question is how many of the well-learned and the less well-learned words are produced.

The results of Cottrell et al. (1968) are shown in Figure 4. When subjects were alone, the well-learned words were not very much more likely to be emitted than the less well-trained words. When in the Audience condition, however, the function sharpens out as would be predicted from the original Hullian formula seen in Chapter 3:

$$_sE_r = {_s}H_r \text{XD}$$

In the experiment there were five levels of sHr: 1, 2, 5, 10 and 25. It was

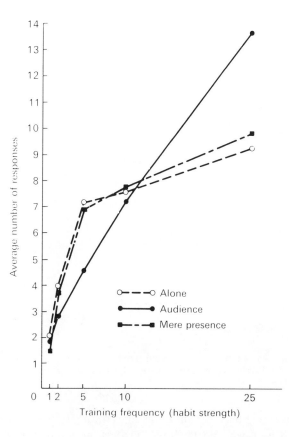

Figure 4. Average number of responses at different training frequencies. Copyright (1968) by the American Psychological Association. Reprinted by permission. (Figure from Cottrell et al., 1968)

therefore shown that having an audience affected the results in a way predicted by an increase in Drive (D). What is interesting is that when the audience was blindfolded the results did not change significantly. Cottrell et al. (1968) interpreted this as supporting the evaluation hypothesis: that the blindfolded audience could not evaluate and therefore did not increase subjects' Drive levels. In Chapter 8 we will see that this is not quite true, since the experimenter was present during the pseudorecognition trials. This means that the mere presence condition was more than mere presence.

A similar idea to Cottrell's was put forward at the same time by Henchy and Glass (1968). They emphasized the aversive drive effects of audiences (Brown and Farber, 1968) and argued that it was the subject's 'evaluation apprehension' which increased drive level. (The evidence now suggests that anticipating positive outcomes does not induce arousal in the same way as

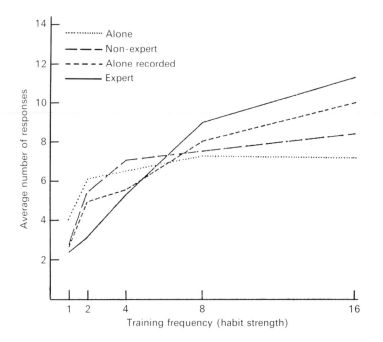

Figure 5. Average number of responses at different training frequencies. Copyright (1968) by the American Psychological Association. Reprinted by permission. (Figure from Henchy and Glass, 1968)

anticipating negative outcomes (e.g., Seta and Hassan, 1980). This has been most recently suggested by Geen and Bushman (1987), although Ferris, Beehr and Gilmore (1978) proposed the opposite. (see Chapter 5.7))

Henchy and Glass (1968) tested their evaluation apprehension hypothesis by comparing an Alone condition with three Presence conditions which varied in the degree of evaluation possible. In one of the Presence conditions the subjects were told that the audience consisted of two students (Non-Expert); in another the audience consisted of two staff members (Expert); and in the third, subjects were told that they were being filmed for later evaluation. The results presented showed that the Recorded and Expert conditions were significantly different from the Alone condition while the Non-Expert condition was not.

The tests again used the pseudorecognition task, but they gave training frequencies of 1, 2, 4, 8, and 16 trials. The results are shown in Figure 5. The main functions are as predicted by the Hullian reaction potential equation, with the well-learned dominant responses becoming more predominant with what is taken to be increased arousal from increased evaluation.

These results, of course, suggested that when evaluation was low, with the

Non-Experts, there was no special facilitation interaction effect. However, as later pointed out by Zajonc (1972b), there *was* a reasonable difference between the Alone and Non-Expert conditions (p < 0.07). So although evaluation clearly had an effect, there was still possibly an influence even with the mere presence of a low evaluation audience.

These two studies led to a very large number of new studies which tried to manipulate evaluative and non-evaluative conditions (see Figure 1). If social facilitation effects could be shown only when evaluation was possible, then mere presence was not a sufficient condition for the social facilitation interaction. Many studies were therefore aimed at constructing audiences with the potential to evaluate and audiences without such a potential, and compared these to Alone conditions. It turned out, eventually, that arranging the non-evaluative audience condition was very difficult. It is very difficult, if not impossible, to have someone else present who cannot evaluate the subject. Some possible guidelines for doing this are outlined in Chapter 8.

The studies which varied the conditions for evaluation and non-evaluation potential did so in many creative ways. Markus (1978), for example, had subjects change into laboratory clothes either alone, with someone there watching them, or with someone working in a corner not watching them. The clothes were either simple to put on or complex. The time taken to don the clothes was the dependent measure, recorded through a secret viewing panel.

On the whole, however, the many studies trying to isolate pure evaluation and pure non-evaluation had little real success. One recurring problem was the difficulty of reducing the possible evaluation when performing in front of others – especially when doing laboratory tasks. It does not take much for people to feel that they are being evaluated. These studies will all be reviewed in Chapter 8.

Group influences on individual performance

While accepting the broad approach of Zajonc, other theorists have looked more generally at how groups might influence the performance of individuals (Foot, 1973; Paulus, 1983; Seta, Paulus and Risner, 1977). Some, as we have seen, attempted to expand the *situational* variables affecting drive increase (Cottrell et al., 1968; Ferris, Beehr and Gilmore, 1978; Weiss and Miller, 1971). Paulus and colleagues attempted to expand the detail of how *group* variables, or social situational variables, might affect performance.

[Still others have tried to expand the *individual* variables that might affect arousal level. Examples of these are test-anxiety and manifest anxiety levels – for reviews see Borden, 1980, Paivio, 1965, and Geen, 1980]

Paulus (1983) suggested that other areas of social psychology find facilitation or inhibition of task performance under somewhat different social conditions. By including these other areas, a more general model of the effects of others was fashioned. For example, research on group size effects, crowding, social loafing, and brainstorming, all seem to bear on the social facilitation conditions.

Three variables were used by Paulus to construct a *general group influence model*. The influence of a group on individual performance was said to depend upon:

(1)   whether simple or complex tasks are performed;
(2)   whether there are increased or decreased consequences from the increased group size;
(3)   whether these consequences are negative or positive.

The combinations of these variables produce eight possible conditions (see Paulus, 1983, Figure 5–1). Some of these eight conditions lead to increased effort, increased arousal, or increased processing of task irrelevant stimuli. These will produce facilitation of simple performance and decrements of complex performance. Others lead to decreased effort, decreased arousal or processing of task irrelevant stimuli. These will produce decrements of simple performance and facilitation of complex performance.

This model, then, predicts over a wider range of group influence situations. What it gains in explanatory power, however, it perhaps loses in testability. Clear manipulation of all the proposed variables is needed, especially what is meant by increased or decreased consequences. The model is a good attempt, though, to 'put it all together', rather than assume the arousal notions will be the same in all situations. Some support has been given to the Paulus model by Griffith, Fichman & Moreland (1989).

4.4 Mere presence effects, fear and alertness

The later extensions to Zajonc's arousal theory (Zajonc, 1980) have already been discussed in Chapter 3. A number of problems were raised there. One was that mere presence was defined in a negative way: when all other effects of evaluation, competition and distraction are removed, what is left is the effect of the mere presence of another person. There was no positive theory of mere presence.

The only definite comments first came in a conference paper (Zajonc, 1972b). There it was suggested that the uncertainty in the other's behaviour led to mere presence effects. Response preparation was needed in the presence of a conspecific in case interaction became necessary. The response preparation consisted of a general increase in arousal level to initiate action.

Nothing more was done with this aspect of Zajonc's theory until 1982, because the theories and experiments had all concentrated on the interaction effect rather than on what might be happening in the mere presence situation. It was then suggested (Guerin and Innes, 1982) that a fruitful approach would be to consider the arousal as due to inherent threat or fear in the presence of another person. When dealing with strangers, the response preparation would consist of being ready for negative outcomes of the encounter. This seems especially likely for non-human animals for whom the sense of vigilance is tied up with response preparation for dangerous interactions. So this explanation also made it possible to tie together the animal and human social facilitation literatures.

It is obvious, however, that while we may be wary of strangers, *every* encounter with *every* other person is not wrought with fear. This means that if we can predict the conditions for fear of other people then these will also be the conditions for mere presence effects. In this way a more positive theory of mere presence effects is possible. Mere presence is no longer just the absence of other more direct effects.

It is not proposed that this account deals with all the social facilitation phenomena. Rather, it is concerned with explaining the possibly hard-wired mere presence effects and the possible similarities between human and non-human animals. The non-human animal literature will be reviewed in Chapter 7. Another feature of this theory is that it is an attempt to break out of thinking purely in terms of facilitation and inhibition of responses. For this reason, other behaviours, such as vigilance or monitoring responses, play a large role.

Alertness to social and non-social stimuli

To account for mere presence effects it is suggested that in the presence of a social being, a being that is animate, unpredictable and which affords social interaction, the basic response is to *monitor* this other being so far as is possible or necessary, rather than immediately being fearful. In this context, monitoring refers to a broad process of orientation (Lynn, 1966), vigilance and attention. Its purpose is to assess familiarity, possible threat, and impending interactions or encounters.

Monitoring social stimuli allows for response preparation in advance of any encounter. This point is made by Norman:

> If potential danger is to be discovered quickly, there must be continual monitoring of possible sources of evidence. Moreover, when danger is detected, the organism must be alerted. (1980, p. 10)

If, as suggested by Zajonc (1972b), social stimuli are the most unpredict-able, then regular monitoring, in the background of other social behaviours,

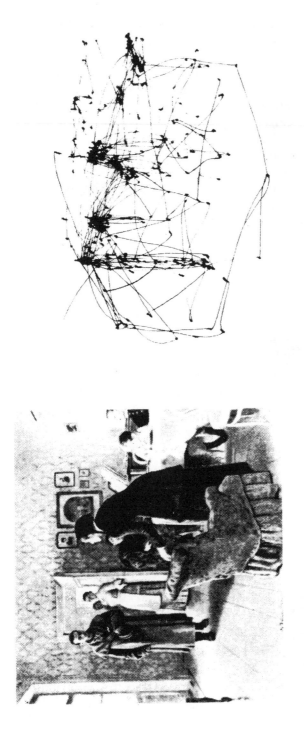

Figure 6. Eye-movements when people are present. Reproduced with permission of Plenum Publishing Corp. (Taken from Yarbus, 1967, Figure 108)

will centre on conspecifics. It is being argued that the mere presence of a social being elicits monitoring. In addition, there will be conditions in which monitoring is not necessary, and there will also be consequences of not being able to monitor when this is impossible.

Before dealing with these, two studies will be mentioned which show the differential attention to social and non-social stimuli. The first is the early eye-movement study of Yarbus (1967), an example of which is presented in Figure 6. The picture is on the left hand side and the eye-movements are recorded on the right hand side. It can be seen that subjects fixate most often on the persons present in a picture, particularly their faces, rather than non-social stimuli. Although these are only pictures of social stimuli, rather than the real thing, the results are certainly suggestive.

Heylen (1978), in an unpublished study supervised by J. Michael Innes at the University of Adelaide, had subjects perform a task in someone's office (supposedly due to lack of laboratory space). There was either no one present or else the occupant of the office worked at her desk paying no attention to the subject. Although subjects in both these groups subsequently remembered about the same amount of detail about the office environment, in the Presence condition attention away from the central task was given to the confederate rather than to the environment.

Further to this, analysis of two levels of task evaluation suggested that there was no reduction in attention to the task-irrelevant social stimulus. Even in the condition stressing very high levels of performance and evaluation, subjects still spent time monitoring the person present. This study, and that of Yarbus (1967), give some evidence that social beings are watched more than non-social objects.

[The study of Heylen (1978) also suggests that the hypothesis of Easterbrook (1959), to be discussed in Chapter 6, does not apply to irrelevant *social* stimuli which are more important. It was also pointed out by Heylen that the only other test of the attenuation of attending to other persons under increased arousal levels had only used pictures of persons (Cohen and Lezak, 1977). This had found an attenuation, and seemed to support Easterbrook's hypothesis for social stimuli. But when Heylen tried this with a real person, rather than a photograph, the effect was not found.]

These results must be treated with caution, since two studies *have* found attention to objects rather than persons (Argyle and Graham, 1976; Krupski and Boyle, 1978). In the first of these, subjects were engaged in a task and it was found that only occasional glances at the other were made. There was though, 'evidence of forces to avoid too much gaze at the other person' (Argyle and Graham, 1976, p. 6). It is likely that monitoring in normal situations will not consist of *staring* if there is a 'rule' against this. Rather, occasional glances will be made.

In the second study, children were found to look more at objects around them than at the experimenter (Krupski and Boyle, 1978). The experimenter, however, was sitting slightly behind the children and watching. So the children had to turn their heads to look and would have met the experimenter's gaze. Given the mutual gaze and head turning involved, it is not unexpected that the children did not gaze more often at the experimenter.

It can be suggested, then, that some evidence does show increased watching of social rather than non-social stimuli. So there is some support for saying that a basic process which takes place in the mere presence of another person is monitoring of that person's behaviour. This helps reduce the uncertainty in their actions (Zajonc, 1980).

Monitorability and alertness

How then does monitoring relate to arousal? It is suggested that monitoring, alertness and arousal are responses to varying degrees of threat, ranging from just the possibility of a threat to a direct attack. A basic response to a stranger is apprehension about possible threat. While there might also be apprehension about evaluation, fear is a more likely base than evaluation for comparing animal and human studies. The conditions for fear and threat, or the conditions for reducing fear and threat, will provide the conditions for mere presence effects. This will also be taken up in Chapter 7.

Factors affecting the communication and perception of threat have been discussed by Marler (1976) and Archer (1976), as conditions which provoke aggression. It seems reasonable, however, that social monitoring for possible or actual threat is an adaptation to aggression, functioning to avoid aggression before it happens. Only if we watch social stimuli can we avoid aggressive encounters.

That is, the first and most frequent response to the presence of a conspecific will be monitoring rather than aggression. It is not that 'every one of our fellow humans is a bearer of aggression-releasing signals' (Eibl-Eibesfeldt, 1978, p. 42). Rather, the mere presence of a conspecific initiates monitoring and not aggression in the first instance (McBridge, 1971). Monitoring, alertness, arousal and attack, can be seen as gradations in responses from neutrality to aggression or fear (Leyhausen, 1979).

The point being made is that a likely response to just the mere presence of a conspecific for both humans and non-human animals is monitoring. For animals, this seems to be monitoring for possible physical threats from the other. In humans, it might be for threats, for talk, or for other types of interactions. To develop this approach to mere presence in both humans and animals it is necessary to know the conditions under which humans might monitor for possible threat. To do this some animal literature will be reviewed briefly.

What conditions, then, suggest possible or actual threat? What conditions lead to increased monitoring and alertness? First, close proximity of the other can be threatening. With other things equal, there is greater danger from someone close than from someone at a distance. Monitoring may concentrate on those close by. There is a large body of evidence to suggest that having others close is alerting or aversive (Altman, 1975; Hall, 1966; Hayduk, 1983; Knowles, 1980; Patterson, 1976).

Second; vocal, facial, postural and gestural communications, are a common source of social unease. Regardless of disputed differences and similarities between species and between cultures, members of a group consistently recognize displeasure and threat by others in their group (Eibl-Eibesfeldt, 1974; Redican, 1975). While a red belly and head down position may be threatening to another stickleback, a raised clenched fist is commonly threatening among human cultures.

A more specific indicator of possible threat is that direction of eye-gaze of the other. It has been shown that humans and other social species have the ability to detect such information (Ellsworth and Langer, 1976; Gibson and Pick, 1963; Lord and Haith, 1974; Martin and Rovira, 1981). If another social being is attentive then there is a greater chance of an encounter. There is also some evidence that eye-gaze indeed can precipitate alertness and arousal (Ellsworth, Carlsmith and Henson, 1972, 1978; Gale, Lucas, Nissim and Harpham, 1972; Kleinke and Pohlen, 1971; McBride, King and James, 1965; Nichols and Champness, 1971).

The final mediating factor to be discussed is one of the most important – novelty or unfamiliarity. Research from a number of different areas suggests that strange or unfamiliar stimuli provoke initial fear, monitoring, arousal and avoidance (Berlyne, 1960; Bronson, 1968a; Scruton and Herbert, 1972), and play a major rôle in any subsequent aggression (Archer, 1976; Marler, 1976).

Unfamiliarity is especially important during social development, as evidenced by research on imprinting (Hess, 1973) and children's fears of strangers (Bronson, 1968b). In later life, it changes into reactions to interaction rituals, rather than to the mere sight of an unfamiliar person. Periodic monitoring, as well as interaction rituals such as hand shaking, are used in adult life to assess changes in friendly behaviour (Eibl-Eibesfeldt, 1974; Goffman, 1963).

Adult monitoring of unfamiliarity has also been found to occur where there is 'stimulus novelty' (Langer et al., 1976; Taylor and Langer, 1977), such as handicaps and non-normal features, attire, or behaviour. It has been found that when given a socially acceptable opportunity to look at such features, they are watched.

Further evidence of adult monitoring of unfamiliars comes from a study by Rutter and Stephenson (1979), who found that during an interaction subjects spent more time looking at the other if a stranger than if the other was a friend. Other studies also support this (Kissel, 1965; Scruton and Herbert, 1972; Swain, Stephenson and Dewey, 1982). There is also evidence from eye-movement studies that attention is directed rapidly to novel features (Loftus and Mackworth, 1978).

In summary, there are a number of social factors which might mediate monitoring. Those who are close, overtly threatening, unfamiliar, or who have uncertain behaviour, require more monitoring. The more predictable the behaviour of the other, the less attention is needed. In this way uncertainty may mediate an arousal reaction to the presence of others.

Predictions of mere presence effects for humans

It is being suggested that an initial reaction to the presence of another person is monitoring of their behaviour. If the purpose of monitoring is to check for possible threat then arousal increases might be explained in this way. Having discussed conditions under which monitored behaviour might appear threatening, predictions can now be made as to when the presence of others will be alerting or arousing and hence produce social facilitation effects even when there is no evaluation possible.

(1)   First, if a familiar other is present and periodic monitoring is possible, then no arousal or alertness increase would be expected. This contradicts the model of Zajonc (1965) for which *any* mere presence will be arousing.

(2)   Second, if another person is present and monitoring is *not possible* then it is predicted that arousal will increase because of the greater uncertainty about possible physical threat.

(3)   Arousal will also increase in the presence of a familiar or an unfamiliar person who is *directly* threatening (although this will not be classed as social facilitation) or when there is some other uncertainty about the other's behaviour. We are alerted to, aroused by, or 'keep on eye on', those around us who are unfamiliar, novel, or threatening.

It should be noted that this model predicts a difference between audience and co-action social facilitation studies, one of the few to do so. In the audience situation, the confederate's behaviour is usually unknown to the subject and the confederate is usually able to change position or change behaviour. Their behaviour is therefore inherently unpredictable and possibly unmonitorable. In co-action studies, on the other hand, the confederates (co-actors) are doing what the subject is doing and so their behaviour is more predictable. It can be predicted from this that mere presence effects would be less likely in co-action settings. This prediction will be taken up when reviewing the empirical studies in Chapter 8.

Three more points about this model will be made. First, it is concerned with possible physical threat and not evaluation threat. This ties it in with the literature on personal space and aggression rather than cognitive functioning. It is not proposed to replace one with the other – evaluation apprehension and threat apprehension may both occur depending upon the circumstances.

Second, it has sometimes been suggested that for humans, at least, evaluation effects are more powerful than any mere presence effects, and the former probably swamp the latter when both are concurrent. While this might be true in some settings, there are easy examples when it will not be true. If you are approached at night by a stranger in a dark alley, for example, how that person evaluates you will probably be your least concern.

A third point is that this model is aimed at a common link between the animal and human research. Although effects of the presence of others may not always be the same for human and non-human animals, this seems to be because of special human adaptations to the same effects (Freedman, 1979; Paulus, 1980; Paulus and Nagar, 1989). That is, the same reactions may be present but humans may have some special adaptations to circumvent them. For example, we may have adaptations, which animals do not, to help us put up with crowded conditions. But in spite of this, crowding is still felt to be aversive.

One adaptation (or strategy for the cognitivists) for reducing the suggested inherent threat from the presence of others, is to form groups of familiar others who need little monitoring because their behaviour is predictable (Bertram, 1978). The time saved can be used for other purposes. For example, monitoring of outsiders can be shared between group members. This has been found many times for human and non-human populations; less vigilance is required in groups than alone (Barash, 1972; Dimond and Lazarus, 1974; Wirtz and Wawra, 1986).

There is also a more direct link with social facilitation along these lines. It has been found that facilitation of eating by some animals in groups is accompanied by an individual reduction in the time spent in vigilance (Bertram, 1980; Hoogland, 1979; Jennings and Evans, 1980; Lazarus, 1979; Smith and Evans, 1973). This may be a cross-species adaptation to reduce threat-related behaviours and so allow a facilitation of other behaviours with the extra time available.

It is suggested, then, that the conditions for mere presence effects will be those conditions for which increases in fear related behaviours are found. If the other animal present is not threatening then no arousal and no mere presence effects will be found. If the other is familiar or their behaviour is predictable then no effects will be found. If the other cannot be monitored, so their behaviour cannot be checked, then effects will be found.

The experimental results for such conditions will be further pursued in Chapter 8, but one example of how such predictions work will be given here. This is done firstly to give an idea of how evaluation effects can be reduced in the setting up of mere presence experiments. Second, it shows how the monitorability hypothesis can be tested. And lastly, other parts of these results will be discussed in Chapter 5.6, on inhibition of behaviour. Readers can therefore refer back to this spot during that chapter.

Guerin (1983) had subjects perform a paired-associates learning task with either simple or complex associations to learn (taken from Cottrell, Rittle and Wack, 1967). In terms of Hullian Drive theory, the simple associates (such as mammoth-oversize and urgent-pressing) would be learned with less errors than the complex associates (such as gypsy-opaque and petite-yonder). Increasing the Drive levels should lead to an increase in errors for the complex task but a decrease in errors for the simple task.

The predictions from the monitoring model (Guerin and Innes, 1982) were that there would be greater arousal levels if the person present was looking directly at the subject or if the subject could not monitor the audience. If the audience was present but could be easily monitored then no difference was predicted to working alone.

One quarter of the subjects in the experiment worked alone in the room, with no other person present and the experimenter out of the room. This is shown in Figure 7 (A). In the Inattentive condition (I), another person was sitting in front of the subject, quietly working, such that the subject could easily monitor what they were doing. In the Behind (B) condition the confederate was sitting directly behind the subject so that the subject's body blocked the computer screen they were working from. Lastly, in the Looking condition (L) the confederate sat in the same place as for the Inattentive condition but sat facing towards the subject and watched the subject about 60 per cent of the time.

The question of evaluation then was one of making sure that the confederate could not evaluate what the subject was doing, or else any changes in performance could be due to evaluation effects rather than monitorability. First, the confederate's presence was explained in such a way that they did not really know what the task was about. After the practice trials the experimenter explained that he had to be near the computer when the experiment was over or else the DecTape (the ancient, but efficient, equipment was run from a programme tape on a PDP-8) could jam and be ruined. It was explained that someone from the adjoining departmental computer section (who knew nothing about the experiment) would sit in to finish everything up when the experiment was concluded.

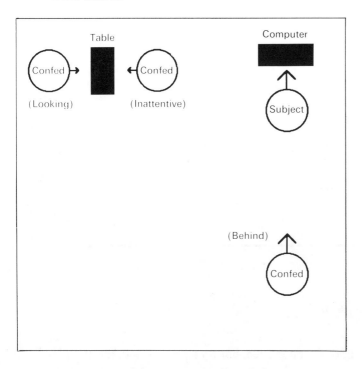

Figure 7. The experimental room used for Guerin, 1983

The next step was to make sure that even a naive confederate could not figure out what the subject was doing and therefore evaluate them. To do this, the confederate was positioned in various ways so they could not see the task. In the Inattentive and Looking conditions the confederate could not see the screen to see the correct associates, so they would not know whether the subject had given correct or incorrect responses. In the Behind condition the confederate was seated behind the subject so the subject's body blocked the screen.

The final consideration was that the subjects' responses (guesses at the correct associates) had to be tape-recorded because it was not possible for them to type the answers into the computer. This constituted a possible source of evaluation (being tape-recorded), but at least it was the same for all subjects across all conditions, even in the Alone condition.

The performance results of this experiment are shown in Figure 8. With the simple task, the predicted effects did not show up with statistical tests of significance. This was partly due to the large amount of variance in the simple associates data. With the complex task, the predicted effect did occur, and there was a significant worsening of performance in the Behind and

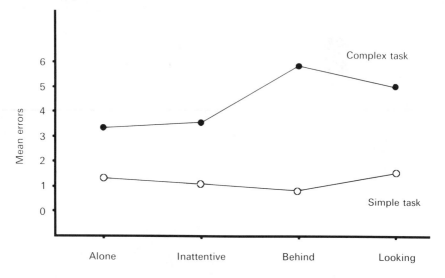

Figure 8. Mean number of errors in paired-associates learning. (Data drawn from Guerin, 1983)

Looking conditions, as predicted, but no difference between the Alone and Inattentive conditions. The two-way interaction across both simple and complex associates and the four social conditions was significant.

The results give support for the monitoring model therefore, except that no effect was found for the simple task. In Chapter 8 all the studies using the paired-associates task are compared, and a similar pattern of responding shown. The purpose here is to point out that only when the confederate was inattentive and the subject could monitor them throughout was no effect found. When the confederate could not be monitored (Behind) or was looking at the subject and therefore could not be monitored (Looking) were effects found. As mentioned earlier, some other results from this study which are even more surprising will be discussed in Chapter 5.6.

There are only three other studies which have directly tested parts of the monitoring model of mere presence effects (Guerin, 1986a, 1989a, 1989b), but others which have set up similar conditions will be reviewed in Chapter 8. It should again be mentioned that the monitoring model is only meant to account for part of the mere presence phenomenon. It does not suggest that evaluation or other social facilitation effects are not also important, just that monitorability plays a rôle in mere presence effects. There could also be other factors within mere presence effects which have not yet been isolated.

5 Social conformity theories

All of the theories in the present chapter have been put together because they relate to a few common points. They all deal with a change in the social valuation of particular behaviours in the presence of other persons. That is, without directing the behaviour of the subject explicitly, the presence of another person can lead to an increased awareness of the *social value* of certain behaviours, of social standards, or of the social consequences of behaviours. This increased awareness can lead to increased conformity to those standards. These theories do not concern 'hard-wired' patterns since the relevant social standards must be learned at some point in the socialization process.

The ideas contained in these theories have all been raised in Chapter 2 when discussing the pre-1965 literature. These include the automaticity of behaviour (Triplett, 1898), the effects of conformity to social norms (Allport, 1924a), changes in self-attention (Ekdahl, 1929; Ruger, 1910), and changes towards looking good in the eyes of others and presenting an impression on them (Burri, 1931; Hanawalt and Ruttiger, 1944; Murphy and Murphy, 1931; Seidman et al., 1957).

These theories are mostly human-specific. With a few exceptions (5.5), it is hard to see how they could be adapted to explain the animal literature. Most of them are also a product of the rise of the cognitive approach in social psychology, although some still retain drive assumptions (5.1, 5.2, 5.4, 5.6). They do not depend, however, upon cognitive assumptions so discussion of the rise of cognitive social psychology will be left until the next chapter.

5.1 Evaluation apprehension

The first example of a social conformity theory has already been discussed in Chapter 4. The learned *evaluation apprehension* models of Cottrell (1968) and Henchy and Glass (1968) are examples of social conformity models because they assume that when performing a task it is socially valued to do as well as possible and to show high task ability. When performing in front of others, therefore, subjects become apprehensive about doing well and try to conform to the expected standards. There would be no apprehension about evaluation if people were not expected to conform to some standards.

As we saw in the last chapter, Henchy and Glass (1968) suggested that negative evaluations from others are especially emphasized in our society, where succeeding in performance and not making a poor show are learned early in childhood. This is also suggested by the interactions found between audience effects and a knowledge of task ability (Geen, 1981a; Sanna and Shotland, 1990; Seta and Hassan, 1980). So even in the *passive presence* of another person, responding can become socially directed, even if the person present does not overtly direct or cue the subject, because there are more general social expectations about how people should perform. Put another way, there is a norm to do well at tasks, and subjects try to conform with this, and they are therefore apprehensive when they are evaluated.

5.2 Objective self-awareness

The second theory of social conformity effects is that of objective self-awareness (Duval and Wicklund, 1972; Wicklund and Duval, 1971). This was also the first theory to attempt a break with drive or arousal mechanisms, although it turns out to rely on a drive-like notion despite this (Geen and Gange, 1977). Since this theory contains elements in common with other social conformity theories which follow, it will be dealt with in some detail. It must be kept in mind, however, that it was designed to account for social phenomena other than just social facilitation, such as deindividuation, opinion change, attribution and helping (Duval, Duval and Neely, 1979; Duval and Wicklund, 1973; Wicklund and Duval, 1971). The theory will be outlined by giving the argument point by point.

(1)   This theory suggested that one effect of the presence of another person was to increase *objective self-awareness*. Objective self-awareness refers to a state of awareness such that attention is given to your self as an object-for-others. That is, you start viewing yourself as others might see you; as an object of attention rather than with a subject's sense of flow. So the presence of others leads people to focus attention on how others perceive and evaluate them.

(2)   It was next argued that the subject's increase in objective self-awareness, attending to how others perceive and evaluate them, involved the subject's appraisal of their own personal ideals, goals and abilities.

(3)   When performing a task in a state of objective self-awareness, people attend to their performance goals. The state of other goals is not considered attention-getting in laboratory task settings.

(4)   It was further argued that we usually fall short of our ideal goals. Our plans for achieving goals do not usually work out as planned, so the ideals we can think about are not usually met in real life.

(5)   The next step argued that falling short of ideals and abilities leads to an aversive cognitive state. We do not like being aware that we are not meeting our ideals, so the objective self-awareness state in these cases will be aversive.

(6)   It was then suggested that this aversive state can act as a motivator to do better. One way of reducing the aversion is to try and do better. Whether or not we succeed in doing this depends further upon the nature of the task.

(7)   For *simple tasks*, the motivation to do better explained the facilitation of performance found in social facilitation effects. People are merely trying harder and therefore do better at simple tasks.

(8)   For *complex tasks* it was argued that we overstep our abilities when trying harder – and this leads to a decrement in performance (Wicklund, 1975).

The objective self-awareness argument includes, then, quite a few processes or assumptions. Combined, they argue that the passive presence of another person is sufficient to increase striving towards valued behaviours. The steps have been spelt out in detail because later theories of social facilitation have used some of the same steps but not all. (Note in passing that this explanation, like most others, tries to explain only the facilitation of simple tasks and inhibition on complex tasks, although room exists to explain other behaviours.) Let us now examine the steps more closely.

Steps (1) and (2) outline the major objective self-awareness tenets. People can be in a state of attending to their thoughts, goals and wishes. This is similar to the later notion of 'state orientation' (Kuhl, 1985).

Step (2) claims that performance goals are foremost when in a laboratory situation. While this step allows for other goals in non-laboratory situations, it ignores other goals and aspirations which might occur in the laboratory, such as impression management towards the experimenter or finishing the task as quickly as possible. These two arguments of Wicklund and Duval do not say whether personal goals or social goals are most relevant or indeed how they might come to be important. The inference is that there is a social valuation placed on trying to do well – or at least giving the impression of trying to do well.

Steps (3) and (4) suggest that people fall short of their aspirations and that this state is aversive. This assumes that people have unrealistic assumptions about what they can achieve. More recent work has suggested that people strategically adjust their aspirations to fit their performance, so the interplay of variables is more complicated than originally suggested by Wicklund and Duval (Bandura, 1977; Deci and Ryan, 1980; Harackiewicz, Sansone and Manderlink, 1985; Mayes, 1978). So while falling short of ideals might be aversive, people can dynamically adjust their goals, or provide excuses, to cover for this. They do not *necessarily* reduce the aversion by trying harder (5 and 6).

It is also of note here that the aversive state is related to drive constructs (Geen and Gange, 1977). Indeed, it is clearly related to dissonance and cognitive inconsistency aversive states. This means that it suffers from the same criticisms as drive theory, which were outlined in detail in Chapter 3.

Steps (7) and (8) are also shared with other theories of social facilitation (Carver and Scheier, 1981a). A point to note here is that while the explanation of simple task facilitation is relatively straightforward, extra assumptions are needed to explain inhibition of complex tasks. Carver and Scheier (1981a) do the same as we shall see in 5.3. (In fact, behaviour inhibition theory (5.6) is the only theory which deals specifically with inhibition of complex tasks. That theory, on the other hand, has to add assumptions to deal with the facilitation of simple tasks!)

While there is nothing wrong with adding extra assumptions to deal with extra cases, these theories lose the elegance of Zajonc's theory – which dealt with both simple and complex tasks in the same assumptions. Once theories start explaining these cases separately, one wonders whether they should even be called a single theory of social facilitation. It also becomes a problem when any result can be explained because there are too many assumptions made by the theory.

While the objective self-awareness explanation has some appeal, it also has shortcomings. In particular, it is difficult to specify which ideals or goals are being attended. It is assumed by the theory that these are the ones set up by the experimental procedure – to perform well at the task – but this cannot be adequately shown. As mentioned above, there might be other goals in the laboratory situation besides performing as well as possible.

This problem is the equivalent theoretical problem to one pointed out for drive theories (3.2). Because the same problem will crop up with most of the theories still to be outlined, it is worth going over it in some detail here (and it will be re-emphasized in Chapter 9).

The problem for drive theories was that of how habit hierarchies can ever be specified in an actual situation, and coupled with this, how can we predict behaviour if we cannot *independently* specify these responses? While experiments such as that of Cottrell et al. (1968) were able to train responses of different habit strengths during a training period, when we come to analysing a real situation we have little idea of what are the responses and what are their relative strengths. We cannot use the social facilitation effects to prove that one response was stronger than another since it must assume this in the first place. Even the experiment of Cottrell et al. (1968) did not have a measure of the hierarchy independent of the social facilitation performance scores.

With objective self-awareness theory, the problem is one of specifying which goals subjects will attend to when objective self-awareness is increased. Wicklund and Duval assume that this will be the goal of doing well at the task, but this has not been shown independently of the social facilitation effects themselves.

An example of the social facilitation research engendered by objective self-awareness theory is that of Wicklund and Duval (1971: Experiment 3). These authors did not directly test that other people increase objective self-awareness, but chose instead to show that the same changes in performance could be found when a non-social source of increased objective self-awareness was manipulated.

To increase objective self-awareness, Wicklund and Duval used a mirror placed in front of the experimental subjects. They argued that the mirror would increase objective self-awareness in much the same way as the presence of other people, and so subjects would think more and work harder in their goal of performing well, and therefore do better on a simple task and worse on a complex task. They also argued that being video-taped would have the same effect. As we shall see (8.4), these manipulations have been widely used since.

For the test Wicklund and Duval only used a simple task. This was to copy German prose from a story. Subjects initially performed this for five minutes while copying the first passage. In front of all subjects was a mirror, facing the opposite direction. Before starting on the second passage the subjects in the Mirror condition had a mirror turned around so it was directly facing the subjects. This did not happen to subjects in the No Mirror condition: their mirror was left facing the wall. (It had been explained to subjects at the start that the mirror was there for a mirror-writing task which was supposed to be the third part of the experiment. This gave Wicklund and Duval a reason for the presence of the mirror.)

Wicklund and Duval (1971) found that on this simple task, the presence of the mirror led to a greater increase between the first copying period and the second. Those in the Mirror group improved their scores by an average of 43.33 words while those in the No Mirror condition only increased on average by 17.65 words. The argument, therefore, was that the facilitation of this simple task was brought about by objective self-awareness and resembled the results of social facilitation studies. They therefore suggested that the same increase in objective self-awareness probably occurs in the presence of another person, although this was not measured directly.

5.3 Control Systems Model

The model of Carver and Scheier (1978)

Perhaps the most developed model of this group is that of Carver and Scheier (1978; 1981a; 1981b; 1982). Their theory is based on a control systems model of self-attention (Carver, 1979). Rather than base self-attention processes on aversive drive reduction, as had Wicklund and Duval (1971), Carver and Scheier (1981a) used a cybernetic or controls systems approach suggested by Miller, Galanter and Pribram (1960). The basis of the control system is a test unit or TOTE (Test-Operate-Test-Exit) which matches an input to a standard, and then goes on to something else. This is a classic negative feedback loop.

For Carver and Scheier (1981a) the standards matched were standards of behaviour, which could come from self or others. The control process was therefore a behaviour standard matching process. Self-attention was assumed to be a periodic control process to test behaviour against a comparison. The system operated in a negative feedback loop to change performance until it matched the standard more closely.

If, for example, you have a standard of doing thirty pushups every morning, then you would also have a periodic check to compare your current behaviour against this standard. If for three mornings in a row you had only done a total of four pushups, then the comparison would trigger you to try and again match your standard – so you would work harder at it the next morning.

Carver and Scheier ingeniously applied this systems model to many applied and basic problems of social psychology (Carver and Scheier, 1981a, 1982), including aggression, reactance, social comparison, deindividuation, expectancy theory, health behaviours, and cognitive dissonance. In each case the focus was upon: (1) how people attend to their thoughts and behaviour; (2) how they discover discrepancies between current behaviour and standards of behaviour (both public and private); (3) how they then operate to decrease the discrepancies.

To apply this theory to the social facilitation setting, it was assumed that the presence of others (or a mirror) leads to an *increase* in self-attention and testing against standards. Like the theory of objective self-awareness, in laboratory situations the relevant standard was assumed to be that of doing as well as possible at the task – the standard induced by the experimenter. The operations to enhance conformity to the standard in the presence of another person leads to the facilitation of performance at a *simple* task. This is not the result of motivation to reduce an aversive state (Wicklund, 1975) but of a control system discrepancy-reducing mechanism (see Carver and Scheier, 1981a, p. 144).

For the explanation of the inhibition of *complex* responses, no single explanation was given. Instead (again like the objective self-awareness explanation), a number of different mechanisms were said to operate. While attending to standards attention is taken away from the task, which can lead to a worse performance on a complex task. It was also suggested that complex tasks have a number of incompatible, competing standards – if subjects try to conform to all of these it can lead to a worse performance. Finally, the subjects' expectancies of doing well at the complex task will be diminished if repeated self-assessments show that the standard is not being matched. This, it was argued, is most likely to happen on a complex task and leads to 'cognitive withdrawal' and an impairment of performance.

In these ways Carver and Scheier predicted the key finding of social facilitation research: a facilitation of simple responding and an impairment of complex responding. No drive state assumptions were necessary, although no reasons were given as to *why* the organism might want or need to reduce performance discrepancies. They were just assumed to do so. So nothing is given to replace the motivational rôle of the aversion reduction used in Wicklund and Duval's explanation. The control system is motivationless in the normal sense.

A further distinction made by Carver and Scheier (1981a) was between private self-attention and public self-attention. The former refers to the self-awareness of private thoughts and feelings and private standards of performing. Public self-attention refers to viewing oneself as others view, with an emphasis on public standards of behaviour.

Originally it was proposed that mirrors and audiences had the same effects (Carver and Scheier, 1980), following on from the reasoning of Wicklund and Duval (1971). Later it was suggested that whereas mirrors increase private self-attention, audiences increase public self-attention (Carver and Scheier, 1981b). With an audience we should compare behaviour with a public standard of performance; with a mirror we should compare with personal standards. (There is some indirect evidence against this, however; see Diener and Srull, 1979.)

In cases where an audience is evaluating an *already internalized standard*, the result should be the same whether private or public self-attention is primed, since the private and public standards are the same. This is what Carver and Scheier had tried to do in their earlier experiments: 'We specifically attempted to choose a situation where it would not matter whether the subjects were trying to do well for themselves or trying to look good for the audience' (Carver and Scheier, 1981b, p. 563). This condition applies to their social facilitation tests.

In cases where the public standards of behaviour are not the same as an individual's private standards of behaviour, mirrors and audiences should have different effects. The audience should lead to attention and behaviour change towards the public standards; the mirror towards the private standards.

In a test of their basic model, Carver and Scheier (1981b) tested subjects with the task (outlined in 5.2) used by Wicklund and Duval (1971) but with an Audience condition included. Subjects were asked to copy a passage of German prose initially without any intervention. One third then repeated this in the same way, another third in front of a mirror, and the final third with the experimenter carefully observing them.

The results showed that subjects in both the audience condition and in the mirror condition improved scores on this simple task over their baseline measures. Those in the control condition did not. Overall, the control group improved by 0.38, the Mirror group by 20.18, and the Audience group by 34.78.

These results suggested that observing audiences had similar effects to mirrors, and it was argued that this was because they both increased self-attention process. As mentioned above, it was later pointed out that this occurred only because the public and private standards of performance were the same in the situation set up by the experimenters. The subjects probably had no interest in doing anything other than following the experimenter's instructions to do well at the task, so the public standards were internalized by the subjects.

It should be pointed out here, as it will be in Chapter 8, that the experimenter was present through all the experiment, but 'retreated to a desk at the far corner of the room outside the subject's visual field, where he busied himself with paperwork.' (Carver and Scheier, 1981a, p. 294) So the subjects in the control Alone condition were not really alone at all. This situation was close to resembling a mere presence (of experimenter) setting, but unfortunately, no true Alone condition was run to look for mere presence effects.

Critical discussion

A number of problems with this model can be raised. In common with most self-attention models it is hard to see how the large animal literature can be explained in this way, even though in principle, control systems theory could be applied to all self-regulating organisms. That chickens have behaviour standards for eating and have periodic self-attentive checks, seems doubtful. It seems clear, though, that Carver and Scheier (1981a) were only interested in human studies and in particular, in explaining the evaluative effects of an observing audience – not mere presence effects (Carver and Scheier, 1978, p.

329). This is also reflected in their explication of drive-theory, where they centre on the Cottrell (1968) and Henchy and Glass (1968) evaluative effects rather than Zajonc's mere presence effects.

A second difficulty is that of specifying which standards are operative. In their experiments, Carver and Scheier assume this to be that of trying to do well at the task, especially if there is social comparison information available to subjects. Even in the laboratory, however, there are social standards concerning how to interact with the person present, how to act like a subject, and personal standards of how to control one's outcomes.

While these standards may be trivial alongside a salient, experimenter-induced, task performance standard, outside the laboratory it is harder to predict the relevant standards which will influence behaviour. Even in the laboratory, subjects may feel strange when they are not allowed to interact with the person present. (A number of studies report, in fact, that subjects try to interact with confederates and have to be dissuaded from doing so.)

This problem is, in essence, the same problem raised earlier for both drive and objective self-awareness theories. Away from the laboratory-induced response hierarchies, it is difficult to rank dominant responses and so predict behaviour. Tests of drive theories needed the artificial induction of response hierarchies; likewise here, testing control systems theory requires the artificial induction of social standards. The problem is not just that these results are ecologically invalid; it is that they may be testing artificial phenomena due to imposing unusually salient and obvious manipulations.

This highlights a further problem with Carver and Scheier's manipulations of behaviour standards. They emphasize that subjects should try and do as well as possible at the task to make salient that particular standard. The *directedness* of this manipulation is unlike the more subtle operation of standards in real life; furthermore, it is likely to lead to competition and other direct motivation effects when other people are present. This does not affect the position of Carver and Scheier because they are interested in any phenomena which arise from self-attention processes. It does mean, however, that their experiments are certainly not dealing with mere presence effects, and are likely to be rich in other social psychological processes.

Despite these misgivings, the model of Carver and Scheier (1981a) is probably the clearest attempt to formulate the processes mediating behaviour changes and the usually unspoken, but ever present, social conformity processes. Indeed, most of the other theories of social conformity and social normative processes which are dealt with here can be explained just as well in terms of the control systems model.

The theories of self are now an important part of cognitive social psychology, and are usually taken for granted. The work of Carver and Scheier (1982) was groundbreaking in this endeavour. They did, however, have something that is presently missing in modern cognitive theories of self-processes, and that is a relationship with motor responding or overt behaviour.

Many of the current self-theories give hypothesized details and models of how self-schemata affect information processing, but few if any get back to how this all affects behaviour on the environment which can then affect perceptual inputs again in turn. One strength of the Carver and Scheier position, as I see it, is that the Operate phase of their TOTE allowed for real changes in behaviour rather than changes in self-schema which somehow are supposed to translate back into action. In this sense it is a pity more social psychologists do not work within the controls systems framework when dealing with self-processes. Like Piaget's cognitive models, the control systems of Carver and Scheier do not get lost in thought because there is an explicit Operate phase.

5.4 Self-presentation models

There are two models of social conformity effects based on the work of Goffman (1959), who investigated the self-presentation or impression management strategies people use to create and maintain an impression to others. For example, people can present themselves as a nice person in order to ingratiate themselves to others; or they might present themselves as a scholar, and attempt to act knowledgeable when they can.

The self-presentation and impression management approach is one which has been used in many areas of social psychology (Baumeister, 1982; Schlenker, 1980; Tedeschi, 1981). It is theoretically situated halfway between the structural models and the functional models of social psychology. It does not deal with many structural details of the cognitive processes mediating self-presentation but with how goals are achieved functionally. Similarly it does not deal with the many details of why this function or that might be important to the person, just with how they are achieved.

For example, if someone wanted to present themselves as a scholarly type of person, it is not questioned why they might do this. Baumeister (1982), for example, puts the motivation for self-presentation down to potential rewards from others and to 'self-fulfillment'. This hardly serves to *explain* the motivation. Similarly, most self-presentation theories are not concerned with how a person cognitively processes the views of scholars, but rather, they look for behaviour and behaviour changes.

One of the two social facilitation models relates self-presentation to drive or arousal notions:

Although the mere presence of others may produce some drive . . . it appears that the evaluative presence of others produces even more drive, which is probably due to concerns with self-presentation.

(Baumeister, 1982, p. 19)

With others present we become involved in self-presentation, and the possible embarrassment from negative evaluation leads to increased drive with subsequent effects. That is, it is the concern of presenting oneself as relatively normal or conforming that underlies these strategies. This view was not developed beyond the suggestion and suffers from the same criticisms as other drive theories, outlined in Chapter 4.

The second account of a self-presentation theory does not use a drive mechanism (Bond, 1982). With this view, facilitation of *simple* responses comes from the subject performing better to 'manage a performance compatible with an image of competence' (Bond, 1982, p. 1043). Only in the presence of others will impression management occur. In performing *complex* tasks in front of others it was argued that loss of face from making errors leads to embarrassment which is 'an indiscriminant incapacitator of continued role performance, an impediment to cognitive and motor control' (p. 1043).

The 'image of competence' suggests that people present themselves in a conforming way so as to avoid negative evaluations. People conform to social or private standards by presenting themselves as such. In this, the theory of Bond (1982) can be seen to be one of a social conformity process with self-presentation as a mediating factor.

Both of the self-presentation views relate closely to the self-awareness theories, the first to the objective self-awareness aversive drive theory (Duval and Wicklund, 1972); the second to the control system model (Carver and Scheier, 1981a). In this latter case, each can explain the other's viewpoint, as will be outlined in Chapter 9. For this reason any experiments purporting to show self-presentation effects on task performance can be explained by the other social conformity theories as well.

The one study which has used self-presentation theory as its basis did not include any independent measures of self-presentation (Bond, 1982). This means that the changes in task performance can be explained in any number of other ways. Just finding changes in performance does not prove that subjects made an active regulation of their public image. Until more direct measures of these processes are made, the results will be equivocal.

5.5 A behaviour analysis of social facilitation

Behaviour analysis has been widely misunderstood by psychologists, and is usually thought of as a slight variation on Hull's behaviourism. It is much more powerful than this, however, and is not closely linked to the work of Hull. Because it is relatively unfamiliar (though most psychologists *think* they know what it is about!), and because it is so powerful as a general psychological foundation, this section will develop an approach to social facilitation in some detail.

The basis for behaviour analysis is the three-term contingency (Sidman, 1986; Skinner, 1938). This analysis looks for the stimulus contexts in which a behaviour occurs, examines the behaviour itself, and looks for the consequences (reinforcers or punishers) which maintain the behaviour and make them more likely to recur. For any behaviour, it is assumed, there are contingent consequences which make them more likely to recur in the same or similar contexts. The contexts are called discriminative stimuli because they discriminate different availabilities of consequences. They are not the same as Hull's stimuli.

In the most simple experimental example, a rat might press a bar in a cage and receive food only when a green light is on. If the animal does not receive any food contingent upon bar pressing when the green light is off, then the green light is discriminative of the consequences of bar pressing. The animal will gradually stop responding when the green light is off, not because it 'realizes' that the green light means food, but because there are no functional consequences when the green light is off (Catania, 1984).

For any behaviours, therefore, we need to analyse the consequences which maintain them and the particular contexts in which they are maintained. This applies to all types of behaviours, not just the obvious motor movements such as bar-pressing. This includes verbal behaviours, thinking, remembering, perceiving, imaging, imagining, and even 'realizing'.

For example, under some circumstances (but not others), people will have a series of thoughts about a topic (cf. 'cognitive responding', Petty and Cacioppo, 1986). To look at what maintains this thinking, the behaviour analyst will look for the consequences which occur with and without thinking. There are obviously many positive consequences of thinking which can make the behaviour more likely to recur (cf. maintenance of cognitive responding, Guerin & Innes, 1990). A behaviour analysis will also look for the contexts in which such consequences occur, their discriminative contexts. The resulting analysis is nothing like a Hullian stimulus-response link, since the context does not trigger the response in any sense, but 'selects' it. This occurs in the same way (metaphorically) as evolution selects; the environment does not trigger an evolutionary change but makes a change more likely to occur again in that context.

This is a very simplified account of behaviour analysis (Catania, 1984). The particular ways in which discriminative contexts control (or select) the production of behaviour can be quite complex, and the consequences which maintain behaviour for humans are usually not as obvious as the food given to animals (Guerin, 1992, in press). The consequences can be intermittent, generalized across many behaviours, and contingent themselves upon other consequences (Catania, 1984; Vaughan and Michael, 1982). In particular, the consequences maintaining social behaviour in humans are usually quite subtle (Guerin, 1991, 1992, in press). In addition, the behaviours themselves in humans are more complex and have special properties (verbal behaviours in particular; Guerin, in press).

A behaviour analysis of social facilitation starts then with the three-term contingency. The presence of another person might control our behaviour in two possible ways: as a mediator of consequences (or establishing operations, Michael, 1982, 1988), or as a discriminative context for other types of consequences.

In the case of a person directly acting to present contingent consequences, this is not covered by our definition of social facilitation, since social facilitation does not include cueing and directing of behaviour by the person present. Such cases must be covered as separate research topics, cooperation, conflict, imitation, and social interaction (see Deguchi, 1984; Hake and Olvera, 1978). This leaves the analysis of social facilitation as an analysis of the person present having been a discriminative context for other consequences in the past.

Other people as discriminative stimuli

As mentioned above, the concept of discriminative stimulus goes well beyond the 'stimulus' of Hullian Stimulus-Response behaviourism. A discriminative stimulus is not a trigger for behaviour, a learned habit, or an association (cognitive or otherwise) between a stimulus and a response. If the presence of another person is a discriminative stimulus it means that subjects have previously learned that in the presence of another person the consequences contingent upon behaviour change in some way. This is important for social facilitation theory because it means that without directly cueing the subject, the presence of others can reliably change behaviour. The problem, then, is to identify the consequences 'signalled' by the presence of another person. These are to be found in the learning history of the individual, not in their heads.

(While it is not a word used by behaviour analysts, we might say here that the presence of others 'signals' a number of consequences. The word is not normally used by behaviour analysts since it is not a primitive term and needs to be further analysed. In particular, it does not imply that a learning history is needed before signals work. But for present purposes it will suffice. For more on this see Michael, 1980, 1982; Peterson, 1982.)

In the case of animals, the rôle of discriminative contexts are easy to test, since the learning history of the animal can be controlled if necessary (e.g., Barrett, 1977). For example, the presence of other birds in the past history of a pigeon will usually have been discriminative of food availability, since flocks tend to congregate around food sources. So in the presence of another bird, pecking has usually been reinforced, whereas it would not have been reinforced as much when alone. In the future, therefore, pecking will occur at a higher rate when in the presence of other birds.

This means that, in general, birds will peck more in the presence of others (Hake and Laws, 1967; Hake, Powell and Olsen, 1969; Wheeler and Davis, 1967). This occurs because, in general, most birds have been reinforced for pecking more when with other birds than when alone. One can experiment with animals by training a different learning history in the presence of other birds, and much more subtle ones (Fushimi, 1990; Hake, Donaldson and Hyten, 1983; Millard, 1979), rather than just relying on the 'natural' generalized consequences which occur in the presence of other birds.

In the case of humans, there are a number of problems with identifying the discriminated consequences. First, we cannot control the past history of humans (Wanchisen, 1990). Only with work on very young children might this be at all possible. This means that we are restricted to studying rather obvious and generalized discriminations which occur in the presence of other people, and in particular, ones that are socially produced and therefore widespread amongst the populations typically used.

To overcome this problem there are only a few research strategies. One can look at the behaviour in another culture which affords different discriminative consequences (see Guerin, 1992). One can also try to get verbal measures of reinforcement histories from the subjects (Chase, 1988). Lastly, one can try and study the effects of training specific discriminative histories with human subjects as far as this is possible (LeFrancois, Chase and Joyce, 1988; Weiner, 1964), although the research is battling against the subjects' lifetime of discriminated consequences. These are not particularly satisfactory methods at present.

A second problem with identifying consequences in social behaviour is that social consequences are notoriously diffuse, and multiply-determined (Skinner, 1957). Reinforcers such as providing money, attention, affection, or positive regard are used by many people in many settings to reinforce many different behaviours. Even negative reinforcers such as avoidance of social disapproval have the same quality: they are multiply-determined.

While this diffuseness of social reinforcers is useful, and probably necessary, to maintain social relations, it provides problems for analysis. It would be far easier for analysis if the control of all social interactions was purely governed by specific demands which had to be met for specific reinforcers which could not be obtained in any other way. But multiply-determined social (which includes economic) reinforcers can control a range of different behaviours. This has properties and side-effects which are important for an analysis of both social and verbal behaviour (Guerin, 1992, in press). It means, for example, that social psychology might only be properly able to deal with very general consequences (Guerin, 1991).

Verbally governed behaviour

There is one other way in which behaviour analysis can make predictions about social facilitation phenomena. For behaviour analysts, the foundations for verbal behaviour and the use of symbolic systems are social (Lee, 1984; Skinner, 1957). This is because the non-social environment has no discriminative consequences for verbal behaviour, so other people *must* be involved in the contingencies if they are to be maintained. This view provides a foundation for social construction and social representation theories of social behaviour (see Guerin, in press; Mead, 1934; Wittgenstein, 1953). The contingency principles for verbal behaviours (including thinking and gestures) are the same as for any other behaviours such as bar-pressing, but the necessity of having others in the contingencies to maintain the verbal behaviours gives them special properties.

An interesting prediction from this is that verbal behaviour will be more likely when other people are around. Some of the social facilitation tests utilizing word associations have indeed found this. We have usually been reinforced for speaking only when other people are present.

There is a more interesting prediction, however. The behaviour analytic view is that verbal instructions can, under some circumstances, control behaviour (Hayes, 1989; Hayes, Zettle and Rosenfarb, 1989; Malott and Garcia, 1991; Skinner, 1969; Vargas, 1988). This applies to both instructions from others, 'wash your hands before eating' and to self-instructions, 'I must wash my hands before eating'. Because of the social basis of verbal behaviour, other people will be needed in the contingencies to maintain the production of instructions and the instruction following. This means people are more likely to produce and follow self-instructions when someone else is present, even if that person does not know about the instructions. The mere presence of another person makes the production of the verbal behaviours more likely.

While this view has not had much testing yet (see Hayes, Rosenfarb, Wulfert, Munt, Korn and Zettle, 1985) it promises to be useful. The importance for social facilitation is that the difference between following self-instructions and other people's instructions corresponds, for the behaviour analyst, to the induction of private versus public self-awareness, except that the basis of the 'awareness' is better spelled out as verbal behaviour. This also fits with a general conclusion from this chapter that the presence of others means an increase in the *control* taken over behaviour. This is equivalent to an increase in verbally governed behaviour for behaviour analysis.

The behaviour analysis of social facilitation suggests, then, that in the presence of others there are two possible effects. First, the presence of the person can act as a discriminative stimulus for certain consequences which have generally, in the past, been reinforced when others are present. Second, the presence of others can lead to an increase in following self-instructions, which might change the consequences being contacted in the situation. (DeGrandpre, Buskist and Cush, 1990; Hayes, Brownstein, Haas and Greenway, 1986).

Behaviour analysis and social conformity theories

Viewing people as discriminative stimuli comes close to the evaluation apprehension and other social conformity models. We learn that the presence of others is a signal for a change in reinforcement schedules, although the outcomes do not have to come from the person who is present – they are just a discriminative stimulus for previously learned consequences. The differences between the social conformity models depend, therefore, on which type of *generalized consequences* have been learned in the past.

With regards to the evaluation apprehension model, the particular consequences signalled in the presence of other people are said to be aversive ones. Other people in the past have signalled that generalized negative consequences are contingent upon the present behaviour: therefore there is an increase in behaviours which have *avoided* these consequences in the past.

There are two differences between the ways that behaviour analysis and the evaluation apprehension model deal with this. First, the behaviour analysis makes explicit an assumption that the evaluation hypothesis relies upon implicitly: that *in general* people have received negative consequences in the presence of others. Only to the extent that this is true will tests show a facilitation effect. In some populations this might not hold true (see Pfiffner and O'Leary, 1987).

The second difference between behaviour analysis and evaluation apprehension lies in the mechanism for the effect. Evaluation apprehension moves from the assumption of learned negative consequences to posit an increase in drive level which in turn causes the facilitation effects. The behaviour analysis makes no such drive assumptions. The organism has emitted various behaviours in the past which have been selectively (Skinner, 1981) reinforced with consequences in the presence of other people. This means that in the presence of others, people will respond more frequently with behaviours which have been strengthened in the past when in the presence of others. A drive construct is not needed to derive this.

It will be obvious by now that the behaviours which have been generally reinforced in the presence of others, and which are multiply-determined, constitute the social conforming behaviours. We acquire conforming behaviours not by applying specific demands to specific behaviours, but by having generalized social reinforcers. So behaviour analysis has points in common with other social conformity theories, but does not make assumptions which rely on cognitive processes. The differences that remain between the different frameworks lie in three areas.

First, the behaviour changes in the presence of others will depend upon the past history of the subjects. We cannot assume that subjects will *always* obey a particular social standard under all circumstances. This depends on what consequences subjects have previously received in similar circumstances. In fact, Carver and Scheier's public and private standards of behaviour are merely verbal descriptions of behaviours which are *commonly* reinforced in the presence of others in our society.

Second, and more particularly, the behaviour changes found experimentally will be those which have been reinforced in the past in situations which are *similar* (stimulus generalization, Catania, 1984) to the experimental laboratory: schools, doctors' surgeries, interviews, etc. The more a situation resembles the experimental testing environment, the closer will be the specific behaviours. So if, for example, a student has usually been punished by peers when trying hard to get good grades on educational exams, then inhibition of performance would be predicted, if tested in the presence of peers only (versus alone).

This means that the most common social facilitation effects found, with eating and task performance, are not universal but depend upon the existence of typical past histories. They work *in general* because they are reinforced *in general* in our society when in the presence of others. People have a long history from childhood of working harder in the presence of others, or at least looking as if they are working harder (hence the reinforcement of self-presentational behaviours).

The third difference to other social conformity theories is that a behaviour analysis predicts that all behaviours previously strengthened in the presence of others will be more likely when again in the presence of another person, not just those called personal or public standards. It is not just the test behaviours which can appear, but others as well. As was mentioned in Chapter 3, usually only facilitation and inhibition of task performance have been measured in human experiments since Zajonc (1965).

5.6 Behaviour inhibition in the presence of others

An interesting approach to social facilitation grew from earlier work on the use of motor movements and symbolic prompts in observational learning (Berger, 1966; Berger et al., 1979). It was found that during the learning process, subjects rehearsed what they were learning if it was a motor movement, and made verbal self-statements or symbolic representations to themselves if it was more abstract. That is, subjects had motor movements and verbal self-talk as functional mediators of the learning process.

Berger and Hecken (1980) showed that in the presence of a stranger, motor mimicry decreased and imaginal or symbolic coding increased. This had been suggested from earlier research as well (Berger, 1966; Berger et al., 1979). 'It seems that observers believe that overt mimicry is socially unacceptable and that they would be embarrassed if they mimicked in the presence of a stranger'. (Berger and Hecken, 1980, p. 2)

To explain the social facilitation interaction effect (Alone/Presence × Simple/Complex), Berger and his colleagues used the earlier result and proposed that in the presence of others, overt rehearsal is inhibited, as compared to working alone. For *complex* tasks this means that performance should be worse, since the functional performance mediators are not used. People avoid rehearsing to-be-recalled words out loud, or gesturing, or counting on their fingers, or talking to themselves. Without these mediators in the presence of another person they do worse on a complex task.

For *simple* tasks, the explanation was a bit trickier. It was proposed that for easy learning, many types of mediators are normally used. These can interfere with the task sometimes, it was argued, if they are being carried out simultaneously and only some are appropriate (Berger et al., 1981). The unnecessary mediators will interfere with the attention given to the main task. Under normal conditions, therefore, simple tasks are not always carried out optimally. It was argued, then, that if the use of some of these overt mediators is inhibited, then the subject can rely more directly on one or two forms only. Presumably, the ones finally used will be the most appropriate, and therefore performance will be facilitated. So it is predicted that the presence of others will facilitate simple performance by simplifying the performance mediators subject use.

Consider the example of learning paired-associates. When learning complex associates in the presence of others the lack of overt rehearsal will impair performance. With easy associates, subjects who are alone might try all of the following: saying the words softly to themselves, trying to find connections between the words, making backchat to themselves about any errors and what to do next time around, making images with both the words involved, and perhaps counting the number of words on their fingers. The point, then, is that these processes can interfere with each other so that their reduction in the presence of another person might *facilitate* learning if only one (most appropriate) strategy were to be used.

It will be seen in the next chapter that this part of the explanation is similar to attention-reduction explanations (Chapter 6.5), except that it is the *range of learning strategies* which are narrowed rather than the number of stimuli which are given attention. A more important difference is that it is not an arousal increase which narrows the mediators used, but a socially conforming inhibition in using the performance strategies.

A problem with this theory is that it does not apply to all forms of social facilitation discovered, only those that can possibly have motor or verbal mediators. It is possible though that extensions could be made to include other types of performance. This is merely a limitation of scope, rather than any logical error.

Another problem with the behaviour inhibition theory is that a lot of assumptions are made which help explanation but which need substantial evidence to back them up. The explanation for facilitation of simple responding in particular needs more direct evidence, plausible though it is.

A further problem is that the conditions under which the social norm applies need more consideration. Why the norm appears at all needs to be carefully established, and conditions under which it will not apply need to be tested. There should, then, be useful theoretical and empirical study of this process still to come. It holds interest as a good (and interesting) explanation for some of the social facilitation findings.

There is some direct evidence of overt rehearsal inhibition in the presence of others and an effect of this on social facilitation (Berger et al., 1980, 1981, 1982, 1983; Bond, 1982; Guerin, 1983). Berger et al., (1981), for example, had subjects learn lists of familiar (simple task) or unfamiliar (complex task) words. Like other social facilitation studies, they found that an audience inhibited complex performance (Experiment 1) and facilitated simple performance (Experiment 2). Concurrently, they found that there was less (self-reported) rehearsal of the words out loud or with lip movements in the audience group. More silent verbal practice was reported by the audience group.

While the rehearsal measures used in this study by Berger et al. (1981) were indirect self-reports, other evidence, to be reviewed in Chapter 8, shows inhibition of other forms of overt behaviour more directly (Dabbs and Clower, 1973; Guerin, 1989b; Kleck et al., 1976; Yarczower and Daruns, 1982). One example of this research will be outlined.

It will no doubt be recalled that at the end of Chapter 4 we looked at the details of an experiment which tested the monitoring hypothesis (Guerin, 1983). This had conditions of Alone, an Inattentive other confederate, a

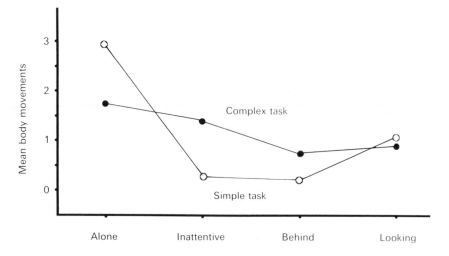

Figure 9. Mean number of body movements. (Data drawn from Guerin, 1983)

confederate who sat Behind the subject, and a confederate who Looked at the subject about 60 per cent of the time. The same study also videotaped the subjects during the experiment and then measured the number of large body movements made by the subjects such as rocking on the chair and leaning backwards, the number of smaller body movements such as scratching and fiddling about, and the number of sounds or vocalizations made by the subjects such as groans, sighs, and laughs. It was of interest whether these would be inhibited in the presence of the confederate, and especially any differences between the different social conditions.

The results are shown in Figures 9, 10 and 11. It can be seen that the presence of the confederate had a marked effect on the movements and sounds produced by subjects. Subjects showed inhibition of their overt movements and sounds when a confederate was present. The effects were not quite as strong for big and small body movements when the confederate could not see the subject – in the Inattentive condition. In particular, the effects are very strong for vocalizations. Subjects kept much more quiet when not alone. Even the inattentive confederate could hear the subjects, of course.

These results clearly show that if subjects do need to make overt sounds to rehearse the material they are learning, then they will suffer when someone else is present, as suggested by Berger and others. This was obviously not the case with the learning materials in this experiment, however, since the subjects in the Inattentive condition did not vocalize very much and yet they made no more errors than those in the Alone condition.

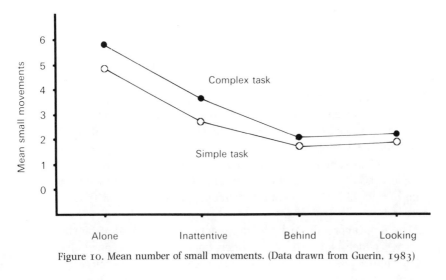

Figure 10. Mean number of small movements. (Data drawn from Guerin, 1983)

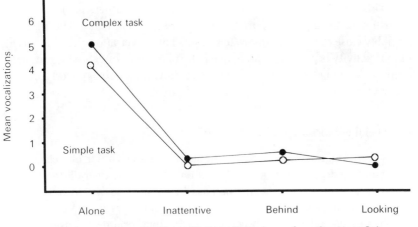

Figure 11. Mean number of vocalizations. (Data drawn from Guerin, 1983)

5.7 Other social valuation theories

Two other models have been proposed which emphasize the rôle of social conformity processes. Ferris, Beehr and Gilmore (1978) used an extension of Hull's theory which was made by Tolman (1932). As mentioned when discussing the drive theory of social facilitation, Zajonc used only the simplest of drive models. Many other variables were added later by Tolman and Spence to account for new phenomena which had been found.

Ferris, Beehr and Gilmore added an extension to the social facilitation drive theory, which dealt with *expectancy*. They suggested that incentive (K) in the social facilitation situation was based upon social approval – the learned expectancy of working in the presence of others. So the effort put into performing a task will be based on the consequences – social approval. The presence of others will increase effort because of this expectancy and so improve simple performance.

This model was developed to apply to organizational performance, rather than as a model of social facilitation effects, so the social inhibition of performance is not accounted for. Neither does the model account for findings of apprehension about evaluation and instead seems to assume that people will only seek others to gain approval. In all, the model brings out another side of evaluation but does not integrate this well with the previous research.

The final approach to be briefly mentioned here is that of Matusewicz (1974) which suggests that wider goals can exert an influence on performance. Increases in performance can come from those conditions which increase the 'consciously functioning guiding of activity' (1974), p. 29). This reiterates that one effect of the presence of others is to gain more control over behaviour, enforcing more directed behaviour. The model is probably close to the controls systems model of Carver and Scheier (1981a), in that activity is guided by an active control process. In behaviour analytic terms, it is saying that verbally-governed behaviours such as covert thinking occur more frequently in the presence of others.

5.8 Social conformity and evaluation

It has been suggested through this chapter that social conformity effects can at present be described in a number of different ways. Overall, the passive presence of others leads to an increase in behaviours which are socially valued. The models all suggest different mechanisms which might mediate this process. While drive theories assume the appropriate responses are well learned and therefore appear more frequently as drive increases, the theories in this chapter assume processes of more direct control over the appropriate response.

So there appears to be a complex of theories all trying to explain why people conform more to social standards of behaviour when in the presence of another person who does not directly instruct them to behave in that manner, nor directly disapprove if they do not behave that way. In the usual laboratory case, subjects are working harder or trying to be seen to be working harder at the laboratory task. These theories can all make similar predictions about this and can explain the similar results. The theoretical relationships between them will be covered further in Chapter 9.

6   Cognitive process theories

The rise of the cognitive approach in psychology can probably be dated to the publication of Miller, Galanter and Pribram (1960), while its position in social psychology was most clearly stated by Zajonc (1968a). Miller et al.'s book did not so much present any new data about psychology, but rather, it gave psychologists permission to speak about events which they could not observe. This was antithetical to the dominant behaviourisms of Hull and Spence, but not to that of Skinner (1974). Giving such permission had some benefits, but it also had some costs which are perhaps only now being appreciated in social psychology.

The benefit of speaking about unobservable events was that such events could be modelled in words, symbols or equations, and predictions made of observable behaviour. Such a strategy had helped the development of nuclear physics, for example, by allowing modelling of (then) unobservable atoms and electrons. Since being applied to social psychology, there has been a rapid proliferation of cognitive models (Markus and Zajonc, 1985).

The problem with cognitive models is that unless strict controls are kept on theorizing (see Skinner, 1950), the models can become underdetermined or indeterminate, such that many different models can be supported by the same observed data. We have, in fact, already seen some of this occurring in the last chapter, when each of the theories could account for the same data in seemingly different ways. One of the conclusions in that chapter was that independent measures of the proposed mechanisms need to be taken: the data which show social facilitation cannot also show the existence of some proposed causal mechanism. This is one of the major points of this book, which will be pointed out once more when reviewing the empirical studies, that the theories of social facilitation are underdetermined and the data support many theories which cannot really be distinguished.

The basis of the cognitive models is to treat the organism as if it were taking in information about the environment, transforming that information in different ways (depending upon how smart the organism is), storing some information away for future use, and acting on the basis of the information previously processed. Most cognitive models in this way *dissect* behaviour into *temporal* stages or processes. This usually includes a sensory or perceptual stage where the information about the environment is 'taken in' or attended to, a working stage where the information is changed in some way, a memory stage where information is stored in some form, and a retrieval stage for getting back stored information.

In such cognitive models the basic processing stages are taken to be unchanging; the variability and flexibility in behaviour occurs from the changing information taken in from the environment and from the previous information stored. This means that if an organism is observed twice, any behaviour change could be due to a changing environment or to a different way of processing due to previous memories. This has led to a conflict between two perspectives about processing: 'top-down', when previous memories are said to be the source of a change in observable behaviour; and 'bottom-up', when the environment is said to be the source of a change in observable behaviour.

(In behaviour analysis these two positions become equivalent, because there is no posited storage of previous memories in the cognitive sense. Rather, the organism is said to be changed when it behaves, in the same way that a battery is changed when current is put into or taken out of it: a battery does not store electricity. The organism does not process with unchanging processing stages: instead the organism is always changed when it interacts with the environment. This position does not deny a top-down approach, but rather suggests that it is a different organism which interacts with the environment the second time. So the top-down and bottom-up approaches merely differ in time-scale.)

The dissection of behaviour into discrete temporal stages forms the basis for the different cognitive theories of social facilitation. Most of these theories deal with the attentional stage of processing, that is, the presence of another person affects how much information is taken in, or what types of information are attended to and taken in. Some of these theories still have a drive mechanism which is said to affect processing. One other cognitive model looks more closely at how the processing stages are affected by the presence of other people (Blank's theory, 6.7). Some of the attention and distraction effects have already been mentioned in Chapter 2, when discussing the work of Allport (1920, 1924a), Dashiell (1935), Ekdahl (1929), Meumann (1904), Pessin and Husband (1933) and Ruger (1910). It is only the more recent theories which are presented here.

6.1 Physical distraction

The first attentional effect will be called *physical distraction*. One effect of the presence of another person may be to watch or monitor them for some reason. In doing this, at least some time will be spent away from the on-going activity. Depending upon that particular activity, the physical distraction of turning the head or body will have different consequences. Time away from the task could be deleterious or beneficial. This factor was specifically mentioned in the early work of Dashiell (1935; Kushnir, 1978).

It might be recalled from Chapter 2 that the opposite prediction was made in the early work of Meumann (1904), who suggested that there may be compensatory processes for distraction such that subjects try harder and do better with increased physical distraction. The question then becomes one of showing with independent measures what mechanisms might account for one or other of these effects from physical distraction.

It is likely that with the experimental tasks presently used little effect of physical distraction would be noticeable. There is usually no over-riding time urgency in most tasks and subjects can occasionally glance at the other person with little detrimental effect. If a high precision visual tracing task were used, however, effects of physical distraction might be more noticeable.

6.2 Cognitive distraction

A second attentional effect, noted by Allport (1924a) and Jones and Gerard (1967), will be called *cognitive distraction*. The presence of another person can be a complex event which requires processing of information about that person. This may be to assess possible threat, to anticipate evaluation, to prepare to respond, or to select socially appropriate behaviours. In association with any other effects of this extra processing, time is taken away from the on-going task, whether or not physical distraction is involved. The effects of this may not be lasting, especially if there is nothing unusual about the other's presence. Again, this effect may not be measurable with the currently used experimental tasks.

6.3 Distraction-conflict

A third attentional effect is *distraction-conflict* (Baron, 1986; Baron, Moore and Sanders, 1978; Groff, Baron and Moore, 1983; Sanders, Baron and Moore, 1978). The distraction-conflict model proposes that in the presence of others there is a conflict between attending to the person and attending to the task. This conflict of attention is arousing or drive-inducing (Sanders and Baron, 1975) so the interaction effect predicted by other drive and arousal models (Chapter 4) is also predicted. So this is an arousal model based upon an attentional process.

As a test of the first element in this theory, Sanders and Baron (1975) found that a non-social distraction could produce the social facilitation effects. Subjects were given a simple or complex copying task (Taylor and

Rechtschlaffen, 1959) to do with or without a non-social distraction. In this case, the distraction was from having to look up at a point on a wall when the experimenter occasionally knocked on the door. The typical social facilitation effects were found with this procedure: that is, facilitation of simple copying and inhibition of complex. Subjects in the distraction condition also reported greater distraction in post-session questionnaires than controls.

One question remaining for distraction-conflict theory was the source of the distraction from the presence of another person. There could be many reasons for being distracted in the presence of another person. Sanders, Baron and Moore (1978) argued that one source of distraction would occur if subjects wanted to get social comparison information from the other person (Chapter 10).

To test this, Sanders, Baron and Moore (Experiment 2) set up the same copying task with three conditions: alone, with another person present doing the same task, and with another person present doing a different task. It was argued that only in the case when the person present was doing the same task could there be social comparison going on, therefore only in this case would there be distraction and the social facilitation effects.

The authors found the typical social facilitation effects only when subjects were doing the same task, which was reflected in correctly copied digits for the simple task (see Figure 12) and incorrectly copied digits for the complex task. Unfortunately, self-reports of distraction failed to show the same results, while a self-report measure of competitiveness showed that any presence of another person increased feelings of competition. Thus it is quite possible that the social comparison itself could have increased motivation to perform better rather than the distraction arising from social comparison checks on the other person. While the different task subjects also felt competitive, they could gain nothing to help themselves from watching the other person. Other evidence also suggests that social comparison is a sign of competitive motivation (Conolley, Gerard and Kline, 1978).

This point raises a general problem with the distraction-conflict model. This is that all models of social facilitation might predict concurrent distraction from monitoring, social comparison, assessing evaluation potential, or whatever. To show that it is the distraction engendered from these effects rather than a direct effect is very difficult. The evidence for this view rests, to a large extent, on self-report data of distraction from subjects obtained after the experiments. Doubts have been raised as to the validity of self-report measures (Guerin and Innes, 1981; Nisbett and Bellows, 1977; Nisbett and Wilson, 1977).

The only positive reason so far tested as to why subjects *should* attend to the other person present is to gain social comparison information about their relative performance. This can only apply in co-acting situations, of course,

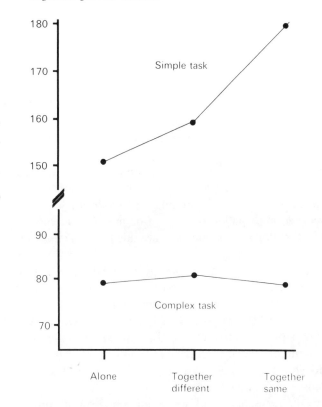

Figure 12. Number of digits correctly copied for simple and complex tasks. Used with permission of authors and Academic Press. (Data drawn from Sanders, Baron and Moore, 1978).

so the many results found in audience settings of social facilitation remain unexplained. Social facilitation effects have also been found previously when no social comparison information was possible. Social facilitation effects have also been found when subjects *could* go slower and attend to both task and confederate. Where such self-pacing tasks have been used, subjects have worked faster, rather than slower with someone else present (Crandell, 1974; Markus, 1978; Rittle and Bernard, 1977; Zajonc and Crandell, no date).

So without denying the existence of some distraction-conflict effects, the model is far from explaining all the results. The effects will be strongest when there is a time urgency, as Baron, Moore and Sanders (1978) point out. It is probably a separate phenomenon, concurrent with others. Other circumstances might also trigger distraction (Collins, 1986). Some new measures of distraction look hopeful of sorting out the measurement problems (Moore, Baron, Logel, Sanders and Weert, 1988) by providing new measures of distraction independent from the social facilitation effects themselves, which do not rely on self-reports.

6.4 Attentional process model

The fourth attentional model is the attentional process model (Sanders, 1981). After reviewing some of the social facilitation models, Sanders proposed a synthesis of the mere presence model, the learned drive model, and the distraction–conflict model. It was suggested that the first two are drive-neutral attending mechanisms: one reflex and one learned. These are seen as two possible antecedents for attentional conflict and distraction conflict. In the presence of others the initial orientation may be a reflexive response or a learned anticipation of positive or negative outcomes. The lasting effects and the direction of influence are due to distraction-conflict, however.

A number of criticisms have been made of this model but will not be repeated here (Geen, 1981b; Markus, 1981). Most of the criticisms of the distraction-conflict model given above also apply to this synthesis. The major problem, though, is that little by way of real detail has been given of the model so far. How the parts interact and the contexts in which they do interact are not mentioned. Further work will presumably elucidate this. The model stands to show a possible way in which a few different social facilitation phenomena may combine.

Another very similar scheme, of an automatic arousal process in conjunction with a voluntary controlling process (effort), has been very roughly outlined by Kushnir (1981). It does not, however, seem to have been followed up.

6.5 Arousal effects upon attention

Another attentional explanation of social facilitation effects stems from a review by Easterbrook (1959), which concluded that an increase in arousal would lead to a restriction in the range of cues which were attended. The explanations for social facilitation effects are as follows, for simple and complex responses respectively.

For *simple* tasks, an increase in arousal means that task-irrelevant cues which might have been attended to are now ignored. As only task-relevant cues are attended to, some facilitation of performance is predicted. For *complex* tasks, the range of cues is narrowed so as to exclude some of the task-relevant ones and performance is therefore inhibited. So if it is assumed that the presence of others increases arousal then the social facilitation interaction can be explained by a narrowing of the range of attention

(Anderson and Revelle, 1982; Bruning et al., 1968; Landers, 1980; Landers, and McCullagh, 1976).

There are some problems which can be raised with this model (see Bacon, 1974; Wachtel, 1967). One of these concerns the meaning of 'task-relevant'. Although fewer task-relevant cues might be attended as arousal increases, it has been suggested that what might be called 'life-relevant' cues gain priority even over task requirements – cues such as scanning the environment. This is a view of 'defence as a problem of distribution of attention' (Wachtel, 1967, p. 419).

Monitoring others is another important behaviour in an unfamiliar environment. Zajonc (1980) suggested that conspecifics are important especially because of their unpredictability. This means that they may need watching even above task concerns. Supporting this is the study mentioned in 4.3, Heylen (1978), which used a task designed to test Easterbrook's hypothesis. It will be recalled that even under high arousal conditions subjects still attended to the person present instead of only task-relevant cues. So if there is an effect of arousal on cue-utilization, it is not always a direct one.

This model is close to the behaviour inhibition model (5.6) except that it deals with the inhibition of cues. The behaviour inhibition model, on the other hand, suggests that the presence of other people leads to a restriction in the range of learning strategies which are used. It also makes no arousal assumptions, relying instead for its motivation by assuming that we have learned previously during socialization not to rehearse out loud when others are around.

6.6 Manstead and Semin (1980)

A further attentional model is a combination of a few of the above explanations (Abrams and Manstead, 1981; Manstead and Semin, 1980). This model suggests that *simple* tasks are routinized and usually performed sub-optimally. With a disruption or with an evaluative audience, *controlled* processing replaces *automatic* processing and performance improves (Norman and Shallice, 1980; Schneider and Shiffren, 1977; Shiffren and Schneider, 1977). With *complex* tasks, attentional demands are heavy so that disruption from the audience accentuates the demands and inhibits performance.

This model uses distraction and attentional demands without the intervening arousal process used in all the models present earlier in this chapter. It fails, however, to say why the audience should increase demands if they are not directive or cue-giving. This needs to be spelt out separately or else the motivation is still lacking.

A very similar version of this position has also been put forward which supposes that it is the distraction-conflict of audiences which increases attentional demands (Moore and Baron, 1983). The overall stance is similar to a conclusion from the social conformity theories given in Chapter 5: that one effect of the presence of others is that stricter control is taken over behaviour. The attentional processes involved in this 'stricter control' constitute the theory of Manstead and Semin (1980), although the details are still dependent on very tightly run cognitive experiments (Schneider and Shiffren, 1977; Shiffren and Schneider, 1977). What is needed now is for independent measurement of attentional demands beyond showing the social facilitation effects themselves.

It can also be pointed out here again that the cognitive position of Manstead and Semin (1980) is very close to the behaviour analysis prediction that there will be more verbally governed behaviour in the presence of another person, since verbal behaviour must be maintained by social consequences. While behaviour analysts have done much research on the effects of verbally controlling behaviour (e.g., Buskist et al., 1984), as opposed to contingency governed behaviour, they have not done much on the conditions which occasion verbally governed behaviour.

6.7 An information processing view

The final model to be discussed was an attempt by Blank (1979) to incorporate both arousal and social factors into an information processing model. Blank suggested that an increase in arousal leads to an initial filtering of stimuli and to a limited working capacity. This was again based on the ideas of Easterbrook (1959) but the way in which the limited capacity was produced was based on a more sophisticated and cognitive model than that of Easterbrook (1959).

Blank's (1979) model was based on information processing systems (Broadbent, 1971) in which pre-response filters exclude whole sets of responses. Which responses are excluded from consideration is based on past experience and stored information, and from social valuations of previous responses. For example, in many situations whole sets of responses are not considered at all in behaving, including socially inappropriate responses and other responses which would lead to negative self-presentations.

Blank proposed that filtering could occur at two points during information processing. First, there could be filtering at the attention stage, and in line with Easterbrook (1959), this was due to arousal increases. Unlike Easterbrook's model, however, it is not just any cues which become narrowed with increased arousal, but cues with specific functions which depend upon previous information processing. The second filtering occurred just before the response was initiated and this was cognitively driven rather than arousal driven. So at a pre-response stage there is 'avoidance or retardation of responses with certain characteristics' (Blank, 1979. p. 15). This second filtering of responses could be changed flexibly by smart information processing, although processing would be slower if much filtering had to take place.

Blank (1979) used the word association task as an example of this information processing model. If there is no response filtering required in the presence of another person (a neutral other) then the arousal increase can increase the speed of producing associations. This means that in certain cases word associations can be faster in the presence of another person. If, on the other hand, the person present has some characteristics which require the response filtering stage then the processing is going to slow down. Blank showed that previously contradictory speed changes in the presence of another person could be accounted for in this way. For example, Ekdahl (1929) found very slow word association times when a prestigious audience was watching.

Before discussing problems with this information processing model, it is well to consider how a more recent cognitive model might explain social facilitation effects. (Given that Carver and Scheier's control systems model is also atypical of modern cognitive theories.) No recent model has been proposed so this will be developed from scratch. Some of the points, however, follow on from points already hinted at in the last chapter.

Cognitive theories now work on the assumption that behaviour is organized by having memories stored as organized units called schemata. The organization is stored in the organism on the basis of previous experience. Schemata relevant to social facilitation would include previous experience with normative behaviours, and 'how to act' in the appropriate situation. The presence of another person would 'prime' certain schemata in the same way that Blank's Information Processing model had pre-response filters. These schemata would then be easily available during processing and would help to make sense of the current situation in order to plan responding patterns. Thus, if socially acceptable or unacceptable schemata of behaviours are primed by a particular audience then they will play a salient role in deciding upon a course of action (see Baldwin, Carrel and Lopez, 1990).

A second way in which the presence of another person could make a difference corresponds to the theory of Manstead and Semin (1980). A lot of the processing which occurs in social and non-social situations is automatic and requires little processing time. In the presence of another person, and in particular a person with special characteristics, deeper, more lengthy, or more controlled processing would occur. This would allow the finer points of socially appropriate options to be weighed before acting. It would also result in slower responding, like Blank's Information Processing model.

Overall, a modern cognitive processing model would explain social facilitation effects in varied ways. With regards to the speed of responding this would be faster when specific responses are primed by the presence of the other person but slowed if controlled processing is required. With regards to the form of the responding, this would arise from the organization of the schemata which are primed by the presence of the other person or by those schemata which are utilized in the controlled processing stage. This can also be summarized by saying that more directed and controlled responding will occur in the presence of another person.

The problems with the information processing models are similar to those of all the arousal and attentional models, and the information processing models come very close, in fact, to the control systems model of Carver and Scheier (1978). There is one problem that is common to all of these, however. Just as it was uncertain how to predict exactly which behaviour standards are operative at any time with the control systems model of Carver and Scheier (1978), so it is uncertain how to predict in advance which particular response sets will be filtered out or which schemata will be primed. Blank's process of filtering out sets of inappropriate responses, and the more recent priming of schemata, correspond *conceptually* to Carver and Scheier's feedback mechanism which matches behaviour more closely to a standard. Both try to address why it is that some responses occur but not others, and they therefore share the same problems. But there is nothing to really decide between the two models since they are underdetermined by the data.

To give an example of this problem, in the standard social facilitation experiment it is claimed that the salient standard of behaviour is to do as well as possible for the experimenter (5.3). We have already seen that there is no adequate answer to the question of why subjects should try to match this standard. Answers rely on weak forms of reinforcement models, with social psychologists usually citing 'hedonistic relevance'. The question of why organisms should self-regulate, and why they do it in the particular ways they do, is not addressed in discussion of these issues (see Carver and Scheier, 1981a, Chapter 18).

This highlights the problem which also occurs for the other attentional models discussed in this chapter. The question is rarely addressed as to why attention *should* change in the presence of others. Distraction-conflict suggests that getting social comparison information is one reason but as was pointed out above, this cannot explain all the effects that have been found. More to the point, finding the motive for attentional changes is vital to making these models predictive, for it is this very motive question which allows them to explain the social facilitation effects. In the same way that

Carver and Scheier (1981a) need to explain why the organism must match its behaviour against a standard, Distraction-Conflict theory must spell out why another organism is distracting, Blank's Information Processing model must explain why sets of responses must be filtered, and modern social cognitivists must explain why certain schemata are formed and why they are primed in certain circumstances.

Until more attention is given to these points, the very answers to these 'why must' questions can equally explain the social facilitation effect without the rest of the models. If, for example, we have to assume that a standard of behaviour is matched because in the past such matching has led to strengthening consequences, then we could adopt the behaviour analytic perspective without the rest of the control systems model. The strengthening consequences can explain the behaviour without the rest of the proposed mechanism of matching standards. And given that there are no independent data to show these matching mechanisms, such a view becomes attractive.

These points can also be clearly seen if we consider the metaphors underlying the control system and cognitive models. The control systems model was based on a self-regulating unit like a thermostat, but the question can be asked of why the thermostat must be set to a particular temperature? With real thermostats humans set the temperature, but if I consider that my behaving rapidly when the experimenter is in the room is a result of my matching my behaviour to a standard, then we still have the question of why that standard is there. This would probably be answered by referring back to socialization during childhood, but that merely puts the question back another stage: to why I should do what society has taught me. It seems that some explanation involving the consequences of our actions will be required at some point.

Likewise, if we consider the metaphor of the computer, which forms the basis of the modern cognitive models, we can see that the computer stores certain information with a certain organization because it is told to by the operator. If, in our case, we ask why certain schemata are abstracted and stored we must again go back to socialization processes. Why should I be primed with 'trying hard' responses when the experimenter is in the room and why should I act on the basis of those primed schemata? Again, some form of behaviour consequence idea is needed here to provide the motivational glue in the computer.

The problem then is not just to reject the cognitive and control systems view, but to look for the independent evidence for the unobservable mechanisms. Given the underdetermined nature of cognitive models, however, discussed at the start of this chapter, we cannot give priority to any one of all these views. This is the negative legacy left by Miller, Galanter and Pribram (1960) and the cognitive revolution: that the freedom of flexible models of unobservable events leads to fully compatible theories with indeterminate differences. It might be time to re-examine the problems of laissez-faire theorizing (see Skinner, 1950).

These questions are complex ones which go beyond just the social facilitation effects, although it is not a coincidence that they re-occur in a discussion about social facilitation. This is because social facilitation concerns the most basic problem about sociality and because social psychology has repeatedly taken on different frameworks of psychology (Innes, 1980) without examining the observable basis of its data to find out whether anything could decide between the different models which happen to be fashionable. As an area of social psychology with a fixed definition relying on a simple interaction effect (Simple/Complex and Alone/Presence), social facilitation has been taken on by all the frameworks adopted by social psychologists.

More will be said about these issues in Chapter 9, after examining the empirical data in the next two chapters. From what has been written here it is clear that the empirical data should not be examined to see whether they support this theory or that theory, since the theories are obviously underdetermined. It will also become clear that social facilitation should not be defined by its effect on people but by the situation in which certain behaviours occur.

III Experimental studies of social facilitation

7   Social facilitation effects in animals

7.1 Introduction

It may be asked: why is there a chapter on non-human animals (called 'animals' from here on) in a book on social facilitation? There are five answers to this. First, the early literature made great use of animal experiments after about 1930, especially within comparative psychology. This was not discussed in Chapter 2 but left till now. So a full understanding of the early arguments about social facilitation requires a look at this extensive literature.

Second, Zajonc (1965) included a lot of animal studies in his major review which was outlined in Chapter 3, and this triggered a lot more animal research after 1965. This was probably helped by the fact that the methodology was so clearly set out that it could be easily applied to animals. Many experiments looking for the social facilitation interaction effect were conducted.

A third reason for including animals is that the theories given in Chapter 5 suggest that animals will not be affected by evaluation apprehension and social conformity. Therefore, if social facilitation effects can be shown with animals, it would mean that social conformity is not a necessary condition for mere presence effects. This would mean that the mere presence idea has some merit.

The fourth reason for including animals is that the mere presence effects discussed in Chapter 4 suggest that such effects would be more important in non-human animals than in humans. Some of the fear reactions of animals have been discussed there, and these reactions seem easier to demonstrate in animals.

The final reason is that there has not been a careful review of the animal social facilitation literature for some time. Clayton (1978) reviewed most of the literature, but included many other phenomena not usually considered social facilitation by social psychologists. This point will be taken up briefly before considering some of the major issues of animal social facilitation.

7.2 General comments about the literature

The animal social facilitation literature includes a large number of studies which use many different species, and which seem to include many different phenomena. The distinctions made throughout this book, between the effects of social facilitation and the effects of competition, cueing, imitation, and direct reinforcement, have not usually been followed in the animal literature. For example, imitation is often called social facilitation (Armstrong, 1951; Hinde, 1953; Robert, 1990). Like the human literature, the experimenter has often been present in the Alone conditions; and the animal has been alone in the Presence conditions.

While this all makes reviewing difficult, it must be kept in mind that comparative psychologists and ethologists have usually been exploring other issues when conducting the studies that will be reported here. Their experiments often set out to make points totally unrelated to social facilitation. This means that in many cases the experiments discussed cannot be interpreted unambiguously. We can only suggest what *might* have influenced the data. It is hoped that these comments will still be useful in planning future experiments.

7.3 The major issues in animal social facilitation

Before discussing the animal studies in detail, some of the major points raised by this literature need to be mentioned. These points will become clear as we proceed, but stating them here will help make more sense of the studies as we go along.

The major problem is that social facilitation has often been taken to mean *any* observed increase or facilitation in behaviour when in the presence of other animals (Crawford, 1939). This means that phenomena such as flocking in birds and schooling in fish have sometimes been included. This review will try to restrict the range of effects covered: social facilitation can no longer refer to (or pretend to explain) any increase in behaviour. The term becomes meaningless if this is done.

In a similar vein, social *inhibition* effects are sometimes excluded, and treated as a separate topic (Clayton, 1978). This ignores the fact, however, that many explanations of social facilitation deal with both simultaneously. The two phenomena are intertwined, and social inhibition cannot be ignored.

A further problem with the animal studies is that different experimental paradigms have been used in many studies. Most frequently, behaviours specific to one animal have been studied: bar pressing in rats; pecking in birds; or building in ants.

The most common exception to this is eating. A lot of research has been done across different species on the amount eaten by a satiated animal when there is another animal near the cage. It is not certain, however, that we are still talking about the same response – 'eating food'. For example, pecking in chickens might be affected by an entirely different set of variables than feeding in fish or armadillos. So while we might assume that the motivation and response topography of eating is similar for all humans, this is less plausible in animals.

But it is not only the behaviour being measured which might be animal specific. A major consideration in the animal literature is that *fear responses* play an enormous role, and that these will vary from species to species. As was shown in Chapter 4, there might be similar fear reactions in humans, but perhaps not with the variety of effects found in the animal literature.

This emphasis on fear has generated a number of considerations about social facilitation which are not usually raised in the human literature (see Archer, 1969; Barnett and Cowan, 1976; Boice and Adams, 1983; Cowan, 1977; Jones, 1987; Jones and Harvey, 1987; Suarez and Gallup, 1981). Six of these will be given here.

(1) First, the effects will depend upon the species used. Vogel, Scott and Marston (1950; and Scott and Marston, 1950) have argued this strongly. They proposed a new term – 'allelomimetic' – for species which tend to do the same thing at the same time. They took this to be '. . . an important type of motivation which may be independent of competition' (Scott and Marston, 1950, p. 135). They predicted that for social facilitation of eating, allelomimetic species (primates, dogs, fish, chickens) would show the effects with or without competition. Non-allelomimetic species (rats) would only show similar results if there was competition. Their review of the extant literature seemed to agree with this formulation.

Species differences will also be reflected in the size of the group. While some animals might be fearful if left alone, others would panic if left with many of the same animals; while still others would panic if *not* left with a large number of others.

(2) Second, the results will depend upon the *familiarity* of the animals with the animal being added as the presence. Different effects are predicted for strangers and familiars because of differences in fear, although this prediction itself may be different for different species. Some animals, perhaps some invertebrates, for example, might be less concerned about familiarity.

(3) Third, the predictions will depend on whether the animals are housed in isolation or in groups. If housed in isolation, then strictly speaking, the effects found are due to the *addition* of another animal in the presence condition. If housed in groups, the effects are due to the *removal* of companion animals in the alone condition. These two types of housing might have very different effects for different animals.

So, because of the fear considerations again, the predictions for animal social facilitation will involve the caging conditions, how long they have been caged in this manner, whether or not they are domesticated, and the 'normal' state of the animal in the wild. Humans normally are assumed to be sociable animals living with others, and not caged in the testing environment.

(4) Fourth, the results will depend upon whether the animal is tested in a familiar environment or not: that is, whether there is a separate feeding (test) and housing area. Animals react to a strange environment as well as to a strange animal. Careful controls are needed to separate these two.

(5) Fifth, the social structure of the animals needs to be considered, since dominant animals may behave differently to subordinates. Similar effects are ignored in human studies.

(6) The final consideration is competition. Since most studies have used eating as the behaviour measured, results will depend upon the availability of food. While human subjects may have some self-restraint or delay of gratification, this should not be assumed for animals.

Given these sorts of constraints in discussing the animal facilitation literature, the plan will be to discuss the available evidence species by species. After this, the general results will be summarized. Each of the six points given above will be raised in connection with particular studies, and they will be discussed again in summary.

7.4 Dogs

Ross and Ross (1949a) found that dogs of two breeds ate less in solitary cages than when in groups. Ross and Ross (1949b) followed this up by testing facilitation of eating after satiation; either alone or in groups. More eating after satiation was found for dogs in groups than dogs alone.

While it was argued that these results showed social facilitation in groups, it can also be argued that they showed inhibition when alone. The dogs had all been raised together, and normally lived in group cages. So the absence of the other dogs might have led to an inhibition in behaviour.

Vogel, Scott and Marston (1950, Experiment 2) found faster running to food in pairs of dogs than alone. This was mainly accounted for by the slower dogs going faster. There could have been a ceiling effect for the fast dogs, however, so it is uncertain whether there was no effect on the faster dogs or simply that an effect could not be demonstrated.

Scott and Marston (1950) tested dogs in *unfamiliar* pairs, arguing that it would be harder for mutual mimicry in these cases. It was also pointed out that this would lead to more competition, since there was novelty and the dogs could not predict which one would get most of the food. Some evidence for this was found: 'An animal may run either better or more poorly with an unfamiliar animal, depending upon the relationship between them.' (p. 138). It was also found that unfamiliar animals provided more *interference* with each other.

It could be, of course, that there was competition in running to the food, since the first dog probably got more food. Scott and McCray (1967) varied the competition, some dogs getting enough food for one after running; others getting enough food for two. It was found that pairs of dogs ran the same no matter what the competition. With competition, in fact, the dogs ran slower overall.

James (1953, 1961) found that dominant puppies ate more after satiation than subordinate puppies. The opposite result, however, was found by James and Cannon (1955) with older dogs. James and Gilbert (1955) fed dogs alone or in groups for the first ninety days after birth. While the dogs which were fed together ate more in groups when later tested, the dogs fed alone took about fourteen days to develop this pattern after testing began. Put together, these three studies show that the increased eating in groups needs to be learned. The same conclusion was found in the results of James (1960).

Lastly, James (1954) found that dogs ate more with either the experimenter or another dog present. The experimenter talking to the dog also raised the amount eaten slightly.

Overall, the results show good evidence for some form of social facilitation in dogs. Dogs ate less when alone, ran faster to get food in pairs, and showed facilitation without competition. Of most interest are the findings that the predictions depended upon the social relationships between the dogs, and that the social facilitation effects needed to be learned.

7.5 Rats

Fear reduction in groups

Davitz and Mason (1955) found that rats were less scared with a non-fearful rat present, as did Morrison and Hill (1967) and Hughes (1969). These results mean, of course, that any increase in responding in groups may be due to a *reduction in fear responses* rather than an extraneous group phenomenon. For example, if the animals are not spending time being fearful, monitoring, or being aggressive, then they can spend more time eating food or interacting. This is the *disinhibition hypothesis* which will be referred to later in this chapter.

One earlier study by Anderson (1939) found no difference between alone and together in an open field test, but all the rats in that sample were not very fearful at all. This was probably because they were kept in group cages and familiar cagemates were tested together.

A more detailed analysis of fear reduction was presented by Moore, Byers and Baron (1981). Pairs of naive rats were no less fearful than alone rats, but rats paired with others which had been pre-exposed to the open field showed less fear. This was interpreted in terms of distraction: that fear reduction was due to being distracted by interaction initiated by the pre-exposed rats.

It could be, however, that there was something about the increased interaction itself which led to the results; for example, the pre-exposed rats might have cued the behaviour to the other. These different effects are hard to separate experimentally, of course, since any increased contact will always lead to some increase in distraction. This same problem with human distraction theories was raised in Chapter 6.

Taylor (1981) found that groups of rats had shorter immobility responses than single rats. A second experiment showed this only occurred for a social stimulus. It did not occur with a non-social stimulus (a hand vibrator attached to the floor of the cage). A third experiment found that stressed animals chose to interact more than non-stressed. It was suggested that reduction of stress was a major reinforcement for attraction in rats.

Taylor's study is also noteworthy because it varied housing conditions (group or individual) and familiarity of the animal pairs. No effects were found of these variables, however, the fear reduction being robust no matter what the housing arrangements. It would be interesting to repeat this with an allelomimetic species. The variables used by Taylor should affect these animals.

Baum (1969) trained rats to avoid electric shock and then prevented them from responding (flooding) to enhance extinction. It was found that the presence of a non-fearful rat facilitated this. It seems likely to have been a cueing effect, and no effect was found by Corriveau, Contildes and Smith (1978) using a different method.

Marina and Bauermeister (1974) found that rats which were alone were no quicker to learn an extinction response than rats with three non-social objects present, but both were slower than others having either three live rats or three anaesthetized rats present. Similar findings were reported by Tachibana (1974a, b).

Overall, the results show a robust finding of fear reduction in the presence of other rats. While Taylor (1981) did not find any effect of some variables which commonly affect fear, such as housing or familiarity, other studies have found that the fear reduction in open field settings depends on having rats which are caged in isolation (Latané, 1969; Latané and Glass, 1968; Latané, Poor and Sloan, 1972; Latané et al., 1971). This means that more needs to be known about the variables affecting fear in rats independently of any social effects. After this has been done, we can find out with more certainty how social conditions affect fearful rats.

Eating in rats

In one of the earliest studies on social facilitation of eating, Harlow (1932) found no evidence for greater eating after satiation in pairs of rats (Experiments 1 and 6). 'Social facilitation' only occurred when there was some form of competition present. It was suggested that social facilitation effects were a form of competition.

Strobel (1972) found less eating in satiated pairs of rats. The time not spent eating was taken up with social interaction, which must have been distracting. There was little inhibition if one of the rats was hungry. This led Strobel to conclude: 'Behavior of the satiated rat can only be predicted if the state of the companion is known' (p. 507). This experiment had removed any competition, so it goes against Harlow's (1932) findings. Since it was more carefully controlled than Harlow's, more weight should be given to it.

Shelley (1965) found that a group of rats ate less than rats alone, using ad lib feeding. The opposite was found by Hoyenga and Aeschleman (1969). They suggested that as Shelley (1965) had fed the rats on the floor, group rats would have more urine on the floor and therefore be less likely to eat contaminated food. A feature of group performance that is often overlooked!

Cooper and Levine (1973) found that deermice ate less in pairs than alone. It was suggested that companion mice huddled when in pairs, which led to conservation of energy and less food intake.

Overall, the results suggest *less* eating in groups of rats than alone – the opposite of what would be expected of dominant responses! All of the authors, however, have mentioned that interaction interfered with eating. So none of the tests have been carried out with only one major motivator present.

An interesting comparison with these results is the report by Drew (1937), who looked at *non-social* conditions for renewed eating after satiation. His conclusion was that any conditions which 'arouse a certain state of excitement in the animals' (p. 105) will lead to the extra eating. This means that if social conditions were shown to lead to excitement, then Zajonc's (1965) idea that the presence of others leads to arousal would be plausible.

The problem, though, is that the experiments have all had some other forms of 'excitement' present, such as social interaction, aggression and competition. This means that clear tests need to do the following: reduce other forms of 'excitement' present; reduce any interfering social interaction effects; and show that there is excitement present in the experimental social conditions *independently* of the social facilitation measures.

While not a social experiment, the results of Premack and Premack (1963) bear on the points in this section. They found that rats ate less when there was a wheel present. It was argued that the presence of the wheel changed the overall behavioural contingencies. On this basis it can be argued that the presence of other rats does the same (cf. Rajecki, Kidd and Ivins, 1976), and that it is the increased social interaction which reduces food intake in groups of rats. For this reason, bar pressing for food would seem to provide a better test of social facilitation effects, since direct interaction is usually not possible.

Bar pressing in rats

Bankart et al. (1974) had rats press a bar for food either alone or with another rat in an adjoining box. The other rats were either naive or previously trained. It was found that an alone condition was no different to having a sophisticated rat present, but that in both these conditions learning to press the bar was quicker than when two naive rats were together. The authors suggested that the distraction from the naive rat interfered. The sophisticated rat was less distracting since it was busy pressing the bar (although it may also have provided a secondary cue with the noise of the bar click).

Exactly the opposite result was found by Deni and Jorgensen (1976a). They found that a trained companion led to poorer performance than either alone or with a naive companion. It was reported that distraction influenced the results. The bars and food troughs were placed at opposite ends of the cage, so the rats were moving back and forth during the trials, especially those which were well trained rats. So there may have been more distraction with trained rats than for Bankart et al. (1974) because of this extraneous factor.

Deni and Jorgensen (1976b) found that both naive and trained rats pressed a bar less than an alone rat when the rats had not been deprived of food. There were low rates of responding overall, naturally. These results are comparable to those given above of eating after satiation. Unfortunately, the authors do not report whether there was interaction between the rats when they were not pressing the bar. This was the interpretation from the satiation studies above.

Zentall and Levine (1972) had rats press a bar under four conditions: alone, with a rat pressing a bar, with a rat drinking, or with a naive rat. It was found that the cueing effect was most strong, the drinking rat did not differ from alone, and with a naive rat there were least bar presses. This suggested that cueing was effective, and that a naive rat was distracting. A similar finding was reported by Henning and Zentall (1981).

Levine and Zentall (1974) used deprived rats alone or with a conspecific. Pairs were better than solitary ones and deprived rats were better than non-deprived. While this latter finding goes gainst Strobel (1972), it can be suggested that there was greater distraction in that study. In this case, only visual contact was allowed. So when distraction or contact is reduced, the effects seem to be clearer.

Gardner and Engel (1971) tested three groups of rats. One group were run alone. The second group learned to lever press for food while a second rat was eating food in the adjoining cage (social facilitation). The third group learned while another rat was pressing a bar for food. It was found that the two experimental groups were no different in learning, but that both learned faster than rats alone.

Wheeler and Davis (1967) trained rats on a DRL 10 schedule: this means that responses less than ten seconds apart are not reinforced. When placed with other rats, they pressed more often than when alone – even though this meant that they received less food reinforcement. It was reported that aggression developed in several cases. So in this instance the other rat led to an increase in responding, even though this meant less reinforcement and the other rat was distracting. This seems to be good evidence for an arousal type of increase.

Delfini and Fouts (1974) tried a new method of testing the effects of social facilitation by training rats to treat other rats as discriminative stimuli. After initial training on bar pressing, rats were trained on a separate task to discriminate reinforcement or not in the presence of another rat. They were then tested on the original task alone or in the presence of another rat. The results were hard to interpret, unfortunately, but the method could be usefully repeated (see Holder, 1958 below).

Treichler et al. (1971) found that rats were more resistant to the extinction when trained alone but tested in pairs. Pishkin and Shurley (1966) found that rats placed in sensory deprivation responded more afterwards if they had been in a group. This suggested to the authors that the companions had lower arousal levels. *All* rats were tested alone, however. More responding still might have occurred in group tested rats.

Overall, there seems to be evidence for mere presence effects in some studies, especially in Wheeler and Davis (1967). The other studies, mostly highlight the problem of distraction, with some finding a trained companion more distracting and some a naive companion more distracting. While these distractions have not been from increased direct interaction with the companion animals, as occurred with the feeding studies, the distraction is still present. Clearly, we need to be able to predict distraction effects independently of their effects on bar pressing before more can be concluded.

Maze running in rats

Holder (1958) paired rats in pre-trial sessions such that some were associated with being rewarded, some associated with no reward and frustration, and some with equal number of trials leading to reward and non-reward. Although there was no alone comparison condition (unfortunately!), rats later performed faster when the stimulus rat had been associated earlier with reward. The non-reward group were worst of all.

Langenes and White (1975) found no evidence of social facilitation in maze running, and even some inhibition. It seems likely that there were problems with the distraction by the social stimulus (p. 643), perhaps exacerbated because the rats were housed individually.

Hamrick, Cogan and Woolam (1971) tested alones, audiences, and mirror audiences in mice. It was found that the mirror group learned a maze faster than the other two groups, but the audience group ran slower than the other two on a runway. Species differences were suggested. Since the mirror is unlikely to have increased objective self-awareness in these rats, a distraction effect could be presumed.

Becker and Franks (1975) ran naive rats in a maze alone, in pairs or in threes. They found that having more rats led to faster performances. Adding a trained rat to a naive rat worked better still; while adding two trained rats had an even greater effect. Their method seems to point to cueing effects causing the results.

The results from this section suggest conflicting effects of rats in maze running. All suffer from the same problem, however: that distraction was not assessed independently of the performance results. Every facilitation and inhibition can be explained by appealing to distraction effects: some have said their experienced rats were more distracting, others their naive rats. Some have appealed to the size of the mazes. As summarized for the last section, until this factor is clearly manipulated no causation can be assigned.

Avoidance and escape in rats

Rasmussen (1939) found that rats in groups took longer to learn shock avoidance than rats alone. Cunningham and Roberts (1973) found that paired rats learned an avoidance response more slowly than individuals. It seems that aggression during shock led to this. The same was found by Benedict, Cofer and Cole (1980) when a spectator rat was used. It was not mentioned, unfortunately, whether the rats attempted to attack the spectator rats as well.

Angermeier, Schaul and James (1959) placed rats with either naive rats or escape trained rats. The rats in the latter condition learned to escape faster. Unfortunately, again, there was no alone comparison made.

Overall, the results seem clear that avoidance and escape responses are inhibited by the presence of other rats. The same has been found for humans (Ader and Tatum, 1963), although the mechanisms are probably quite different. Most of the rat studies mention that aggression occurred when in pairs. This was not reported for the human subjects of Ader and Tatum (1963), although there may have been some 'animosity' towards the experimenter from the electric shocks!

So once more the interaction engendered by putting the rats together has probably led to the effects, although the interaction was negative rather than positive in the present cases. Moreover, it is almost impossible to separate out the mere presence effects from the interaction effects.

Miscellaneous behaviour in rats

Simmel and McGee (1966) found that pairs of rats explored more than alones. They suggested that an earlier study (Simmel, 1962) had not found this because there were insufficient trials. This result was replicated by Hughes (1969).

Lepley (1937) and Bruce (1937) found that pairs of rats did *not* run more than rats alone. Lepley (1939) also found no effects. Bruce (1941) found no evidence for any imitation or social facilitation effects beyond what could be explained by competition. Since few details were given for these studies, we do not know whether the rats were housed together or whether there was much interference or distraction present.

Observing sexual behaviour in rats, Larsson (1956) found that while the number of intromissions was no different between groups of rats or a single pair, the number of ejaculations increased in groups. No alone condition was possible in this case, of course.

Rivero (1971) found that rats ran for longer on a treadmill in pairs than alone. The criterion was collapse from exhaustion. Lastly, Paul et al. (1973) studied hunger-induced killing in rats, but all their rats were tested alone. There were no special facilitation conditions at all.

7.6 Primates (excluding Homo sapiens)

While a lot of research has been done on social attachments in primates, especially in isolating animals from birth, little has been done which can be explicitly attributed to social facilitation. For example, a test by Wechkin (1970) was really a test of imitation and observational learning. Imitation was found when the observer was familiar with the demonstrator. There was no alone comparison, however. This was also true for Lepoivre and Pallaud (1985).

Stamm (1961) tested pairs of monkeys, which were housed together, either alone or as pairs. More responses were made when tested in pairs. One unusual effect was that the dominant monkeys seemed to press less when alone. The time was taken up instead with emotional behaviours, such as pacing, jumping, and yelling. These were not present when the subordinates were there. So in these animals caged together, the effect occurred when isolated rather than paired. It was interesting that this occurred only for the dominant monkey.

Harlow and Yudin (1933) had earlier tested monkeys not housed together, and had found the same result. More food was eaten by pairs than by alones. The non-competition condition may still have had residual competition, however, especially since trails were alternated.

Gunnar, Gonzalez and Levine (1980) removed rhesus monkeys from their home cages and placed them in different social conditions. After half an hour, animals with a familiar peer had lower plasma cortisol levels than animals with either an unfamiliar peer or alone. The effects disappeared after twenty-two hours. This supports fear reduction interpretations.

A final point which is relevant is the report by Caine (1990). She found that the experimenter's presence affected the time her tamarins entered their nestbox. It was later with a familiar or unfamiliar observer, and later when the observers were either facing away or towards the monkeys. When a video camera was used the monkeys nested earlier. Caine attributed this to anti-predator behaviour.

7.7 Invertebrates

Ants

Chen (1937) found that ants in groups moved more earth than single ants. They also began work more quickly. Sakagami and Hayashida (1962), on the other hand, found less work in groups.

Two reasons will be suggested for this discrepancy. First, Sakagami and Hayashida (1962) had the ants working in small tubes, which may have added coordination problems to the animals working in groups. The second reason is that Chen (1937) kept the ants in colonies, whereas Sakagami and Hayashida (1962) kept them isolated between sessions. The latter also reported that a lot of time was spent in social interaction when in groups. So the physical distraction when interacting with conspecifics may have led to less work in groups.

Like Sakagami and Hayashida (1962), Sudd (1971, 1972) found less work in pairs of ants. The rate of digging was the same for both conditions, but there was more time spent in social interaction when in the groups. Unfortunately, he did not report whether the ants were kept in colonies or isolated. Based on the explanation given for the earlier discrepant ant results, it would be predicted that they had been kept isolated.

Cockroaches

Gates and Allee (1933) tested running in cockroaches. Isolated animals were quicker than paired animals, which were quicker than groups of three. Fewer errors were made by the isolated animals. The authors do point out at the end of the paper (p. 357) that the cockroaches were distracting each other and that there was group interference (p. 356).

In a test of the drive theory of social facilitation, Zajonc, Heingartner and Herman (1969) ran cockroaches in easy or hard mazes, alone or with a co-actor or audience. It was found that simple performance was facilitated and complex performance was inhibited with any other animal present (see also Zajonc, 1968b). A second experiment seemed to suggest that mirrors and odours were a distracting influence.

Other invertebrates

Connolly (1968) tested drosophila flies preening alone or with an 'audience' of ten other flies. More preening, and more time spent preening, was found for groups, especially for female flies. Order effects were not checked, however, and all animals were tested alone before the group.

Hosey et al. (1985) found a facilitation of both latency to move and running time for centipedes on a simple runway when there was an audience, but not when co-action. There were problems with the control groups, however, which make interpretation difficult. Two very similar control groups showed markedly different patterns which places some doubt on the reliability of the results of the other groups.

7.8 Fish

Bauer and Turner (1974) tested goldfish with a clear view of another fish, no view of another fish, or with a mirror. General activity levels slowly increased for fish either with a mirror or another fish. No effect on eating was found. It was suggested that competition is essential for social facilitation.

Warren et al. (1975) found that goldfish acquired an avoidance response quicker in groups than alone (see rats in 7.5). Trained fish did not further facilitate learning. This had been found previously by Welty (1934), who also found that the fish ate more in schools. Welty's fish lived in the aquarium, unlike the fish of Warren et al. The schooling which occurred in a novel environment may have allowed more cues from the other fishes' behaviour. Unlike Welty, Warren et al. did not find an advantage to having a trained fish in the group. There was possibly a ceiling effect.

Hale (1956) found that grouped green sunfish learned a simple maze quicker than individual fish. Allee et al. (1948) found that grouped fish grew faster than both isolated fish and fish in visual contact. Olla and Samet (1974) found that fish viewing feeding fish took less time to start feeding themselves; isolated fish were in the middle; and fish viewing a non-feeding school took even longer to start feeding.

Gleason, Weber and Weber (1977) found that while groups of five fish took less time to learn avoidance responses than individuals, pairs of fish took longer than individuals. It was suggested that pairs showed more aggression and this may have disturbed them. Alternatively, if the groups showed a cueing effect, then the larger group would have been more likely to have had some good learners amongst them.

In a series of studies, Uematsu (1970, Uematsu and Ogawa, 1975; Uematsu and Saito, 1973) found that fish ate more in larger groups. This worked with a variety of different fish species. In two other studies, Uematsu (1971a, b) found an increase in eating and also evidence that it was the visual stimulus of another fish which led to the increase, rather than seeing others eating, learning, or imitation.

The results from all the fish results are interesting to compare with the rat studies. The fish seem to have less interaction when put in groups, and seem to utilize observational cues better than the rats. For these reasons the opposite result to rats was found with avoidance learning: groups of fish learned faster than individuals. In the only case where inhibition of avoidance learning was found (Gleason et al., 1977: pairs condition), it was reported that interaction (aggression) interfered with feeding in the zebra fish.

7.9 Birds

Chickens

(a) Feeding

Tolman (1964) found that chicks raised in isolation ate less than those raised in pairs. Partial isolation had no effect. Social interaction seemed to be a *necessary* condition for social facilitation. Tolman and Wilson (1965) also found that social interaction was required for social facilitation effects, at least over a longer period. A reduction in fear could not account for the results. This was also suggested by another finding of social facilitation effects even with pre-exposure to the testing situation (Tolman and Wellman, 1968). Tolman (1965a) found that with a short test, and with an unfamiliar testing area, the reduced fear in chicks with a companion led to greater eating. Tolman (1965b) found that a mirror was enough to increase eating (cf. Gallup et al., 1972).

This suggested that the social facilitation effects might be different for short and long terms: over a short time, the fear reduction in the presence of a companion leads to facilitation; over a longer time (Tolman and Wilson, > 1 hour), interaction is necessary for social facilitation – which perhaps suggests that some effect of cueing is utilized or learned arousal is generated.

Tolman (1967a) found that pairs of chicks pecked more than singles, and that an added tapping sound increased pecking as well. There was no interaction of the two. Tolman (1967b) used a surrogate model of a hen and found an interaction between pecking and tapping. The sound of tapping alone did not increase pecking rate. Silent pecking increased pecking rate, but pecking with tapping increased it even further.

Tolman (1968a) found that the amount of deprivation in a companion chick affected rate of pecking. When more deprived, and therefore presumably eating more, the test chick also pecked more. It made no difference whether free interaction was possible or not. A second experiment found that a companion check led to more pecking, even if there was no free interaction, and even if the other was not eating at all. In the non-feeding condition, there was a slight tendency to reduce pecking, it should be noted.

A third experiment found that the non-feeding companion led to an increase in feeding over the presence of a dead companion. The presence of a dead companion was no different to being isolated. So it seems that just another animal behaving is enough to get facilitation effects in chicks.

Overall, the results suggest that while the non-feeding behaviour of a companion is sufficient for social facilitation, feeding behaviour is certain to get the effects. This was also found by Tolman (1969). The other experiments suggest that this is probably due to cueing by the companion chick.

(b) Other behaviours

Smith (1957) found that chicks learned a runway quicker if with companions. They did better still with a trained companion, but only when this companion was familiar. So again there seems to be a disinhibition effect: the reaction to unfamiliars is inhibiting, so cueing or other mere presence effects can only take place if a familiar other is the model. So the effects are a mixture of disinhibition and cueing.

Frank and Meyer (1970, 1974; Meyer and Frank, 1970) showed that *learning of pecking* can be socially facilitated in chicks. This appears to go against Zajonc's hypothesis that learning is inhibited in social contexts. However, the original statement was that simple or dominant responses were facilitated. It is likely that pecking and imprinting in young chicks are simple innate responses, which will be dominant even in young chicks. Frank and Meyer (1974) also found that the pecking extinguished more slowly when trained with companions.

A number of studies have found that it is not the presence or absence of other chicks which facilitates but the similarity of the setting to the setting in which the behaviour was learned (Brown, 1978; Brown and Kiely, 1974; Hogan and Abel, 1971; May and Dorr, 1968; Strobel, Freedman and MacDonald, 1970; Strobel and MacDonald, 1974; Turner, 1964; Wilson, 1968). If chicks are imprinted alone or with a group then facilitation of eating occurs when alone or in a group respectively. This gives good support for the disinhibition hypothesis.

Rajecki et al. (1975) tested three different hypotheses for social facilitation effects in animals: imitation, arousal and disinhibition (see Tolman, 1968b). To do this they used two responses: drinking and eating (see Rajecki, Wilder, Kidd and Jaeger, 1976) and deprived their animals of either food or water.

If imitation or cueing underlies social facilitation then the test chick should increase whatever behaviour the other was performing. If the arousal hypothesis is correct then they should increase whichever response satisfies their deprivation (dominant response). If the disinhibition hypothesis is correct then all responses should increase when less fearful in the presence of a companion – not just the deprived response.

Rajecki et al. (1975) found that even when pairs of chicks were performing different responses, there was facilitation. These results support the disinhibition hypothesis over the other two. Rajecki et al. (1975) also found more distress calls when chicks were isolated in a second experiment, lending even more support to the disinhibition explanation.

Franchina et al. (1986) also found that drinking could be facilitated with a non-drinking companion. These authors also tested some effects of familiarity with the drinking tubes. Evidence was found for both cueing from the co-acting chicks and an increase in arousal level.

Further studies suggested that rather than a general increase in drive affecting the response hierarchy, the presence of others can change the response hierarchy itself (Rajecki, Kidd and Ivins, 1976). While chicks pecked more with companions than when alone or with strangers, different types of response hierarchies were emitted. In particular, there were distress calls when alone and tonic immobility – which cannot be equated with an 'arousal' increase.

In an excellent series of experiments, Karakashian, Gyger and Marler (1988) varied the types of audience and compared these with alone. They measured the alarm calling in male chickens. Subtle changes in the audience affected the results, such as the sex of the audience, their social relationships with the subjects, and other species of chickens. Cueing from the audience animal was excluded. This fine detail is perhaps a model for the way future research in animal social facilitation should go.

Other birds

Clayton (1976a, b) found that for social facilitation of eating in ducks, the others had to be deprived. He suggested that the others drew attention to the water, so acting as a cue. All the ducks were tested in groups, however, so there was no actual alone condition. Facilitation of eating in the presence of food-deprived others was also found by Mason and Reidinger (1981) for red-winged blackbirds.

Walk and Walters (1984) found some interesting results for ducklings. More ducklings on a visual cliff descended when alone than when in pairs. It was suggested that previous 'reckless' behaviour of single ducklings found in such experiments may have arisen from the distress of being separated from companions.

Three studies have used pigeons. Zentall and Hogan (1976) found that a pigeon alone pecked less than in the presence of either a non-pecking companion or an eating companion. Both these also pecked less than with another key-pecking pigeon present.

Hake and Laws (1967) found that the presence of another bird inhibited avoidance suppression. This worked even though there was no competition and the others were unfamiliar. Hake, Powell and Olsen (1969) found that this occurred mainly at the higher voltages of shock. They also only found it if the other bird was eating. These results indirectly support the fear reduction hypothesis.

Bruder and Lehrman (1967) found that ring doves incubated more when in pairs than individually. Allee and Masure (1936) found that pairs of parakeets performed worse in a maze than single birds. If trained alone they were better even if later caged in pairs. Lazarus (1979) found that weaverbirds fed more when there were more of them, even if these others were not feeding. Deni (1977a, b) found inhibition with quails when they could see each other. The birds in both studies had been caged alone, so the test may have been a stressful event. Bruen and Dunham (1973) found that birds built fewer nests alone than if they could hear and see other birds.

Alones were no different to only hearing other birds. This replicated the result of Morris (1954).

A large number of other bird studies will not be reviewed since they deal with effects of synchrony and large or small flocks, rather than individuals versus groups of birds. Most have not used an alone condition (e.g., Mason and Reidinger, 1981). Measures have included dustbathing (Borchelt and Overmann, 1974), egg-laying (Victoria and Collias, 1973), nest building (Collias, Brandman, et al., 1971; Collias, et al., 1971), weight of testes (Brockway, 1964), reproduction (MacRoberts and MacRoberts, 1972), clumping (Evans, 1970), mobbing (Lombardi and Curio, 1985), behaviour synchrony (Birke, 1974), vigilance (Inglis and Lazarus, 1981) and hatching (Vince, 1964).

7.10 Miscellaneous animals

Winslow (1944) tested cats in a runway with food at the end. His experiment, although interesting, tested for competition effects, not social facilitation. He found that the cats were on average slower to run in pairs or threes than alone. This probably is due to social interactions interfering with this solitary species during the running. Indeed, he remarks that the loser in a paired trial almost always attacked the winner. No wonder they were more cautious when in pairs!

Platt et al. (1967) found that armadillos ate more when placed together. Sessions were alternated randomly, and all lived together in the meantime. There was no effect of repeated trials. The same was essentially found by Platt and James (1966; Platt et al., 1968) for o'possums, except that the difference between solitary and social feeding increased with repeated trials. They are normally gregarious when young but become less sociable as they get older. The same o'possums were tested at 140 days. Those that had been separated showed social facilitation; those kept together did not. As found by James and Gilbert (1955 and James, 1960), the social facilitation effects seems to be learned.

Lindsay et al. (1976) measured mounting and ejaculation in rams. It was found that an audience of rams did not affect the dominant rams' mounting or ejaculations, but that subordinate rams mounted and ejaculated more when alone than when dominant rams were watching. Nothing was said about interaction with the audience, except that the audience seemed 'interest' and 'agitated' (p. 820).

Boice, Quanty and Williams (1974) reported that larger groups of frogs ate faster. It did not matter whether they were habituated or not, although all unhabituated groups ate slower overall than those habituated.

Carr and Hirth (1961) found that more young turtles reach the surface from their eggs if there are more of them. The observations reported suggest that this is more a coordination and cueing problem than anything remotely to do with social facilitation, as here defined.

7.11 Conclusions

It is now time to draw out some conclusions from this wealth of material. First we will look at the fear considerations mentioned in 7.3. Then we will cover four major consistencies in this literature.

On the whole, there is support for the fear considerations which were tested, although this was not always done across all species. First, there seem to be fear effects (independent of any social facilitation) when testing animals in environments which are unfamiliar (for example, Brown, 1978; Brown and Kiely, 1974; Hogan and Abel, 1971; May and Dorr, 1968; Moore, Byers and Baron, 1981; Strobel, Freedman and MacDonald, 1970; Strobel and MacDonald, 1974; Turner, 1964; Wilson, 1968).

Second, most research has found stronger fear effects when the other animal was a stranger (James, 1960, dogs; James and Gilbert, 1955, dogs; Scott and Marston, 1950, dogs; Smith, 1957, chicks), but not all (Taylor, 1981, rats).

Third, the effects sometimes seemed to depend upon whether the animals were housed in groups or in isolation (Chen, 1937, ants; Deni, 1977a, b, quails; Latané, 1969, rats; Latané and Glass, 1968, rats; Latané, Poor and Sloan, 1972, rats; Latané et al., 1971, rats; Ross and Ross, 1949a, b, dogs; Sakagami and Hayashida, 1962, ants; Stamm, 1961, monkeys), but not always (Taylor, 1981, rats).

So apart from Taylor (1981), the results suggest limitations on ever finding pure social facilitation effects in animals because of fear reactions. This suggest that more needs to be done with rats to find out where the discrepancy appears in Taylor's work. Although the difference could be put down to procedural or rat strain differences, the studies of Taylor seem clear and robust enough that they should not be dismissed merely because they go against the pattern.

The other conclusions will be handled in five sections.

The effects of social interaction

A large number of the studies reported changes due to the two animals interacting. This had three types of outcome.

First, sometimes there was direct interference or coordination problems because of the animals interacting in close proximity (Cooper and Levine, 1973, deermice; Cunningham and Roberts, 1973, rats; Gleason, Weber and

Weber, 1977, fish; Rasmussen, 1939, rats; Scott and Marston, 1950, dogs). This came about through competition (Scott and Marston, 1950, dogs), huddling (Cooper and Levine, 1973, deermice), and aggression (Cunningham and Roberts, 1973, rats; Gleason, Weber and Weber, 1977, fish; Rasmussen, 1939, rats; Winslow, 1944, cats).

Second, frequently there were distractive influences reported (Bankart, Bankart and Burkett, 1974, rats; Deni and Jorgensen, 1976a, rats; Gates and Allee, 1933, cockroaches; Henning and Zentall, 1981, rats; Langenes and White, 1975, rats; Moore et al., 1981, rats; Strobel, 1972, rats; Zentall and Levine, 1972, rats).

The third effect of social interaction was that of disinhibition: there was less stress and therefore facilitation of other behaviours (Hake and Laws, 1967, Hake et al., 1969, pigeons; Rajecki et al., 1975, chicks; Smith, 1957, chicks; Tolman, 1965a, b, chicks).

On the whole, it seems that the effects of increased social interaction are positive for chicks but negative for other animals, particularly the rodents. Chickens seem to take up responses such as feeding when less fearful, whereas fear reduction in rats seems to lead to increased distraction through social interaction.

Fear reduction in groups

There was good evidence for group fear reduction across a wide range of species (Baum, 1969, rats; Davitz and Mason, 1955, rats; Gunnar et al., 1980, rhesus monkeys; Hake and Laws, 1967, Hake et al. 1969, pigeons; Hughes, 1969, rats; Marina and Bauermeister, 1974, rats; Moore et al., 1981, rats; Morrison and Hill, 1967, rats; Rajecki et al., 1975, chicks; Smith, 1957, chicks; Tachibana, 1974a, b, rats; Tolman, 1965a, b, chicks; Taylor, 1981, rats; Walk and Walters, 1984, ducklings).

Clearly, it is a major influence in animal social facilitation settings for most of the species considered. As mentioned above, just reducing the fear does not help predict what behaviours will fill the gap. For rats it seemed that distractive social interactions appeared; for chicks, it seemed that on-going responses such as eating (re)appeared.

Cueing effects

For some species, there were obvious influences from the other animal giving cues about how to behave (Angermeier et al., 1959, rats; Baum, 1969, rats; Becker and Franks, 1975, rats; Clayton, 1976a and b, ducks; Gleason et al., 1977, fish; Olla and Samet, 1974, fish; Smith, 1957, chicks; Tolman, 1964,

1986 7a, 1968a, 1969, chicks; Tolman and Wilson, 1965, chicks; Warren et al., 1975, goldfish; Zentall and Hogan, 1976, pigeons; Zentall and Levine, 1972, rats).

This seemed an especially important influence both for schools of fish and for bar pressing with rats. Indeed, most of the fish studies implicated cueing effects of some sort or another. Uematsu (1971a, b), however, found that the visual *stimulus* of another guppy led to the effect rather than seeing the other's feeding behaviour.

The learning of social facilitation

Some studies investigated the learning of social facilitation effects. Some looked across the developmental span of an animal's life (James, 1960, dogs; James and Gilbert, 1955, dogs; Platt and James, 1966, o'possums; Platt et al., 1968, o'possums), while one looked at how conspecifics could become discriminative stimuli for reinforcement (Holder, 1958, rats). All found significant learning of social facilitation. It was something which developed rather than an innate behaviour pattern.

Mere presence effects in animals

A curious point about this literature is that there are few mere presence studies. This is probably because most animals do not react well to complete isolation and, as we have seen, it is difficult to arrange a presence condition without interaction, cueing, or distraction of some sort. In addition, audience conditions are of little applied interest with animals. So, except for using dead animals (which will have other fear effects!), another animal is almost never a *mere presence*. And arranging tests in which they are merely present leads to side-effects. ˊ

Despite this, there were some studies which seemed to find effects when the other animal was engaged in a different behaviour, which might be about the closest approximation (Benedict et al., 1980, rats; Franchina et al., 1986, chicks; Hosey et al., 1985, centipedes; Lazarus, 1979, weaverbirds; Rajecki et al., 1975, chicks; Tolman, 1968a, chicks; Zajonc et al., 1969, cockroaches; Zentall and Hogan, 1976, pigeons).

The problem, then, is that we might *never* be able to find out if there are residual effects of another animal's presence besides distraction, cueing and fear reduction. If this is true, then it becomes important to explore the distraction, cueing, and fear reduction phenomena themselves, rather than continue searching for 'pure' social facilitation effects. Perhaps once this is done, a new way of getting at residual effects might become possible.

7.12 The effects of one animal on another

A large number of effects have been raised in this animal literature, all of which can evoke similar facilitation or inhibition effects: competition, direct reinforcement, cueing, general arousal increase, fear reduction effects, disinhibition, contagion, imitation, and learning of discriminative stimuli.

One major conclusion from this literature is that a single experiment cannot decide between these mechanisms. To do that, there must be knowledge about the mechanisms involved, the motivation of the behaviour, and its origin. This is clearly absent from the animal literature in most cases. So before any social facilitation studies are conducted, the background to particular species needs to be carefully explored. The work of Scott (1968), James (1961), Tolman (1968b), and Karakashian et al. (1988) is exemplary in this respect, and firmer conclusions can be made from this type of research.

More importantly, evidence for these mechanisms must come from sources independent of the measures of facilitation and inhibition. For example, one must be able to recognize whether an animal has utilized cues from another animal independently of noting an increase in that behaviour. Few of the studies have done this, and almost all therefore turn out to be ambiguous with regard to the mechanisms involved.

The motivations for each type of behaviour have been assumed to be different, but no independent measures of them are taken. To help sort this out, in a small measure, some clarifying remarks on the different proposed phenomena will be given.

(1) Competition

This refers to situations in which there is a limited resource for which the animals are motivated, such that if one animal gains the resource, the other misses out. The motivation for engaging in competition is to gain the scarce resource. The method for obtaining the scarce resource may come from any number of sources, even from cues of the other animal, so the different effects might be hard to show independently.

(2) Imitation

One animal does what another is doing despite no obvious source of motivation for behaving that way. The term seems to be used whenever a behaviour is copied for 'intrinsic' reasons. There may be an innate mechanism for imitation (which therefore remains hypothetical), or else imitation may have been reinforced in the past history of the animal. The imitated behaviour might be almost anything, although presumably the behaviour once imitated is reinforced or else it stops.

This all means that labelling a behaviour as imitation, merely avoids the questions of motivations and mechanisms. Calling a behaviour imitation does not tell us the function of the imitation, nor the mechanisms by which the animal came to imitate. It cannot therefore be used as an explanation unless these aspects are independently assessed.

(To put this another way (see 6.5), imitation is a term used when researchers have wanted to talk about animals having a *generalized reinforcer*, such that a variety of behaviours are copied without any obvious direct reinforcement.)

(3) Contagion

As for imitation but where many animals join in. Like imitation, labelling an event 'contagion' does not imply any one motivation or mechanism. It is likewise only a descriptive term, and does not explain anything.

(4) Cueing

These are cases for which one animal seems to utilize aspects of the behaviour of the other animal for a particular end. This is different to imitation only in that the cueing behaviour itself appears to be motivated independently: the other animal merely provides information sufficient to carry it out. This means that it is not clearly separable from imitation unless the source of the motivation can be shown independently. For example, an animal could use cues from another animal to better compete with it, so competition could act as a mediator of cueing.

Uematsu (1971a) called this 'the feeding behaviour recognition effect' as opposed to just the visual stimulus of another animal – 'the presence recognition effect' (p. 48). He only found the latter in guppies.

(5) Fear reduction

This refers to a reduction in fear responses when conspecifics are present. As indicated above, this needs to be established independently of measures of facilitation. It also does not establish what happens once the fear is reduced. This seems to be different for different species (7.11). If the fear reduction is not assessed independently then what is measured might be a result of behaviour filling in the time not spent in fear responses.

(6) Fear induction

Clearly with some animals (cats, for example), placing them with others increases fear responses. This will usually stop responding, which might otherwise have occurred. Finding this out, like fear reduction, requires previous knowledge of the animal. Social facilitation studies with no independent measures or background ethological research on the animals will not elicit this information.

(7) Distraction

Distraction effects will clearly be present with the addition of a conspecific in almost all species. Almost all the other effects (cueing, imitation, social interactions, fear reduction, fear induction, competition) will entail concomitant distraction. It is therefore exceedingly difficult to independently assess the impact of this variable. It will almost certainly play a causal role, but the present author is doubtful that it can ever be really assessed independently.

7.13 Implications for human social facilitation research

The last thing to do in this chapter is to draw some implications for human social facilitation research. On the whole it has been stressed that the responses of animals to the presence of conspecifics need to be researched independently before commencing the social facilitation research. The major point here is that with humans, researchers have either assumed that they know the background behavioural assessments (human ethograms?), or else they ignore them.

With competition, for example, researchers can either try to reduce the effects of competition in social facilitation research, or ignore it. In the former case they need to actually know a great deal about competition in order to do this, with adequate sorts of pretesting in the same setting. Where competition has just been ignored instead, it has usually been done on intuitive grounds. The researchers have arranged things so there did not *seem* to be much competition present. (These same researchers would be horrified if competition researchers intuitively guessed, with no independent evidence, that social facilitation effects probably were not present in their experiments!)

In the latter case, when competition effects are just ignored, we can always wonder how much they played a rôle in any 'social facilitation' effects. This was raised extensively in Chapter 2. But even in doing this, it is only possible by assuming many things about the species in question.

The conclusion then, for both animal and human studies, is that for such subtle effects as social facilitation, if we wish to find the effects separate from competition, cueing and the like, then we need to independently know the behaviour of the animal first. Background psychological and ethological studies are needed to assess any effects of any proposed mechanism. You must 'know your animal' first, whether this is a human or an armadillo. We do not know at present how much competition humans are likely to engage in when merely put with another person.

Mere presence effects

What we *do* know of the behaviour of humans suggests that there are some obvious differences to animal behaviour. First, much social behaviour is governed by generalized reinforcers (5.5) rather than specific motivators. This is why we can find a generalized social conformity effect in humans, but nothing quite comparable in animal behaviour (except perhaps innate imitation mechanisms?).

This leads to an important conclusion for mere presence effects. If mere presence effects are those effects that are residual after more obvious, externally motivated, effects are removed, then only two things are left: 1) innate responses to conspecifics, and 2) effects of any generalized reinforcers.

This means that mere presence research should be directed to finding innate social responses in animals, and generalized reinforcers in humans. This latter will depend on the culture, the language, the particular personal history, etc. (Skinner, 1957). There might also be innate social responses in humans too, of course.

Social interaction effects in humans

Another interesting difference between the animal and human literature is the lack of social interaction effects in the latter, which were omnipresent and problematic for the animal studies. It would seem that social interaction in humans, at least for the populations used, is less disruptive. Subjects need only say hello to the confederate, and they can ignore them after that.

In general, subjects are dissuaded from talking or interacting during experiments. This suggests two ways that social interaction distraction can arise: from monitoring the other person (see Chapter 4) and from more subtle social interactions, such as social comparison (see 6.3). So if direct interaction effects can be reduced in humans, but not in animals, then mere presence, as defined, can probably only be shown experimentally in humans.

The subtlety of human social interaction effects can be seen by comparing the effects presented in Chapters 5 and 6, with the directness of the animal effects presented in this chapter (cueing, imitation, aggression, huddling, fear reduction, fear induction, competition). Again, human social interaction can proceed without immediate external motivators because the consequences maintaining behaviour are intermittent and generalized.

8 Social facilitation effects in humans

8.1 Mere presence effects in humans

Introduction

The large number of theories of social facilitation were reviewed in Chapters 4, 5, and 6. It was suggested there that although most theories have been supported by some experimental evidence, the evidence presented has usually been consistent with other theories as well. To ignore this in a review leads to misinterpretations.

More than this, the many poorly designed studies need to be separated from the more carefully controlled ones. This is especially important with the subtle conditions necessary for tests of mere presence. As was pointed out in Chapter 2, many studies have had the experimenter present in the 'Alone' condition; to include these in the total review would be to blur the better studies.

The present chapter reviews the experimental literature on mere presence and other social facilitation effects. To do this, a situation-specific analysis was made of the literature. That is, each study was 'taxonomically' analysed according to a number of criteria which categorized the situation of the experiment. Each was then examined to see what effects, if any, were found. To carry this out, criteria were needed to define what will be meant by a *well-controlled* mere presence study and a *poorly controlled* one. This has not been made explicit before in the literature. The criteria which were formulated will be outlined below.

This way of reviewing the literature differs from traditional reviews which add up the number of studies finding a particular effect, those finding the opposite effect, and those finding no effect (Glaser, 1982; Kushnir, 1981). Such reviews have usually not been exhaustive in their literature search and have often been selective. When they have been exhaustive, they have usually included numerous poorly run experiments on equal footing with better studies (Glaser, 1982).

The present review also differs from the forms of meta-analysis which put studies into categories and calculate effect sizes (Bond and Titus, 1983). Such reviews can suffer from a number of faults (Cook and Leviton, 1980; Green and Hall, 1984). These include dubious categories, rough categorizations which ignore other aspects of the results found, and again, the inclusion of poorly controlled studies. The readers can carry this out for themselves if they wish, based on the information presented here.

The review used parts of both these types of reviews. This was the method used: the entire literature was searched for every study; explicit criteria were defined to separate the good studies from the others; each good study was analysed for the specific situation of the procedure; and this was related to the effects found. One advantage to this method is that if a criterion is disputed, then the information is there to re-examine the studies affected. That is, the review is not closed. A further advantage is that by examining the procedural details of each study in detail the review becomes exploratory. New connections can be found which have been missed in other reviews.

Initial review of studies

For the initial data collection stage (Cooper, 1982), any study comparing the behaviour of people performing alone with people performing while others were present was obtained. These came from the *Psychological Abstracts* as well as the references of all previous reviews and experimental reports on social facilitation. At this stage studies were excluded if they clearly involved group discussion, imitation or the exchange of reinforcements. This left 313 studies. The review also left out about thirty Dissertation Abstracts. This was done because they provided few details of the experimental procedure – which was of prime concern for the present review.

For the first round of the analysis, all studies were carefully examined and those with the following design problems were excluded:

(1)   if interaction was allowed between the subjects and the other persons present;
(2)   if there were instructions allowing for imitation, competition, cooperation, cueing, or other directive effects;
(3)   if there was no clear Alone condition in which the subjects were physically alone. Studies were excluded if the experimenter had been present in the Alone condition;
(4)   if there was no clear Presence condition with at least one person present not directing the subject. Excluded here were a number of studies using mirrors, one-way mirrors, and computers and videos;
(5)   if the studies had more general design faults such as the lack of a control group or if sufficient detail was not available.

With these criteria applied only 91 studies remain. These constitute the clear tests between people behaving alone and people behaving in the presence of a passive, non-directive other. Details of the 222 studies rejected are given in Table 2. The most frequent fault was having the experimenter present in the Alone condition. This was despite the early warning from Ekdahl (1929) who had shown effects of the experimenter's presence.

While the remaining studies are the clear social facilitation experiments, they still do not constitute clear tests of mere presence effects. A number of further criteria are needed for this (Markus, 1978; Zajonc, 1965, 1980). If mere presence effects exist independently of evaluation effects, then all sources of evaluation should be taken into account.

One principal source of evaluation in the remaining studies is from the use of the experimenter as the person present. It is likely that the experimenter will be treated as evaluative since they know what is expected of subjects and they will evaluate the performance after the subject has finished. A second source of evaluation is from the person present being able to observe the subject. Where observation is possible then greater evaluation should be expected. Rather than just assume that experimenters and observers are felt to be evaluative by subjects, we will review the actual results of such studies later in this chapter.

Altogether four reviews will be made: first, those studies which test the more stringent criteria for mere presence; second, the effects of behaving in front of a passive experimenter compared to behaving alone; third, the effects of passively being observed; the final section will deal with manipulations which have used mirrors, videos, one-way mirrors, or computers rather than the presence of another person. These have never been reviewed before despite there being a sizeable social facilitation literature on them.

Mere presence studies

To review the mere presence studies a number of further criteria must be used. For example, the subject must be truly alone and not with the experimenter partially concealed. Chapman (1974), for example, reported the same effect for a partially concealed experimenter and an experimenter fully present. It made no difference to the subjects.

The following seven criteria were used to further define mere presence. These were used in addition to criteria 1 to 5 given above:

(6)   there should be no obvious emphasis on evaluation by the instructions or by the situation;

(7)   there should not be any differential emphasis on evaluation between the Alone and Presence conditions. Any inherent task evaluation in the Presence condition should also occur in the Alone condition;

Table 2. *Studies not used for review of experimental studies*

Studies	Reason for Rejection
Abel (1938)	Ss with subnormal IQs used
Ader & Tatum (1963)	Ss could interact
Allport (1920)	Rivalry implicit
Amoroso et al. (1972)	Not enough detail given
Amoroso and Walters (1969)	No Alone condition
Andersson and Brehmer (1977)	Interaction allowed
Athey and McIntyre (1987)	Not enough details of situation
Baldwin and Levin (1958)	E present
Bargh and Cohen (1978)	E present
Baron (1971)	Ss had prior experience of shocks
Baumeister and Forehand (1970)	Retarded subjects used
Beasley (1958)	Cooperation allowed
Beatty (1980)	Not enough detail given
Beck and Seta (1980)	Competition effects
Bell et al. (1982)	Subjects could easily compete
Bell and Yee (1989)	E present
Bennett (1946)	Not enough detail given
Bergum and Lehr (1962)	Interaction allowed
Bergum and Lehr (1963)	Interaction allowed
Bird (1973)	E present
Bode & Brutten (1963)	E present
Bowman and Dunn (1978)	E present
Brockner and Hutton (1978)	E present
Bruning and Mettee (1966)	Competition allowed
Buck and Parke (1972)	E in contact throuhout
Burger (1987)	No Alone condition
Burri (1931)	E present
Burtt (1921)	E present
Burwitz and Newell (1972)	E present
Carlin et al. (1972)	No Alone condition
Carment (1970a)	Rivalry implicit
Carment (1970b)	Rivalry implicit
Carment and Hodkin (1973)	E present
Carron and Bennett (1976)	Competition
Carver and Scheier (1981b)	E present
Chapman (1973b)	E present
Chapman (1975)	Cueing involved
Chapman and Wright (1976)	Cueing and interaction involved
Chevrette (1968)	E present
Church (1962)	Competition
Clark and Fouts (1973)	Results not given for Pretest
Clower and Dabbs (1974)	No Alone condition
Cohen (1979)	E in contact throughout; video in Alone condition
Cohen and Davis (1973)	E present
Colquhoun and Corcoran (1964)	E present
Cottrell, Rittle and Wack (1967)	E present
Cox (1966)	E present
Cox (1968)	E present
Craig, Best and Reith (1974)	No Alone condition
Criddle (1971)	No real audience
Dabbs and Clower (1973)	No Alone condition
Davidson and Kelly (1973)	Interaction allowed

Table 2. (*cont.*)

Studies	Reason for Rejection
Davis et al. (1968)	E watching in Alone condition
Deffenbacher, Platt and Williams (1974)	E present
Dey (1949)	Competition from familiarity, defined time limits, and ease of checking performance afterwards
Donoghue, McCarrey and Clement (1983)	Cueing and videotapes
Duflos (1967)	E present
Duflos, Zalenka and Desportes (1969)	E present
Elliot and Cohen (1981)	E present
Epley and Cottrell (1977)	Ss probably aroused by shocks; cues available from confederate
Farnsworth and Behner (1931)	Interaction allowed
Farnsworth and Williams (1937)	Interaction allowed
Forgas et al. (1980)	No Alone condition
Fouts (1979)	Not enough detail given
Fouts (1980)	Not enough detail given
Froming, Walker and Lopyan (1982)	No Alone condition
Fuller and Sheehy-Skeffington (1974)	No real audience
Gabrenya and Arkin (1979)	Small N used
Ganzer (1968)	No real audience
Gastorf, Suls and Sanders (1980)	Competition
Gates (1924)	E present
Gates and Rissland (1923)	Interaction allowed
Geen (1971)	E present
Geen (1974)	No Alone condition
Geen (1976a)	No Alone condition
Geen (1985)	Highly evaluative task
Glass, Gordon and Henchy (1970)	Not enough detail given
Good (1973)	No real audience
Gottlieb (1982)	E present
Greenberg and Firestone (1977)	No Alone condition
Greer (1983)	Interaction present
Grush (1978)	E present and interaction allowed
Gurnee (1937)	Cooperation allowed
Gurnee (1939)	Cooperation allowed
Gurnee (1962)	E present
Haas and Roberts (1975)	E present
Hake, Vukelich and Kaplan (1973)	Ss explicitly videoed throughout
Hamberger and Lohr (1981)	E present periodically in Alone condition to check electrode
Hanawalt and Ruttiger (1944)	E present
Harkins et al. (1980)	Cooperation allowed
Harper and Sanders (1975)	No Alone condition
Harrell and Schmitt (1973)	Cueing and competition present
Hartnett et al. (1976)	No Alone condition
Hatfield (1972)	Interaction allowed
Hicks (1968)	Interaction allowed
Higgs and Joseph (1971)	E present
Hillery and Fugita (1975)	E present
Hormuth (1982)	E present
Houston (1970)	E present
Hrycaiko and Hrycaiko (1980)	No Alone condition
Hunt and Hillery (1973)	E present

Table 2. (*cont.*)

Studies	Reason for Rejection
Husband (1940)	Cooperation allowed
Hutchinson and Cotton (1973)	E present
Innes and Sambrooks (1969)	E present
Isozaki (1979)	E nearby throughout
Jackson and Latané (1981)	No real audience; No Alone condition
Janssens and Nuttin (1976)	No Alone
Johnson and Davis (1972)	Competition from cueing; Ss given incentives
Johnson and Baker (1973)	Interaction allowed
Karst and Most (1973)	E present
Kawamura-Reynolds (1977)	E present
Keating and Latané (1976)	Not enough details given
Khalique (1979)	No Alone condition
Khalique (1980)	No Alone condition
Kieffer (1977)	No clear Alone condition
Kiesler (1966)	Competition allowed
Kissel (1965)	E in contact throughout
Kleck et al. (1976)	No real audience
Kljaic (1974)	Not enough details given
Knowles et al. (1976)	Recorder present in Alone condition
Kohfeld and Wietzel (1969)	E present
Kozar (1973)	Competition implicit
Kumar and Bhandari (1974)	Not enough details of E's position, order effects, or the task
Kumar and Kriplani (1972)	Not enough detail given
Laird (1923)	Interaction allowed
Lambert and Lowy (1957)	E present
Landers, Bauer and Feltz (1978)	E present
Landers, Donna M. (1975)	E present
Landers and Landers (1973)	E present
Laughlin et al. (1972)	E present
Levin et al. (1960)	No Alone condition
Levy and Fenley (1979)	Interaction allowed
Livingstone et al. (1974)	E present
Lombardo and Catalano (1975)	E present
Lombardo and Catalano (1978)	E present
Mallenby (1976)	E present
Malpass and Fitzpatrick (1959)	Administrator present
Manstead and Semin (1980; Exp.1–4)	No real audience
Martens (1969a)	E present
Martens (1969b)	E present
Martens and Landers (1969)	E present
Martens and Landers (1972)	E present
Martin and Knight (1985)	E present
Marx, Witter and Mueller (1972)	No Alone condition
Mash and Hedley (1975)	E present
Mayer (1904)	Competition
McCullagh and Landers (1976)	E present
McGhee (1973)	E present
Meddock et al. (1971)	No real Alone condition
Meglino (1976)	Cooperation; no Alone condition
Meumann (1904)	Interaction allowed
Michaels et al. (1982)	No Alone condition
Mintz and Collins (1985)	No social presence

Table 2. (*cont.*)

Studies	Reason for Rejection
Miyamoto (1979)	E present
Moore (1917)	Interaction allowed
Moore et al. (1988)	Highly evaluative task
Morrissette, Hornseth and Sheller (1975)	Competition implicit
Mukerji (1940)	Order effects not controlled
Noble et al. (1958)	Competition
Paloutzian (1975)	Cooperation involved
Passman (1977)	E present
Paterson, Philips and Pettijohn (1980)	E present
Pattinson and Pasework (1980)	No Alone condition
Pederson (1970)	E present
Pennebaker (1980)	Cueing present
Perl (1933)	Interaction allowed
Perlmutter and Montmollin (1952)	Cooperation allowed
Pessin and Husband (1933)	E present
Pines (1973)	E present; No Alone condition
Porter (1939)	unusual population used
Poteet and Weinberg (1980)	E present
Quarter and Marcus (1971)	E present
Query, Moore and Lerner (1966)	Interaction allowed
Rittle and Bernard (1977)	E present
Rosenquist and Shoberg (1968)	E present
Rule and Evans (1971)	No Alone condition
Sanchez and Clark (1981)	No real test made
Sanders (1984)	E present throughout
Sanders, Baron and Moore (1978)	T-S subjects encouraged to compete
Sapolsky and Zillman (1978)	Interaction allowed
Sasfy and Okun (1974)	E present
Scheier and Carver (1983)	No Alone condition
Scheier and Fenigstein and Buss (1974)	Victim present in Alone condition
Schramm and Danielson (1958)	Competition
Seidman et al. (1957)	E present
Sengupta and Sinha (1926)	E present to time Ss
Seta et al. (1988)	E present in room
Shaw (1932)	Cooperation allowed
Shrauger (1972)	E present
Siegel and Haugen (1964)	E present
Silver et al. (1986)	E present
Simmel, Baker and Collier (1969)	Interaction allowed
Simpson and Molloy (1971)	E present
Singer (1965)	E present
Singer (1970)	E present
Sommer and Sommer (1989)	No Alone condition
Sorrentino and Sheppard (1978)	No Alone condition
Soukup and Sommervill (1979)	E present
Steigleder et al. (1980)	Ss had prior experience; told about observation variable; E's presence unknown
Stotland and Zander (1958)	No Alone condition
Street (1974)	Competition implicit
Strube, Miles and Finch (1981)	No real Alone condition
Terris and Rahhal (1969)	E present
Thayer and Moore (1972)	E present
Thelen, Rehagen and Akamattsu	Interaction allowed

Table 2. (*cont.*)

Studies	Reason for Rejection
Travis (1925)	E present
Travis (1928)	Unusual population used
Triplett (1898)	Rivalry present
Wankel (1972)	E present
Wankel (1975)	E present
Wankel (1977)	E present
Wapner and Alper (1952)	E present
Watson (1928)	Interaction allowed
Wegner and Zeaman (1956)	Cooperation allowed
Weston and English (1926)	Test forms not controlled
Williams (1976)	Spouses used as presence
Williams, Harkins and Latané (1981)	Cooperation; no Alone condition
Wirtz and Wawra (1986)	No real Alone condition
Wolfgang (1967)	Competition probable
Worringham and Messick (1983)	No real Alone condition
Zajonc et al. (1970)	Ss given incentives; possible competition from cueing
Zucker (1978)	E present

(8)   the person present should not be the experimenter, who is likely to be perceived as evaluative;

(9)   the other person present should not be there to observe the subject, as this must be at least potentially evaluative;

(10)   the task used should not be inherently evaluative, such as the word association task which most subjects have heard of in connection with psychiatric diagnosis;

(11)   the subject must be truly alone and not with the experimenter partially concealed;

(12)   only one or two others should be present as it is likely that performing in front of large crowds will have other effects and would not constitute mere presence.

Criteria 6 to 10 emphasize that all sources of evaluation should be reduced to a minimum. This might, in fact, remove all mere presence tests, since all have used a laboratory task which subjects know will be evaluated by the experimenter. For this reason criteria 6 and 7 were added: there should be no *obvious* evaluation taking place, and any evaluation should also be present in the Alone condition.

With studies removed using criteria 6 to 12 there remain only eighteen tests of mere presence. Details of the seventy-three good social facilitation studies which did not meet the mere presence criteria, with some indication of the limitations, are given in Table 3, along with the eighteen mere presence

Table 3. *Studies used for review of experimental studies*

Abrams & Manstead (1981)	Evaluative task; nonevaluative audience could still listen
Aiello and Svec (in press)	Computer and observer presence
Anderson (1929)	Small sample size
Barefoot and Kleck (no date)	Other close and back-to-back
Baron, Moore and Sanders (1978)	Observers were used
Berger et al. (1983)	E was the presence
Berger et al. (1982)	E was the presence
Berger et al. (1981)	E was the presence
Berger and Hecken (1980)	E was the presence
Berkey and Hoppe (1972)	Observers were used
Blank (1980)	Evaluative task used
Blank, Staff and Shaver (1976)	Evaluative task used
Bond (1982)	Observers were used
Borden, Hendrick and Walker (1976)	Observers were used
Borden and Walker (1978)	E was the presence; observers
Bray and Sugarman (1980)	Easily evaluated task
Brown et al. (1973)	Observers were used
Bruning et al. (1968)	E was the presence
Carment and Latchford (1970)	E was watching
Carver and Sheier (1978)	Observers were used
Carver and Sheier (1981b)	E was watching
Chapman (1973a)	Observers were used
Chapman (1974)	E was the presence
Chatillon (1970)	Observers were used
Cohen (1980)	E was the presence
Cottrell et al. (1968)	Observers used; E in contact
Dashiell (1930)	Large groups; observers used
Desportes and Dequeker (1971)	E was the presence
Desportes and Dequeker (1973/74)	E watching
Desportes and Lemaine (1969)	Observers were used
Dua (1977)	Observers were used
Ekdahl (1929)	E was the presence
Evans (1971)	Coaction and easily monitored
Farnsworth (1928)	Highly evaluative task
Ferris and Rowland (1980)	Observers; E was the presence
Fouts (1972)	E was the presence
Fouts and Jordan (1973)	E was the presence
Fouts and Parton (1974)	E was the presence
Fraser (1953)	E was the presence
Geen (1973)	E was the presence
Geen (1976b)	E was the presence
Geen (1977)	Observers; E was the presence
Geen (1979)	E was the presence
Geen (1981a)	Evaluative task; E presence
Geen (1983)	E was the presence
Gore and Taylor (1973)	Observers were used; large groups; highly evaluative
Groff, Baron and Moore (1983)	Observers were used; E present
Guerin (1983)	Varied monitoring
Guerin (1986)	Observers and mere presence
Guerin (1989a)	Varied monitoring
Guerin (1989b; Exp. 1)	E was the presence
Guerin (1989b; Exp. 2)	Varied monitoring
Hall and Bunker (1979)	Coaction

Table 3. (*cont.*)

Harkins (1987)	Coaction
Henchy and Glass (1968)	Observers were used
Heylen (1978)	Mere presence
Huntermark and Witte (1978)	E was the presence
Innes (1972)	Coaction
Innes and Gordon (1985)	Mere presence
Innes and Young (1975)	Mere presence and mirror
Klinger (1969)	Coaction
Knowles (1983)	Observers were used
Knowles et al. (1976)	Observers were used
Kobasigawa (1968)	E was the presence
Krueger (1936)	Large coaction group
Kushnir and Duncan (1978)	E was the presence
Laughlin and Jaccard (1975)	Observers were used
Manstead and Semin (1980; Exp. 5)	E was the presence
Marchand and Vachon (1976)	E was the presence
Markus (1978)	Observers and mere presence
Martens (1969c)	Large audience; E interrupted
Matlin and Zajonc (1968)	Highly evaluative task
Miller et al. (1979)	E was the presence
Musante and Anker (1972)	Small sample used
Musick, Beehr and Gilmore (1981)	E was the presence
Newman, Dickstein and Gargan (1978)	Observers were used
Paulus and Cornelius (1974)	Observers were used
Paulus and Murdoch (1971)	Observers were used
Paulus et al. (1972)	Many observers were used
Pessin (1933)	Observers used; E was presence
Putz (1975)	E was the presence
Rajecki et al. (1977)	Observers and mere presence
Sanna and Shotland (1990)	Observers and E present
Schmitt et al. (1986)	Observers and mere presence
Shaver and Liebling (1976)	Small sample used
Smith and Crabbe (1976)	E was the presence
Sorce and Fouts (1973)	Explicit evaluation
Van Tuinen and McNeel (1975)	Coaction
Weiss et al. (1971)	Observers were used
Yarczower and Daruns (1982)	Observers were used
Zajonc and Sales (1966)	Observers were used

studies. Many of these were not conducted to investigate mere presence effects but are still useful studies. As mentioned earlier, a number of the studies in Table 3, which did not meet criteria 8 and 9, will be reviewed later in this chapter since they show other effects.

The eighteen mere presence studies are shown in Table 4 with some details of their procedures and results. Of the eighteen, eleven found evidence for mere presence effects and seven did not. So the model of Zajonc (1965), that mere presence is a sufficient condition for social facilitation effects, seems not to hold in a strong form. Mere presence alone was not enough to have an effect on all the tasks used in these varied experiments.

Table 4. *Experimental studies of mere presence*

Effects found	
Barefoot and Kleck (no date)	Other back-to-back; no monitoring
Guerin (1983; Behind)	Behind condition; no monitoring
Guerin (1986a)	Other was behind; no monitoring
Guerin (1989a)	Other was behind; no monitoring
Guerin (1989b; Exp 2)	Other was behind; no monitoring
Harkins (1987)	Coaction but no monitoring
Innes and Gordon (1985)	Other was behind; no monitoring
Innes and Young (1975)	Other was behind; no monitoring
Markus (1978)	Other was behind; no monitoring
Rajecki et al. (1977)	Blindfolded other; distraction?
Schmitt et al. (1986)	Blindfolded other; distraction?
Effects not found	
Carment and Latchford (1970)	Coaction; easily monitored
Evans (1971)	Coaction; easily monitored
Guerin (1983; Observer)	Inattentive other; easily monitored
Heylen (1978)	Inattentive other; easily monitored
Innes (1972)	Coaction; back-to-back
Klinger (1969)	Coaction; easily monitored
Van Tuinen and McNeel (1975)	Coaction; easily monitored

The results do seem to fit, however, with the predictions of the monitoring model outlined in 5.3. For nine of the eleven studies which found mere presence effects, the person present was behind the subject and could not be monitored. Markus (1978) in fact writes that her mere presence condition was designed to 'make it difficult for the subject to attend directly to the audience' (p. 396). So in nine of the mere presence studies for which effects were found the subjects could not keep an eye on the other person present.

Of the studies for which the effects were not found, five were co-action studies in which the co-actors were easily monitorable. It was also argued in Chapter 4 that the behaviour of co-actors is more predictable and so less effect would be expected.

Only two studies which did not find effects were not co-action settings. In both of these the confederate was facing the subject and was purposely inattentive – working at a desk. So the confederate was presumably not seen as threatening, was easily monitored, and no effects were found, as would be predicted.

The two studies which do not fit into this pattern are those of Rajecki et al. (1977) and Schmitt et al. (1986). In both these cases a blindfolded person was sitting to the side of the subject, purportedly to adapt their eyes to darkness ready for another experiment. As for Cottrell et al. (1968), discussed in Chapter 4, no arousal and therefore no social facilitation effects would be expected in this condition since the subjects were able to monitor the other person who was blindfolded and had predictable behaviour. Both of these studies did find effects, however.

As post-hoc explanations for these studies, it might be suggested that the *novelty* of having a blindfolded person present might have increased alertness. It might have been that there was increased effort to compensate for the increased distraction (see Meumann, 1904).

Another suggestion is that because they were small blindfolds there was some arousal increase from the uncertainty of the other's behaviour. The other person could have easily slipped the blindfold off or looked underneath and so possibly interacted. For Rajecki et al. (1977) there was also possible interaction from the other person talking.

The final suggestion is that perhaps the effects of monitorability are not the bottom-of-the-barrel for mere presence effects. While the overall results suggest a rôle for the predictability of the other person's behaviour, and hence for the importance of monitorability, there may still be other factors. Perhaps even the remote chance that the person may have taken off their blindfold and earphones and interacted may have been enough to get subjects a little more alert than they would have been otherwise. This needs to be pursued further. There might be another phenomenon present in these two studies which needs exploring.

Whatever the reason for these results, the eighteen studies suggest a rôle for increase in alertness due to unpredictability, especially in the form of unmonitorability. It may be argued that evaluation mediates these results, but in five of the eleven studies finding effects, the other behind could not evaluate the performance (Barefoot and Kleck, no date; Guerin, 1989a; Innes and Gordon, 1985; Markus, 1978; Schmitt et al. 1986). So the unpredictability explanation is preferred. The relation of this to possible physical threat is also suggested by the effects being found in one study only when the other person was near but not when the other was far away (Barefoot and Kleck, no date).

So there is some evidence that there are mere presence effects in humans independent of evaluation effects or social conformity. While we have suggested that they have a defensive basis, the exact meaning of this is unclear, as was pointed out in Chapter 4. Other effects might still be apparent in the mere presence situation, such as the novelty effects suggested above to explain two findings which did not otherwise fit. The problem, then, is how to experimentally dissect these different effects. This question will be addressed later.

8.2 The effects of the presence of the experimenter

Of the studies in Table 3, thirty-seven were good studies but they had used the experimenter as the person present. These are outlined with some details in Table 5. Rather than assume a *priori* that these will have an evaluative effect, this section will analyse them. Reports with two different conditions are

Table 5. *Experimental studies with the experimenter present*

Effects found

Berger et al. (1983)	Less overt practice with E in room; Alones recalled more
Berger et al. (1982)	Effects of E watching; less overt responding with presence
Berger et al. (1981)	Effects of E watching; less overt responding with presence
Berger and Hecken (1980)	Less mimicry when E watched
Borden and Walker (1978)	Better recall when watched by E
Carment and Latchford (1970)	Effects of E watching; more responding with E present
Carver and Scheier (1981b)	More letter copied with E watching
Chapman (1974)	Effects even from concealed E; behaviour of E unpredictable and 'occasionally watched'
Desportes and Dequeker (1971)	Effects of E watching
Desportes and Dequeker (1973/74)	Effects of E watching
Ferris and Rowland (1980)	Effects of E watching
Fouts and Jordan (1973)	E present and listening inhibited idiosyncratic associations
Fouts and Parton (1974)	Less novel complex behaviours with E watching than working in another room
Fraser (1953)	Better vigilance with E present
Geen (1973)	Effects of E watching
Geen (1976b; Exp. 3i)	E watching inhibited anagram task
Geen (1976b; Exp. 3ii)	E watching inhibited complex task
Geen (1976b; Exp. 3iii)	E watching inhibited anagram task; Effects of 3i to 3iii mitigated if the observation was to help the subjects
Geen (1977)	Observing E had same effect as negatively evaluating E; both Alone and positively evaluating E different again
Geen (1979)	Observing E inhibited after failure on earlier task; facilitated after earlier success
Geen (1981a)	Observing E increased persistence at task after positive feedback but inhibited after negative feedback; probably confounded with earlier task
Geen (1983; Looking)	Effect of observing E; less if helpful
Guerin (1989b; Exp 1)	Inhibition of behaviour
Huntermark and Witte (1978)	Better vigilance with E present
Kobasigawa (1968)	E inhibited children's play (Control condition)
Kushnir and Duncan (1978)	Effects of E watching
Marchand and Vachon (1976)	Effects of E present but not watching same as E watching
Miller et al. (1979)	Effects even when E present but not able to evaluate
Musick, Beehr and Gilmore (1981)	Facilitated simple task with E and observer watching
Pessin (1933)	Effects of E watching
Putz (1975)	Better vigilance with E watching
Smith and Crabbe (1976)	Learning inhibited by observing E

Effects not found

Fouts (1972)	No difference; E watching or working elsewhere; possible novelty and ceiling effects

Table 5. (*cont.*)

Effects not found	
Geen (1973)	E facing away busy at work; no different to Alone; different to watching
Guerin (1988b; Exp 1)	No effect on task performance
Sanna and Shotland (1990)	E's behaviour unpredictable and close by in all conditions
Smith and Crabbe (1976)	No effect of busy disinterested E
Related studies	
Aiello and Svec (in press)	Experimenter monitored by computer
Burger (1987)	Evaluating E same as non-evaluating
Chapman (1973b)	Lower EMG when E could not listen; E could observe; no Alone
Deffenbacher, Platt and Williams (1974)	E watching; different to E facing away busy at work; no Alone
Geen (1974)	E watching different to E facing away busy at work; no Alone
Stotland and Zander (1958)	Nonexpert E still rated competent

counted as two studies. Six other studies which varied the experimenter's presence, but which had other problems, have still been included, making a total of forty-three studies to be examined. These six were included because they show some interesting effects of the experimenter's presence.

There were another four studies in Table 3 which dealt with the experimenter's presence but have been left out because of problems with interpretation. Sorce and Fouts (1973) quite explicitly evaluated subjects in both the Alone and Presence conditions, which may have swamped any other results. Cohen (1980) had statistical results which were very hard to interpret. Ekdahl (1929) had sessions separated by two weeks and gave few details in any case, especially concerning the subjects used. Manstead and Semin (1980: Experiment 5) had erratic response slopes in the Alone condition compared with four previous successful replications of the same result. This may have been due to distraction or anticipated evaluation from the video cameras and monitors which were present in the Alone condition. Subjects in this Alone condition did rate themselves half-way along a scale measuring evaluation.

Of the forty-three studies to be reviewed, one gave direct evidence that experimenters are viewed by subjects as experts, and therefore probably evaluative (Stotland and Zander, 1958). This experiment had subjects work in the presence of either an experimenter who claimed to be an expert or one who claimed to know little about the research area. Although the former were rated as the more competent of the two, the latter were still rated as quite expert on the scale used.

Twenty-seven of the experiments had the experimenter *watching* the subjects, and *all* found social facilitation effects. This may be due to effects of evaluation apprehension, self-presentation, self-attention, or mere presence arousal. So even without direct cueing, the presence of the experimenter can affect performance.

For three of the studies which found effects, the experimenter could not observe the subject's performance and so could not be *directly* evaluative (Chapman, 1974; Marchand and Vachon, 1976; Miller et al., 1979). If it is argued that the results are still due to evaluation apprehension, then the implication is that just the experimenter's presence is sufficient for subjects to be aware that their performance will be evaluated. This did not occur, however, in another four studies which found no effect of just the experimenter's presence (Deffenbacher, Platt and Williams, 1974; Geen, 1973, 1974; Smith and Crabbe, 1976). A possible explanation for this will be given below.

To summarize so far: of the studies that have found effects, the majority have had the experimenter watching the subject. These results could be due to evaluation apprehension or self-attention effects. Other studies have found an effect even when the experimenter could not watch the subjects. This suggests that if evaluation is the main cause of experimenter effects then just the passive presence of the experimenter is sufficient to cause evaluation effects. A number of other studies, however, have found no effect of the experimenter's passive presence, which suggests that other mediating variables are present.

Five of the studies shown in Table 5 found no effect of the passive presence of the experimenter. For one of these it is very likely that there was a ceiling effect (Fouts, 1972). Ten-year-old children were pulling a handle at a rate of thirty to forty pulls per minute. It is unlikely that much difference between conditions could be shown with such a task. In the one minute the task took, the children were probably still aroused from the novelty of the task. If it had been spread over three to four minutes more might have been found. Another study had the experimenter come in and out of the room regularly (Sanna and Shotland, 1990). This means that whether the subjects were alone for a short while or had an observer present, the experimenter's presence was probably always there. As we shall see, even the possibility that the experimenter will come into the room can affect results.

Two studies were based on a third which did not find effects (Geen, 1973). In the Mere Presence condition of this study, the experimenter sat away from the subject and was busy with work. So the experimenter's behaviour was predictable, and was unlikely to interact with the subject. The two related studies had the same situation, but did not have an Alone condition for comparison (Deffenbacher, Platt and Williams., 1974; Geen, 1974). When

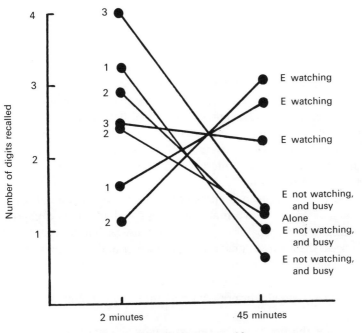

Figure 13. Number of digits correctly recalled with short and long delays. Reproduced with permission of authors and Academic Press. (Data drawn from Geen, 1973, 1974 and Deffenbacher et al., 1974. Figure taken from Guerin, 1986). 1 = Deffenbacher et al, 2 = Geen, 1973; 3 = Geen, 1974.

all three studies are plotted together, however, the results for the shared conditions are very similar. It is suggested that the Alone condition of Geen (1973) can be used as a comparison for the studies of Deffenbacher, Platt and Williams, (1974) and Geen (1974).

These three studies are all plotted together in Figures 13. It can be seen that the effects of the experimenter being present but working busily on something else is no different to being alone. So it might be again suggested that when the other person present has *predictable* behaviour and will obviously not be interacting, then no effects will be found – even when this is the experimenter. The same was true for Smith and Crabbe (1976) who used a different design.

This view is also supported by the studies of Miller et al. (1979) and Chapman (1973b). In these cases the experimenter was not engaged in any work and could have interacted at any time, and effects were found as would be predicted. With Chapman (1974) also, the concealed experimenter gave little indication of what would occur and even occasionally glanced through the screen.

So if the Geen (1973) results are robust, and the two partial replications suggest that they are, then experimenter effects may not be due to observation and evaluation potential alone. The effects in the first instance seem to depend upon whether or not the experimenter's behaviour is predictable. Where it has not been predictable then effects have been found. When the experimenter has been explicitly observing and evaluating subjects their effects have also been found. When the experimenter has been present, but would obviously not interact until after the task was completed, then no effects have been found.

Only one other study seemed to find an effect of the experimenter. Burger (1987) found a difference between an observing E and an E who could not evaluate. In this latter case, pains were taken to assure Ss that the E could not evaluate. Indeed, the E was a substitute experimenter and results were kept anonymous, which they were not for the observing (real) E. So this study confounded a lot of manipulations of evaluation and accountability and is therefore hard to interpret in the present terms, interesting though the results are.

This does raise the question, however, of why the uncertainty in the experimenter's behaviour should have an effect. It might be due to some inherent threat in the experimenter's unpredictable behaviour or it might be due to the possibility that the experimenter would come over and evaluate the performance. The mere presence results with strangers suggest a rôle for the threat interpretation (see 8.1). The same may be true for experimenters. Other results in this section, on the other hand, suggest that experimenters are likely to be seen as evaluative. If their behaviour is unpredictable then they may come over and evaluate. Only in cases where the experimenter has been working at a desk busily have no effects been found.

In this regard one other study will be mentioned here, although there was no actual experimenter or anyone else present in the 'Presence' condition of interest. Aiello and Svec (in press) had conditions under which subjects performed a computer task having been told that either they would not be monitored through the computer or else that they would be monitored. A third group had an observer present behind them. The 'electronic presence' group presumably had the experimenter evaluating them although no experimenter was physically present.

Aiello and Svec (in press) found that the 'electronic presence' led to worse performance on the complex task, as did having a real person behind them. This suggests firstly that monitoring does not have to be done in person, and secondly, that it must have been evaluation effects which were mediated by monitoring in this case, rather than any type of threat, since the electronic presence could not have been physically threatening. So a version of the monitoring model which mediates evaluation might also be plausible, as suggested for the Geen (1973) result and its replications.

8.3 The effects of an observer

It has been shown above that there are effects from the mere presence of another person who cannot evaluate only when their behaviour is unpredictable or when they cannot be watched. It has also been shown above that experimenters are seen by subjects as evaluative, and that if there is a chance that they may evaluate performance during the experiment, then effects on task performance will be found. If they are busy with something else, on the other hand, or are unable to engage in evaluation, then no effects will be found. This suggests that the exclusion from Table 4 of studies using the experimenter in the Presence condition was justified. There is more evaluation attached to an experimenter than to another person – even an expert (Miller et al., 1979).

The second review is of those studies of Table 3 which had the person in the Presence condition *watching* the subject. It was suggested in the earlier part of this chapter that such studies also confound evaluation. The first section here will review these studies. The following section will relate all these studies to the theories of mere presence and social facilitation.

The observer studies

Table 6 presents the thirty-four studies from Table 3 which used an observer. The majority of tests had significant results, which suggests that it is a robust effect. In the four tests which did not find an effect, the observer in each case was not in a position to evaluate the subject's performance. Desportes and Lemaine (1969) had used student observers who could not evaluate the task. For Groff, Baron and Moore (1983) the observer was not able to evaluate the performance, and for Markus (1978) the behaviour was one that could not easily be evaluated.

For Miller et al. (1979), there was no effect of an expert being present when they could not see the task. It will be recalled that for the same study there *was* an effect of the experimenter being present whether or not they could not see the task. So the experimenter obviously has an effect over and above being able to see the task.

The thirty studies which did find effects of an observer will be further discussed according to the *task* which they used.

Three of the observer studies used the *pseudorecognition* task. This involves exposing subjects to different nonsense words a different number of times

Table 6. *Experimental studies with observers present*

Effects found	
Baron, Moore and Sanders (1978)	Observer facilitated simple task; no effect on complex task
Berkey and Hoppe (1972)	Observer inhibited complex task; no effect on simple task
Blank (1980)	Less objectionable associations with observer present
Blank, Staff and Shaver (1976)	Less unique associations with observers present
Bond (1982)	Less responding with observers; no effects on overall simple task; effects on overall complex task; all responses worse with observer; ceiling effect on simple task?
Borden, Hendrick and Walker (1976)	More attitude change when alone
Brown et al. (1973)	Short pornographic viewing time with observers present
Carver and Scheier (1978)	More self-references with observers
Chapman (1973a)	More laughter with another child present; possible visual cues?
Chatillon (1970)	Less tracing errors with observers
Cottrell et al. (1968)	More well-learned pseudorecognition responses with observer
Desportes and Lemaine (1969)	Higher estimates of points with evaluative observer present
Dua (1977)	Avoidance response acquisition inhibited by observer; extinction facilitated
Ferris and Rowland (1980)	More quantity with E watching; no effect of task familiarity
Groff, Baron and Moore (1983)	Faster pressing with attention-conflict and observer present
Guerin (1983; Looking)	Less complex learning with observer
Hall and Bunker (1979)	Externals worse in coaction; internals better
Henchy and Glass (1968)	Effects of nonexpert watching; stronger for expert
Knowles (1983)	Effects of number of observers, not distance from Ss
Knowles et al. (1976)	Subjects moved further away with more observers
Laughlin and Jaccard (1975)	Complex learning worse with highly evaluative observer
Matlin and Zajonc (1968)	Less unique associations and shorter latencies with observers
Miller et al. (1979)	Effects of expert watching
Newman, Dickstein and Gargan (1978)	Effects of observers with eleven-year-olds but not younger
Paulus and Cornelius (1974)	Better gymnasts worse with evaluative observers; possible ceiling effects
Paulus et al. (1972)	Better gymnasts worse with audience
Rajecki et al. (1977)	Faster maze with observer
Weiss et al. (1971)	More agreement if observers present
Yarczower and Daruns (1982)	Less facial expressions with observers present for children
Zajonc and Sales (1966)	More well-learned pseudorecognition words with observers present

Table 6. (*cont.*)

Effects not found	
Desportes and Lemaine (1969)	Student observers had no effect
Groff, Baron and Moore (1983)	No effect of mere observer who could not evaluate
Markus (1978)	Observer no different to mere presence for nonevaluative task
Miller et al. (1979)	No effect of experts when they could not watch the task

respectively and then getting them to guess the words after a subliminal presentation. It is thought that the more frequently seen and more well-learned words will be dominant responses and should be said more often when another person is present (Zajonc and Sales, 1966). All the studies using this task have found more well-learned responses with observers present (Cottrell et al., 1968; Henchy and Glass, 1968; Zajonc and Sales, 1966). Henchy and Glass found a stronger effect still when there was an expert watching the subject.

Four studies used a *paired-associates learning* task, using simple and complex associates. Baron, Moore and Sanders (1978) found a facilitation of the simple task and no effect of the complex task with an observer present, whereas Berkey and Hoppe (1972) and Guerin (1983; Looking condition) found an inhibition of the complex task but no effect of the simple task. Bond (1982) found no overall effect of observer for the simple task but found an inhibition of the complex task for both the complex items and the embedded simple items. Bond used a different task from the other three studies, however, so direct comparisons cannot be made.

The results of Baron, Moore and Sanders (1978), Berkey and Hoppe (1972), and Guerin (1983) can be reconciled by considering the relative levels of performance. The subjects in the first study did much better than those in the other two. The overall mean errors to criterion for simple and complex associates, respectively, were 0.96 and 2.99 for Baron, Moore and Sanders, 4.1 and 7.6 for Berkey and Hoppe, and 1.59 and 5.04 for Guerin. All the subjects of Baron, Moore and Sanders did well on the complex task while all of the subjects of Berkey and Hoppe and Guerin did poorly on the simple task. So there may have been a floor effect in Baron, Moore and Sanders, and a ceiling effect in Berkey and Hoppe and Guerin. Different levels of performance between different populations have been found on this same task before (Katahn, 1966).

Three studies have used a *word association* test. Since there are special problems with this task, discussion of the studies will be left until the next section.

Nine of the observer studies used *motor tasks* of different sorts. Chatillon (1970) found that children made less tracing errors with an observer present. Ferris and Rowland (1980) found subjects did better on a video game when observed by the experimenter. Hall and Bunker (1979), using a 'roll-up' game, found that internal locus of control subjects did better co-acting whereas externals did worse. They interpreted this result as showing that externals need more social reinforcement than internals. It is not certain, however, whether competition played a rôle in these results. Evaluation was discouraged, but not competition. The results could also be explained in terms of both arousal and attentional differences between internals and externals.

Rajecki et al. (1977) found that subjects performed a simple maze task quicker when observed, but made no more errors. Knowles (1983) found worse maze performance when subjects had eight persons watching them. There was no effect of how far away the people sat. Miller et al. (1979) found that subjects did a simple rotor-pursuit task better with an expert watching. Groff, Baron and Moore (1983) found greater motor responses of squeezing when there was greater attentional conflict, although they had no true Alone condition for comparison. The experimenter was nearby in each case. The effect was an immediate one – in the first trial block only.

Paulus and Cornelius (1974) and Paulus et al. (1972) found that gymnasts performing in front of observers did worse than when performing alone. This effect was greater for the better gymnasts. The result might be due to a number of things. First there could have been a ceiling effect which would be consistent with a drive interpretation (Broen and Storms, 1961). The result might also have been due to the large size of the audience. The distraction and other effects of seventeen people watching may have overloaded subjects and led to a decrement in performance. The results may have even been due to self-presentation effects and trying to show off within the club. Last, there is a good chance that the gymnasts were competing between themselves and the effects were due to competition rather than passive observation.

The other eleven studies in Table 6 used a variety of tasks. Both Borden, Hendrick and Walker (1976) and Weiss, Miller, Langan and Cecil (1971) found more attitude change and persuasion when someone was observing their subjects. While the results can be interpreted in terms of a neo-Hullian Drive theory (Weiss et al., 1971), they might best be seen as conformity responses with subjects going along with the persuasion. Brown et al. (1973) found that subjects looked for less time at pornography when observers were present. This can also be seen as a conformity or self-presentation effect with subjects not wanting to show themselves as interested in something like pornography, at least in front of an observer.

Carver and Scheier (1978) found that subjects made more self-references with an observer present than when alone. While they interpreted this as showing greater self-awareness and self-focus with someone present, it could also be due to self-presentation effects. With someone else there, subjects may have been more concerned with how they presented themselves and so produced more self-references. As mentioned in Chapter 5, both these theories seem to be able to make similar predictions. It was also suggested in Chapter 5 that self-references are certainly dominant responses so more can also be predicted with observers present by a drive or arousal interpretation.

Desportes and Lemaine (1969) found that subjects made higher estimates in a guessing task with observers present. Laughlin and Jaccard (1975) found that subjects did worse on a complex learning task with an observer present. Newman, Dickstein and Gargan (1978) found that eleven-year-old children did better at the WISC Object Assembly task with an observer present but that an observer had no effect on younger children. They suggested that social learning only begins at this age, so such social effects would not occur before this. A number of other studies, however, have found effects on children less than eleven years old (Chapman, 1973a; Chatillon, 1970; Fouts and Parton, 1974; Yarczower and Daruns, 1982).

Dua (1977) found that the acquisition of an avoidance response was slower when subjects were observed, suggesting that they wished to try fewer novel responses. This is perhaps interpretable in terms of social conformity, with subjects trying not to do anything which is not obvious or conforming. Knowles et al. (1976) found that subjects veered more around confederates sitting to the side of a path when there were more confederates present. This was interpreted in terms of a personal space theory (Knowles, 1980).

Chapman (1973a) found that children laughed more when another child was watching. Although this may be due to a self-presentation strategy there may have been other cueing effects in the situation, one child providing a cue for the other to laugh. Yarczower and Daruns (1982) found that children made more facial expressions when alone than when being observed. Again, the children may have been trying to present themselves in a good light with the others present.

Word association studies

There have been a number of tests of social facilitation which have used a word association task. Whereas the tasks described in the last section were mostly standard ones and easily interpretable, this is not true for the word association studies. For this reason they will be discussed in greater detail.

Some of the studies are poorly controlled and will not be discussed: Allport (1920) likely confounded rivalry in his conditions; Travis (1928) used stutterers who cannot easily be compared to the other studies; Kljaic (1974) does not present enough details to make comments; Good (1973) did not have a proper Presence condition; and Ekdahl (1929) used the experimenter as the person present.

The use of word association tasks since Zajonc (1965) came about because for the word association task, the more common associations could be easily classed as the dominant responses. This meant, according to Zajonc (1965), that more should be emitted in the presence of others compared with associating alone.

The results of the social facilitation word association studies have been confusing, partly because of the different measurements used to rank the commonness of responses (see Blank, 1979). Matlin and Zajonc (1968) ranked the *frequencies* of response words, the most frequently used word having a rank of one. They called this 'response commonality'. The mean response commonality for each subject was computed. Matlin and Zajonc (1968) also had a measure of 'uniqueness', which was the number of words per subject which *did not* appear in the Palermo-Jenkins association norms (Palermo and Jenkins, 1964).

Blank, Staff and Shaver (1976) used three measures of commonness. Their 'response commonness' measure was the raw frequency score for each word across all subjects. If a subject received a score of one then this indicated that they were the only person to produce that response. The measure of 'response uncommonness' for Blank, Staff and Shaver was the same as Matlin and Zajonc's response commonness score: the rank of the frequency. The third measure of Blank, Staff and Shaver was that of 'uniqueness', which was different to the 'uniqueness' of Matlin and Zajonc! In this case it was simply the number of *idiosyncratic* responses a subject made.

There were also some problems with experimental design. Matlin and Zajonc (1968) used a within-subjects design in which the confederate left halfway through the experiment. Blank, Staff and Shaver (1976) criticized this, suggesting that subjects might have been disillusioned by the unexplained walkout. There was also no return to baselines which would be required with such a design (Sidman, 1960).

With regards to the results of these studies, Matlin and Zajonc (1968) found that subjects gave more common responses with an observer present. Blank, Staff and Shaver (1976) found instead that subjects gave less idiosyncratic responses with an observer present. All of these suggest either that there are less subordinate responses or more common responses in the presence of others.

It can be suggested that these results show more socially conforming responses in the presence of others. That is, the idiosyncratic associations can be interpreted as less conforming responses. So the two theories can make identical predictions. This is also supported by the results of Blank (1980), who found that subjects gave less 'objectionable' associations with an observer present.

Matlin and Zajonc (1968) also found that subjects had shorter latencies in the presence of an observer (although only in the condition where the confederate walked out halfway). But the latency finding has failed to emerge in a number of studies (Blank, 1980; Blank, Staff and Shaver, 1976; Zajonc, unpublished data, referred to in Staff and Shaver, 1976, p. 727). So there is some doubt about the validity of this finding. It might have had something to do with the walking out.

The theories of observer effects

What do all these studies of observer effects show? They seem to show that the presence of observers, especially evaluating observers, has a large impact on a variety of behaviours, since similar effects have been found on many different tasks. What is more difficult is to find one overall explanation for all of the results.

Drive theory is consistent with all but four of the studies (Bond, 1982; Brown et al., 1973; Knowles et al., 1976; Yarczower and Daruns, 1982). With some changes it could include Bond (1982; see Sanders, 1984) and Yarczower and Daruns (1982). If it were assumed, for example, that lively facial expressions are subordinate responses then it could be predicted that there would be less with observers present.

Self-presentation, social conformity, and self-awareness theories are consistent with all but a few of the studies and even these can be included with a few added assumptions. If it were assumed, for example, that one self-presentation strategy is to say the most common words or the ones least likely to be wrong or to sound silly, then the pseudorecognition results can be explained. (This was also suggested for word associations in the last section of this chapter). To try and do as well as possible and to try and look as good as possible, subjects would guess more of the well-learned words of which they were certain. This is the result that has been found. Similarly, if it is assumed that there is a public standard of behaviour not to move close to strangers, and if subjects would look bad if they did, then the results of Knowles et al. (1976) can be explained.

The only study which these theories do have trouble explaining is that of Groff, Baron and Moore (1983). It is hard to see why subjects should squeeze harder on the ergograph measure, which was an incidental task, if either of these two views are taken. It was, however, a short-lived effect, occurring only in the first trial block. It would be useful to replicate and extend this finding, however, to see whether any other phenomena might be present.

The Distraction-Conflict and Attentional Overload theories, on the other hand, have trouble explaining most of the results *except* Groff, Baron and Moore (1983). The Alone condition of this study was not adequate, so the results do not exclude other explanations. In most of the other studies where effects were found there was often little time pressure or overload so that subjects could have slowed down and done better if this was the case. So the Distraction-Conflict and Attentional Overload explanations are not *necessary* conditions for observer effects, although they seem to be sufficient in some cases.

One task in which they might be useful is that of the paired-associates learning task. Here subjects are under some time constraint. Baron, Moore and Sanders (1978) found a correlation of some distraction measures with performance at this task, but the correlation could have been due to other mediating causes. If the effects were due to something other than Distraction-Conflict or Attentional Overload, then one would expect some concomitant distraction in any case.

8.4 Other manipulations

There remains in this chapter, a need to review studies which have used mirrors, one-way screens, one-way mirrors, and video cameras as their manipulation of presence or evaluation. These have been introduced into social facilitation studies for a variety of reasons, usually to manipulate either evaluation or self-awareness without having a person physically present.

Mirrors

Ever since Wicklund and Duval (1971) proposed that both the presence of other people and mirrors increase objective self-awareness, mirrors have been employed in social facilitation studies. The original idea was that if mirrors could produce the same performance effects as having people present then this would be evidence for the objective self-awareness interpretation without having all the other effects of someone being present. Later, Carver and Scheier (1981b) proposed in the terms of their control systems model that mirrors induced *private* self-awareness whereas the presence of other people induced *public* self-awareness.

After weeding out studies with design problems (Table 2), the empirical evidence for mirror effects is mixed. Some have found similar performance effects with mirrors and other people (Carver and Scheier, 1978, 1981b; Hormuth, 1982; Wicklund and Duval, 1971), while others have not (Abrams and Manstead, 1981; Borden and Walker, 1978; Guerin, 1989b,

Experiment. 1; Innes and Gordon, 1985; Innes and Young, 1975; Paulus, Annis and Risner, 1978). Explaining these different findings is very difficult, since the theoretical differences expected are vague, and the manipulations used are not comparable in most cases.

With regards to the theoretical interpretations, many differences can, and have been, suggested between mirrors and the presence of another person. We have seen that Carver and Scheier (1981b) introduced private (mirror) and public (audience) self-awareness as a difference. The problem is still one of clearly specifying the conditions for each of these, and also being able to recognize when they are occurring or not in a situation. For most of the experiments, we could not begin to decide whether subjects were following personal standards, public standards, or even both, and there is certainly no measurement of these standards independent of the performance effects themselves. This is the problem which has been mentioned a number of times in Chapters 4, 5, 6 and 7, that of clearly measuring the response hierarchies, the standards of behaviour, or the sources of distraction in a way which is independent of the social facilitation performance measurements. One study which did this, found the opposite to Carver and Scheier's equating of mirrors and private self-awareness, audience and public self-awareness (Diener and Srull, 1979).

Some authors have suggested other mechanisms whereby the mirrors might have their effects. Some have suggested that the mirrors are distracting and might take time away from the task, especially for ego-involved subjects (Innes and Young, 1975; Liebling and Shaver, 1973a). While this has some merit, the problem is that no clear analysis of all the mirror-induced effects is available, let alone evidence for a distraction effect. Further testing of mirrors needs to be carried out if they continue to be used.

To help explain the empirical evidence that mirrors affect performance, one post-hoc suggestion will be made here, although there is no direct evidence for this suggestion at present. In all the cases where differences have been found between Alone and Mirror conditions (whether in the expected direction or not), the mirror was very large and salient and/or the experimenter made a point of uncovering it for the subject, sometimes without explanation (Borden and Walker, 1978; Carver and Scheier, 1978, 1981b; Hormuth, 1982; Innes and Young, 1975; Paulus et al., 1978). In the three cases where no significant differences were found, the mirror was either small or not obviously in front of the subject (Abrams and Manstead, 1981; Guerin, 1989b; Innes and Gordon, 1985).

So this might suggest that a salient mirror is needed to get the effects. Unfortunately, this raises even more clearly the question of whether the effects are due to distraction by a salient mirror, private self-awareness, or some other effect.

Videos and one-way screens

Like mirrors, a number of studies have used video cameras of one-way screens to manipulate evaluation and audience presence. It should be noted that a lot of these studies have had the experimenter present in all conditions (see Table 5). The manipulations have been used to induce evaluation pressures without the presence of a person. Video cameras have also been used as manipulations of self-awareness.

For one-way mirrors, an early study (Wapner and Alper, 1952) showed that decision time was shortest when the experimenter was present, next shortest when an audience could be seen through a wall panel, and longest when there was an audience which had not been seen (one-way mirror). Most of the studies have found an effect when using one-way mirrors (Cohen and Davis, 1973; Criddle, 1971; Ganzer, 1968; Kleck et al., 1976; Putz, 1975). One study not finding any differences, used measures other than task performance (Van Heerden and Hoogstraten, 1981). It is not certain, therefore, how to interpret the results or to compare them with the other results. Davis et al. (1968) found only some predicted effects of a one-way mirror observation, but the experimenter was present in the control condition. This means that a complex interaction might have been present.

The results for video recording are more straightforward: all the studies published have found the effects (Cohen, 1980; Cohen and Davis, 1973; Geen, 1973; Henchy and Glass, 1968; Laughlin et al., 1972; Laughlin and Wong-McCarthy, 1975; Putz, 1975; Wicklund and Duval, 1971). It should be noted that Laughlin and Wong-McCarthy (1975) found no difference between the effects of video recording, filming, or audio recording.

While an analysis of why video recording affects subjects is not altogether clear, Cohen (1980) interestingly found that video recording only affected subjects when the recording was permanent: that is, when it was actually being put onto tape for later viewing. This would perhaps be predicted by evaluation apprehension theories, but not by self-awareness theories, since the camera and filming process itself is supposed to elicit the process. More theoretical and empirical analysis of this manipulation is obviously needed. It may be that the *consequences* of filming are important in getting the effects which could support a behaviour analytic view.

Computers

Computers have only been used in a small number of social facilitation studies, either to check for experimenter/computer differences in running experiments (see Orcutt and Anderson, 1974), or to reduce presence effects by having the subjects work alone with a computer. While the latter conditions might reduce the presence of another person, they do not necessarily reduce evaluation apprehension.

Johnson and Baker (1973), for example, found no performance differences between such a pair of conditions, but they found less variance with the experimenter running the experiment. The major differences were between low and high ability subjects. Martin and Knight (1985) found that it was the external locus of control subjects who performed better with a human than a computer. Internal locus of control subjects did equally well in both conditions. The experimenter was, however, present in each case.

It should be concluded that although the methodology holds some promise, little is really known of the effects of using a computer to run a social facilitations study. Like mirrors and videos, more theoretical analysis is needed of what differences might be expected, and why. Does a computer induce self-awareness? Perhaps only with a new computer or a novel setting? Does typing into a computer terminal in a laboratory task induce evaluation apprehension (see Schmitt et al., 1986)?

Some progress has been made in this area recently. With the increase in the use of computers in offices and at home, researchers have turned to studying communication by computer in more detail. These studies will be discussed in Chapter 10.

One paper using a social facilitation framework (Aiello and Svec, in press), which was mentioned in 8.2, had subjects perform a complex task on a computer under varying degrees of being monitored (and presumably evaluated). Subjects had to complete difficult anagrams on the computer terminal. Of most interest here is the comparison between those who had the 'electronic presence' of a master computer monitoring their performance and those who had an observer present watching them from behind. Both of these groups performed worse at the complex task than subjects who were told that their performance would not be monitored by the computer. This effect was reduced in other conditions which allowed subjects to turn off the electronic surveillance or which pooled the subjects' performance results. Some support exists, then, for a monitoring model of evaluation effects: that we monitor others to find out about their evaluation.

8.5 Conclusions

Many suggestions have been made in this review of the empirical studies of observer effects. While it is uncertain exactly what mediates the effects, there do seem to be clear and strong effects of the passive presence of another person who does not watch or evaluate. As we saw earlier in this chapter (8.1), there is some support for the notion that the inherent threat the person poses relates to the effect. In particular, whether or not the person's behaviour is predictable and whether they can be watched if it is not predictable seem to be important.

There also seem to be definite effects on behaviour from being watched and from being evaluated. This seems to be inherent in an experimenter's presence, although it can be attenuated if the experimenter is seen to be busy elsewhere and not about to intrude. How these effects are explained is more tricky. It is possible that several independent effects actually exist including increased drive from anticipation of evaluation, self-awareness effects and self-presentation effects. It was suggested in Chapter 5 that these latter two can be viewed as different aspects of the same effect – a social conformity response.

What emerges is experimental evidence for one sort of effect which may be hard-wired and deals with drive and arousal levels, personal space and threats, and physical social and non-social contingencies from another person; and evidence for another sort of effect which deals with public, personal, societal or standard forms of behaviour, or in behaviour analytic terms, the other person acting as a discriminative stimulus for social consequences (Guerin, 1992). In the presence of others, people are likely to conform more closely to these standards for the purpose of making a particular impression and thereby gaining social approval.

The social facilitation literature, then, suggests two basic responses which people have towards other people. One is to become more alert or aroused, probably in preparation for interaction. This has some concomitant effects upon other behaviours, such as the distraction-induced effects. The second basic response towards other people is to control behaviour and direct it towards more socially approved forms of behaviour. This also has several concomitant effects upon other behaviours.

One implication of these summary results is that much of the detail of the mechanisms mediating these processes, and the conditions under which these basic responses do and do not occur, will depend heavily on the situation in which the episode occurs, the make-up or learning history of the person involved, and the relationship between the two persons. This further suggests that social facilitation might only be defined through the setting in which it is tested, rather than through the responses measured in the subjects.

IV The place of social facilitation in social psychology

9 Integrating the theories of social facilitation

9.1 Some connections between the theories of social facilitation

There are a number of relationships between all the social facilitation models. With so many theories all trying to explain the same experimental interaction effect, many links must be possible. Some of these have already been mentioned in passing through the last five chapters.

A first point is that most of the mere presence and social conformity models must also predict concurrent attentional changes. If arousal arises in some fashion from the unpredictability of others (Guerin and Innes, 1982; Zajonc, 1980) then these others must be watched, at least briefly. If a behaviour standard matching process influences behaviour then subjects must have attended to their internal standards or to the external cues for the appropriate behaviours. This means that there must be epiphenomenal changes in attention with both arousal and social conformity models, so it is not clear whether attentional differences found between Alone and Presence conditions might be products of other differences in arousal or standard setting rather than causes in themselves.

A second point specifically concerns social conformity models which all suggest that in the presence of others certain socially approved behaviours are more frequent and socially disapproved behaviours more infrequent. The different theories conceptualize the source or storage of these socially valued behaviours in slightly different ways: as social standards, response sets, social schemata, or learned self-presentation strategies. The point here, though, is that each assumes that these behaviours can be described and predicted in different contexts. As suggested above, it is not clear that this can be done in practice independently of the social facilitation measurements.

The only behaviour standard which has really been tested is that of doing as well as possible at a task: conforming to the experimenter's instructions, perhaps with regards to a personal standard as well. This corresponds to both a self-presentational strategy of trying to look competent to the experimenter, and to a behaviour standard of doing as well as possible at tasks. The response set explanation is less well developed but presumably would involve the pre-response filtering out of responses inappropriate to the task. The point to note, which will appear again later in this chapter, is that all these explanations seem to be either different ways of talking about the same phenomenon, and hence interchangeable, or else talking about different aspects of the same phenomenon.

A third point concerns some links which can be made between the arousal models and the self-attention models. Arousal models suggest that in the presence of another person the level of general arousal or alertness increases. It is suggested by self-attention models, however, that when there is an increase in general activation level, or bodily activity, people become more self-attentive (Carver and Scheier, 1981a; Wegner and Giuliano, 1980). This means, of course, that if there is an increase in arousal from the presence of others then one should also expect an increase in self-attention. So the empirical increases in self-focus found when in the presence of others might, in fact, be explained easily by arousal theorists. It is problematic to try and separate these and say which caused which.

A further complication to this argument is that it is reasonable to assume that self-referencing and self-focus are dominant responses. We tend to think more about ourselves than about others. This assumption means that arousal theories also predict that an increase in arousal will lead to an increase in self-reference and self-focus, as has been found many times. Indeed, it was the evidence of self-reference which provided the experimental foundations for self-attention theories. But arousal theories can easily make the same prediction!

The three points above all suggest, as was noted in Chapters 4 and 6, that most social facilitation theories are underdetermined – they can each explain the major results and make similar predictions. Even worse, the conditions under which they do and do not apply, and the methods of predicting which behaviours will increase or decrease, are not well developed in *any* theory. It has been mentioned repeatedly in these last chapters that most of the experiments in social facilitation have had no *independent* measures of the response hierarchy, the dominant responses, the social or personal standards which will be matched, the features or cues which will be attended to, or the aspects of the self or social stimuli which will be attended to.

This problem is not disastrous, however, because we still have the basic empirical results to guide future theorizing. What it means, though, is that there is no good evidence for any one of the theories of social facilitation. Which is used in explanations depends solely upon the framework of words one wishes to use. This in turn must depend upon which is most useful and this probably rests on the coverage or extent of the framework. From this very pragmatic view we must favour the control systems theory, behaviour analysis, or cognitive frameworks because they cover more of the psychological phenomena than, say, behaviour inhibition or monitorability. Each of the three frameworks can encompass the effects on physical behaviour, attentional processes, and covert events, which all reliably occur in the presence of another person.

Putting together the complete argument given in this section suggests that we should deal with social facilitation theorizing within a general psychological theory, and that we do not need to develop special social facilitation theories. The three major frameworks which have been mentioned are also probably equivalent in the long run, since links have been developed between control systems theory and cognitive theory (Carver and Scheier, 1981a; Miller, Galanter and Pribram, 1960), between behaviour analysis and controls systems theory (McDowell and Wixted, 1988; Ray and Brown, 1975;), and between behaviour analysis and cognitive theories (Guerin, in press; Hayes, 1986, 1989; Rachlin et al., 1986; Skinner, 1985).

For this reason the present book has thought it wise to focus separately on the theories and data of social facilitation. As has just been summarized, the theories and their support depend largely upon the framework one adopts, and as has been mentioned earlier, social psychology is fickle in its adoption of different frameworks from psychology (Innes, 1980).

Turning to the empirical studies of social facilitation, most have been directed at showing *more* or *faster* behaviour in the presence or absence of another person (usually depending on the task complexity). Measurements of other behaviour changes has only occurred for theoretical reasons, such as sweat changes to show arousal increases. A major conclusion from reviewing the animal literature in Chapter 7 was that the background or baseline behaviours need to be established first before any other measurable changes make sense. In the case of animals this is the process of constructing an ethogram. If a rat decreases feeding in the presence of another rat we need to know what rats do together when not feeding in order to make sense of this finding.

In the case of humans, we need to know the baseline rates of competition, arousal in laboratory settings, reactions to experimenters, etc., before we can make proper sense of finding that subjects do more anagrams alone. We especially need to know these baselines if we are to measure some other event to prove the existence of a predicted mechanism.

While these conclusions might sound like a major disappointment, that is only so for those who want to keep producing theories specific to social facilitation and not see the broader patterns in the theories. The conclusions strike this author as quite exciting, in two different ways. First, what they mean is that we have to place social facilitation back into a general framework of social behaviour and psychology in general. This means comparing social facilitation with the other social psychological phenomena and not just treating it as a basic building block, such that social loafing,

cooperation, or competition are somehow constructed on the social facilitation atoms. The two social facilitation phenomena are not simple events
which underlie our other social behaviour. They are complex events which
include our learning about the standards of society and how to behave. They
must be studied *with* other social behaviours, not before them.

The second way in which the conclusions are exciting rather than
disappointing is in their call to explore behaviour changes other than just
increases or decreases in performance, and the speed of performance. This
comes out clearly from reviewing both the animal (Chapter 7) and human
(Chapter 8) empirical literatures. We need to study the entire behaviour or
organisms in their settings before making conclusions about particular
mechanisms. We have done enough studies on facilitation and inhibition of
performance at tasks to make conclusions. Before we can better explain why
these effects occur we need to go back and see what else is going on. If we
draw on any of the three major psychology frameworks to get our
assumptions, control systems theory, behaviour analysis, or cognitive
theory, we can explain any new event discovered in the social facilitation
setting. What is more important now is to catalogue the events which occur,
and the conditions for their occurrence.

With regards to the phenomena we already know about from previous
social facilitation studies, it seems that there are at least two general social
facilitation phenomena which can be talked about in several different ways
and which can encompass all the findings. These are the alertness effects and
the social conformity effects.

9.2 The alertness effects

The first type of social facilitation effect is the alertness or mere presence
phenomenon. This would appear to be a reaction to just the mere presence of
another person, and may involve an alerting mechanism which prepares the
organism for a social encounter. In particular, threatening encounters would
seem to produce the strongest reactions, and might be similar across different
species.

This effect will be expressed differently for different species. With humans,
some of the considerations have been dealt with already, in 4.4. While
hard-wired mechanisms have been suggested, they are purely speculative. A
generalized discriminative response (see 5.5) is equally plausible. The further
development of theories in this area should be to get down to more specifics,
such as descriptions of any flight responses, reactions to personal space
invasions, and the details of arousal mechanisms. Evidence from autistic
people could provide information on whether a basic alertness towards
others is learned or hard-wired in some way.

The alertness effect causes a number of other effects such as distraction, attention to the other person, changes in task performance, and increased thinking or cognitive responding. The exact changes in task performance depend upon the task used and can be talked about in several different ways. While palm sweat evidence seemed to confirm talking in terms of arousal, it has been argued above that controls systems theory also predicts sweat increases (Carver and Scheier, 1981b), and behaviour analysis could do the same.

The evidence for the alertness effects being distinct from social conformity effects comes from three sources. First, there is the evidence for physiological changes in the presence of another person. As was seen in Chapter 3, however, the evidence is dubious, since the validity of the different measures is in question (Moore and Baron, 1983). Also, anxiety over whether or not you are behaving with appropriate behaviour standards might also predict increases in physiological measures.

The second source of evidence comes from studies which have tried to avoid any social conformity effects by the experimental manipulations. These were exhaustively reviewed in Chapter 8. Particular attention was paid to whether there were still social facilitation effects when evaluation effects and conformity effects were reduced. Several studies (Table 4) suggested that when social conformity effects were reduced, either experimentally by manipulation or by making them equal in the Alone and Presence conditions, there were still social facilitation effects found.

Third, the animal literature suggests that there were effects which were not due to social conformity. The animal literature (also in 4.4), suggested further that there might be many forms of such effects. Rats, for example, monitored each other by social interaction of an active kind, rather than by 'fear' or 'caution'. This in turn had concomitant effects on their feeding behaviour. Again, the behaviour of the organism needs to be better known (and this includes humans) before making strong conclusions from the single-measure social facilitation studies.

9.3 The social conformity effects

The second phenomenon is seen when behaviour is controlled in the presence of others so as to match more closely some social or personal standards. As mentioned above, this has usually been shown by subjects performing harder at a task with the experimenter present. While this could be manipulated by varying the social or personal expectancies, such a manipulation has not been usually done. Usually the standards are argued *a priori*. If subjects in previous experiments have, in fact, been trying to do well at the task for the experimenter, then we need to know the conditions under which this increases or decreases.

The theories of social conformity effects in minimal social conditions have been outlined in Chapter 5. It has been suggested that there might, in fact, be little contradiction between the theories except for the words used. This section argues that they can be seen as applying to different levels of the same social conformity effect (Carver, 1979), and one theory cannot completely subsume another. The difference between them lies in the part of the social conformity process they explain.

At one level, subjects conform to the experimental task in order to gain social approval or to avoid social disapproval. At another level, to explain how they go about achieving these ends, it is argued that the subjects present themselves as trying harder, by engaging in self-presentation strategies (Bond, 1982). One way of describing this whole process at an internal level is to posit a mechanism which acts to reduce any discrepancy between the internalized social norm and current behaviour. The subjects engage in self-presentational strategies *in order to* match their personal or social standards. So the difference between these theories might only be that between internal and external aspects of the same phenomenon, or between functional and causal aspects.

This way of construing the theories means that even if there is no arousal basis to evaluation apprehension, it might still have a rôle to play in explaining the social conformity effects. It elucidates one of the two higher level functions or goals (Matusewicz, 1974) of conforming – the avoidance of social disapproval. The other function of conforming was to gain social approval (Ferris, Beehr and Gilmore, 1978). It should also be noted here that with the phenomena of stage-fright and audience anxiety, Carver and Scheier (1981a) might be premature in abandoning an arousal basis to evaluation apprehension.

Putting all these points together gives one the following two views. From the control systems perspective first of all, the reason for engaging in self-presentation strategies in social facilitation settings is to reduce a discrepancy between a standard of behaviour and current behaviour. Any change in self-presentation can therefore be explained as part of trying to conform. Self-presentation theory, on the other hand, can argue that any change towards a behaviour standard occurs because the subjects are trying to present a particular impression. So both theories can account for the same results and make similar predictions. Control systems theory describes one internal mechanism for achieving an external self-presentation strategy.

The lack of theoretical discrimination is worse still, however. It is also possible to apply the same argument just given to the two Drive models of social conformity effects (Baumeister, 1982; Wicklund and Duval, 1971).

Gaining approval or avoiding disapproval leads to an increase in arousal (Baumeister, 1982). One way of explaining the mechanisms by which this occurs is to assume an objective self-awareness process which acts to reduce any discrepancy between performance and ideal by trying to reduce the aversive arousal which has been produced from gaining approval or avoiding disapproval (Wicklund and Duval, 1971).

So the two Drive theories of social conformity might also be seen as two aspects of the same process. One could also mix the arousal and non-arousal theories up as well, since there is no definitive evidence that autonomic arousal increases occur. The theories, then, are underdetermined and cannot make separate clear predictions.

As hinted in Chapter 5, perhaps the most general statement which can be made from all these theories is that greater *control* is taken over behaviour when another person is present. This control of behaviour is oriented (unless there are possible threats) towards gaining social approval or avoiding social disapproval. This might be achieved by creating an impression in the other person of being competent. This impression might be mediated by attending more closely to performance and reducing discrepancies between actual performance and the standards expected.

The problem remains, then, that the theories cannot be pitted against another in the falsification style because they are underdetermined. Only the rôle of arousal can differentiate between some of them, and then not perfectly (see above). The empirical studies as presently conducted cannot provide evidence for or against any of these theories. They can, however, show whether alertness effects exist independently from social conformity effects, and the three sources of evidence for this were given above.

9.4 The functional basis of social facilitation motivation

Most theories of social facilitation have been structural, in the sense that they describe a psychological structure which, when activated, produces an effect. Once described, the structures are usually taken to be fixed, and might even become reified. For example, control systems theory proposes a mechanistic structure which acts to reduce discrepancies between current behaviour and standards of behaviour. The matching structure itself is talked about as an object and does not change; only the behaviour standards change to cater for changing environments. Likewise, given the assumption of cognitive structures, the effects follow from different information being processed by the essentially unchanging cognitive processing structures.

What has been developed in this chapter so far is a move towards a functional view, where the functions of these structures is questioned. For example, it was suggested above that: 'The subjects engage in self-presentational strategies in order to match their standards.' It can also be asked what the function of matching to behaviour standards might be: Why do people match their behaviour to personal or social standards? As another example, we have already seen that Zajonc did not just outline a structure for arousal increase, but he also asked the question of why arousal might increase in the presence of others (Zajonc, 1980). The monitorability model (4.4; Guerin and Innes, 1982) was one way of answering this functional question in more detail than Zajonc had, who talked about the inherent uncertainty in organisms' behaviour.

There are two aspects we can look at to pursue the functional questions: the immediate function of an hypothesized psychological structure and the ultimate function.

Looking first at the *immediate* motivations for social facilitation effects, we find the following: that for Zajonc's Drive model and the monitorability model, the immediate source of the organism changing its behaviour is an increase in arousal or drive; for evaluation, apprehension and objective self-awareness models, the immediate source of motivation is an increase in aversive drive; for the control systems model, the change in behaviour is due to an operation which matches behaviour to some standard; self-presentation has people trying to present a particular image to the other person; for behaviour analysis the functional consequences following previous similar behaviours in similar settings provide the immediate source of motivation; behaviour inhibition puts the change onto an inhibition of rehearsal processes; distraction-conflict has the person distracted for different reasons (the only one tested is the gaining of social comparison information); Manstead and Semin's model produces the effects as the result of greater control taken over behaviour; and the cognitive processing models have the behaviour change because of what has been previous processing which has been stored in memory (very similar to behaviour analysis but put inside the head).

When we come to the *ultimate* functions there is more speculation. Zajonc's model says that we are aroused in order to prepare for encounters, and presumably we are prepared because doing so has paid off before either for the organism or for its progenitors (if hard-wired, as suggested by Zajonc). The monitoring model spells out these ultimate functions of being prepared for encounters in more detail, especially the ones to do with defending oneself. Evaluation apprehension suggested that we have learned in the past that other people can provide negative consequences when we perform in front of them, so several functions are possible. First, it might have been that being apprehensive or alert has helped improve performance in the past. Second, being anxious might have helped us escape from such situations in the past. Or third, the effect might be a mixture such that by being apprehensive when someone else is present we have been able to escape if doing a complex task or do better if a simple task. If true, then the functional problem for test-anxiety or performing in front of audiences is that the escape is not possible and we have little practice of doing complex tasks in front of others.

Objective self-awareness does not really suggest why we might examine our ideals in the presence of others. Whatever the source, it might be the same as for social comparison or competition: in the presence of others we examine our ideals and plans in order to compare with others. As put by Festinger:

> Persons try to find out what they can and cannot do in the environment in which they live. This represents a kind of exploration of themselves which is essentially similar to the exploration of the environment. Taken together we can say that the human being attempts to know what his possibilities of action are in that world. (Festinger, 1964, p. 140)

This still does not tell us, however, the function of trying to learn the possibilities of action.

The control systems model must answer the question of why people should try and match their behaviour to public or private standards. The answer to this reflects closely the behaviour analytic answer. People probably try to match *personal* standards because they have proved beneficial in the past when followed (although behaviour analysis would word this quite different-ly for good reasons). People probably try to match *social* standards, on the other hand, because of social reinforcement, even though this might be irrelevant to the actual behaviour performed (Guerin, 1992). Behaviour analysis has pursued the functional reasoning one step further and proposed three types of 'selection by consequences' which are the ultimate functions (Skinner, 1981).

Self-presentation theories implicitly suggest that the reason for trying to present oneself in a particular way is to ingratiate oneself, and the reason for doing this is because of the payoffs from the other person present. This might be generalized praise or attention, or else avoidance of some negative consequences. Behaviour inhibition seems to have a rigid arousal mechan-ism such that any other person will increase arousal and thereby inhibit performance rehearsal. The ultimate functions of this are therefore probably similar to those of evaluation apprehension, to avoid negative evaluations.

Distraction-conflict and the other attentional models all suggest that attending to the other person present is functional because it has paid off in the past by specific exchanges, by giving social comparison information, by preparing for an encounter, or because monitoring the person reduces arousal. The theories differ in whether the information obtained when attention is increased causes the effect (such as helping in competition), or whether the effect is indirect (such as distraction-conflict). Manstead and Semin's model suggests that it is beneficial to control attention in most instances. There must be advantages to controlled performance, or rule-governed performance for behaviour analysts (Hayes, 1989), over automatic processing if it continues.

Cognitive information processing models have to explain why the schemata used in processing are ultimately functional. Presumably they would argue that this is based on previous functional past memories, and also that schema processing is an efficient way for the organism to operate, since it reduces cognitive demands (Bartlett, 1932).

All these questions need to be explained in order to derive the motivational sources for social facilitation effects. Some theories differ only in the level of function they deal with. It must be concluded again that the choice of framework or theory will depend on pragmatic considerations rather than empirical ones. The three major contenders are control systems theory, behaviour analysis, and cognitive theory.

9.5 How the specific behaviours are predicted

The last part of this chapter will put together some comments made throughout the book about the specific predictions from social facilitation theories. What is found in studies is that there is variability in behaviour such that different behaviours occur when alone and when in the presence of another person. To predict this variability, different theories have relied upon different theoretical constructs.

Many of the theories which followed Zajonc (1965) assumed a dominance hierarchy of responses from which to predict changes in behaviour. With increasing arousal, the more dominant responses would become more frequent. The monitoring model and the evaluation apprehension models assume this, as well as the distraction-conflict model and the attention/ arousal models based on Easterbrook (1959). The dominance hierarchy had the advantage that the behaviour prediction did not depend on the loose statement that 'the subject will try harder at the task'. Instead, artificial response hierarchies were usually manipulated (e.g., Zajonc and Sales, 1966). In order to predict behaviour from these theories, therefore, the hierarchy of responses needs to be known.

Objective self-awareness is trickier in this respect because although it is an arousal model, the predictions about the actual behaviour depend upon which strategies are used to reduce the aversive arousal state. This probably depends on the type of goals or ideals which are being considered at the time.

It was usually assumed that the strategies operative in the experimental setting were to do with improving performances.

The control systems model depended for its predictions of behaviour on the standards of performance and the operations used to get a closer match to those standards. Some progress was made in this respect by distinguishing between public and private standards of behaviour, but in the experimental setting there was still the assumption that subjects would somehow operate to try harder at the task. Again, the particular details of these behavioural operations were never spelled out and independent measures of the standards were not tried.

The self-presentation theory's predictions of behaviour clearly depend upon the various self-presentation strategies, which have been spelled out in some detail over the years (Breckler and Greenwald, 1986; Goffman, 1959; Guerin, 1991; Jones and Pittman, 1982) but not measured in experimental work. As noted above, these strategies provide more detailed functions for the matching to standards operations of the control systems model. In order to match to standard, the person can engage in the self-presentation strategies. The strategies, in turn, need to be predicted from the learning history of the person involved in similar settings, in order to predict behaviour in the social facilitation setting.

Behaviour analysis would also predict the exact behaviour from a knowledge of the person's history of reinforcement in similar settings, and their social reinforcement in particular (Chase, 1988; LeFrancois, Chase and Joyce, 1988; Wanchisen, 1990; Weiner, 1964). On top of this, previous behaviours generalize to other similar settings and people, so novel behaviours can occur.

Behaviour inhibition's predictions of behaviour depend upon the severity of the inhibition of rehearsal. How much someone inhibits their behaviour in the presence of another person depends on their previous history, no doubt. Likewise, for Manstead and Semin, how much behaviour is controlled in the presence of others will depend on what has been learned in the past. Some people have learned more control over their cognitive processes (rule-governed behaviour for behaviour analysts) than others (Broadbent, Fitz-Gerald and Broadbent, 1986).

Finally, the predictions from cognitive theories depend either on the schemata which have been learned in the past or the pre-response filters (Blank, 1979) which have been learned. These will in turn depend on the outcomes or consequences of processing in a particular way in the past. This again shows that ultimately the control systems model, the behaviour analytic approach, and the cognitive approach rest on very similar assumptions. The decision between frameworks cannot be decided by experiment.

The major problem with all these ways of predicting behaviour in a social facilitation setting is that independent measures are not usually taken. It is common to assume that, for example, an increase in responding is evidence for social facilitation *and* for a proposed mechanism: arousal, a behaviour hierarchy, a standard of behaviour, an attentional change, etc. Empirical work in this area will not improve until independent measures are taken. With this also goes the point (7.13) that we need to know the background behaviours of an organism before we can decide whether there has been a change and whether the change supports any of the theories.

9.6 Conclusions

In conclusion, this chapter has argued that there are two general social facilitation phenomena; that most of the theories can explain the data which are available; that the theories have similar assumptions if looked at closely, especially their immediate and ultimate functions; that theories specific to social facilitation should be superseded by the larger frameworks of psychology; that the functions of social facilitation effects need to be looked at closely; and that when it comes to predicting which behaviours will occur in a social facilitation setting, the major frameworks each make similar suggestions.

Put together in this way, these conclusions suggest that the traditional method of studying the social facilitation effects will no longer suffice. Coming up with newer ways of talking about the same phenomena, and trying to test between differences which exist only in words, is not the way. As suggested earlier, exploring a more diverse approach to measurement in the social facilitation situation would be more fruitful than testing 'mini' theories which can make similar predictions. Looking at the social facilitation phenomena in the light of other social phenomena will also be useful. Some of this has already commenced in the literature and will be reviewed in the next chapter.

The hypothesis and testing strategy, extensively used in the experimental social psychology literature, has produced some interesting results since Triplett (1898), but is probably not working any longer. The principal reason for this, mentioned several times, is that the theories and hypotheses have become too underdetermined. Most of the different ways of speaking about our social phenomena can predict the same events, and there is little by way of evidence which can distinguish between them.

The next chapter will look at related research areas to suggest how social facilitation research can be intertwined with other social phenomena. Finally, Chapter 11 will suggest how social facilitation research might go from here. The main conclusion is to look at *social facilitation as a type of setting which produces behaviour rather than as a type of behaviour.*

10 Related areas of psychology

We have seen in the last chapter that one way for social facilitation research to develop further is to integrate the phenomena or events taking place in the social facilitation setting with other social psychological phenomena. This will lead us to the view that there is nothing special about social facilitation as a group of responses (facilitation or inhibition in the presence of others) but rather, that social facilitation is distinguished only by the particular setting that is used. If we change the social facilitation setting slightly we get similar effects, but ones which are labelled as separate phenomena with separate literatures.

The final point of this argument (in Chapter 11) is to ignore the labels 'social facilitation', 'social loafing', or 'deindividuation', and instead look more closely at the events which take place in different settings with different consequences. Response facilitation and inhibition can be produced in several ways, and it might be artificial not to treat these together.

Social facilitation is closely related to a number of other areas in social psychology. These are areas dealing with people alone versus people with others present, but with some other variable added as well or some slight difference in the setting. While some of these areas have already been compared to social facilitation by other researchers, this chapter looks at some other links which can be made as well. The major criterion for inclusion is that there is minimal social interaction or direct influence from between the subject and the persons present. The phenomena to be discussed, then, are ones in which there is another person present who does not directly try and influence the subjects.

The first two areas to be discussed add the variable of having a group of other people present (audience effects and deindividuation), and bring together the discussions of conformity processes which have appeared throughout this book. The third area is different to social facilitation in that the people present are engaged in the same task for a group result (social loafing), such that the consequences of their individual actions are not identifiable. The next section looks at how people use the others present in social facilitation-like settings to get comparison information which then guides their own performance in some way (social comparison theory).

Following this, competition effects are discussed since they have also been implicated in social facilitation effects and the setting is similar to that of social facilitation (Table 2 and Chapter 2). Next, we will look at some work on implicit audiences: how we might carry other people around with us. This is tied up with both cognitive models (audience schemata inside our heads) and behaviour analysis (as our social reinforcement history). Finally, we will pursue further a topic touched upon in Chapter 8: the effects when a computer is present rather than a person. There is interesting work being done on telemeetings and electronic communication networks which bears on the social facilitation setting effects.

In each of these areas we will try to pull out the key phenomena or events that are taking place rather than review all the theories which have been proposed or all the empirical data. In each case, then, we are looking at how changing the controlling variables slightly from the social facilitation setting can change behaviour in interesting ways.

10.1 Performing in front of an audience

There would seem to be a connection of some sort between the social facilitation phenomena and the phenomena of test anxiety and stage-fright. Many people report reluctance to speak or perform in front of groups of others, and many report unpleasant feelings, verbal chatter in their head, or the proverbial 'butterflies in the stomach' if they are made to speak. Performing in the presence of others has many marked effects.

While the effects of an arousal increase, also seen in social facilitation research, would seem to be obvious in settings with larger audiences, it is hard to see how social conformity effects might directly lead to the sorts of phenomena reported with audiences. It would seem to mean that there was a norm to act nervously when performing in front of a large crowd. This seems unlikely in most cases, except in cultures where you are expected to act somewhat shy in front of audiences. Social conformity effects are likely to have *indirect* influences in such settings. In a large crowd there are probably many expectations and norms, as well as a greater number of negative social consequences from giving a poor performance. This would have cognitive distracting effects, and possibly physical distracting effects as well if the performer needed to attend to the members of the audience. So although the effects of performing in front of a large audience seem closely related to arousal and autonomic nervous system mechanisms, social conformity influences should not be dismissed out of hand. We will see some indicators of this presently.

There has been much research in settings of test anxiety, which is very close to the social facilitation setting, but the evaluation is made explicit with real consequences and there is usually a personal history of such settings. Some of the best work on this has been done by Geen (see 1989, 1991; Schauer, Seymour and Geen, 1985). Geen (1985), for example, rated subjects as high or low test anxious on the basis of the Sarason Test Anxiety Scale. He then gave them hard anagrams to solve, which they did in one of three conditions: alone, in front of an experimenter who just quietly and passively observed them, or in front of an experimenter who explicitly made it clear that he was constantly evaluating them.

It was found that there was little difference between subjects on the number of anagrams attempted, except that high test anxiety subjects attempted somewhat less anagrams when being passively observed and many less anagrams when being explicitly observed. Geen (1985) also had subjects give self-reports of anxiety before and after the task. These measures showed that the high test anxious subjects increased their ratings of anxiety before and after the task more than the low test anxious subjects. Those high test anxious subjects who were observed, increased their self-reports even more than those alone.

Studies such as Geen (1985) suggest that the same phenomena as occur in social facilitation studies are occurring here, and that they have a relationship to state anxiety levels. The results suggest that an arousal increase is leading to self-presentation effects. If the arousal acted as mere presence would predict then more anagrams would be attempted (though done worse). So the measured test anxiety state suggests that these people have *learned* to attempt less during their personal history, presumably because this self-presentation strategy has worked in the past. Geen called this 'response withholding' (Geen, 1985, p. 38). It again emphasizes the complexities and interdependencies of the theoretical positions in social facilitation.

What is interesting in this literature is that we see the switch from arousal increase to response withholding, which shows that the subjects have learned to manage their arousal increases. In the terms of Chapters 5 and 6, we can say that when these subjects discriminate a situation of evaluation and anxiety, more control is taken over their behaviour (called 'rule-governed behaviour' by behaviour analysts) and less is left to automatic processing (Geen, 1991; Manstead and Semin, 1980). This strategy must have been learned at some point in their lives. In this case the control is probably not a socially learned standard for behaviour (such as being taught by our elders that 'When you get nervous, slow down') but an individually learned strategy. In behaviour analytic terms, the verbal control is said to be by 'tracking' rather than by 'pliance' (Hayes, Zettle and Rosenfarb, 1989).

Turning now to *speaking* in front of audiences rather than performing a test, there is also good evidence that the same social facilitation effects occur here. There are increases in autonomic nervous system activity, facilitation of simple tasks and inhibition of complex tasks, physical and cognitive distraction effects, and further distraction effects from the time-pressure engendered by the other effects (see Borden, 1980).

Jackson and Latané (1981), for example, found in a laboratory study that as the size and status of an audience increased, the performance apprehension increased as a power function. As the number of co-performers increased, however, the apprehension decreased as a power function. This supported the 'social impact' theory of Latané (1981): that the impact of others increases as the number of others increases, but that the impact becomes increasingly less as the number of co-performers increases.

The same result was found 'in the field' at a university Greek Week talent performance, where students performed acts in front of about 2500 others. Jackson and Latané asked the performers about their nervousness and tension before and after their acts. The acts themselves varied from one to ten participants, so the effects of a varying number of co-performers could be tested. Strong support was found for the social impact power function. Performers who were with ten others rated about two on the scale of tension (very low), whilst those who were in groups of four rated at about ten on the same scale, and those who performed alone rated at over sixty! The power function can be seen in the results of those who performed in pairs: they rated themselves at about sixteen. This means that adding just one other performer had a very large impact in reducing tension, while adding more performers after this had less and less of an impact.

Another approach was taken by Seta, Wang, Crisson and Seta (1989), who looked more closely at the composition of the audience and compared the impact of high and low expert audiences. Psychology students were asked to rate how tense they would be to perform in front of faculty staff (high status), graduate students (middle status), and high school students (low status). To stop other effects occurring the subjects were shown photographs of such people rather than having the people actually present with them. While this does reduce the interference of other effects such as social interaction and unpredictability, it loses ecological validity and makes it harder to compare to other results.

Seta et al. (1989) found that the felt anxiety was greatest for two faculty members and two graduate students, less for just two faculty members, and lowest for two faculty members and two high school students. Thus while adding more people sometimes increased tension, this was not always the case, especially when high and low status members were mixed. Seta et al. (1989) suggested that the results could be interpreted as showing an 'averaging' effect across the number of others and their status, so adding high school students reduced the impact of the two faculty members even though the audience was larger. In this regard it would have also been interesting to run another condition with four faculty members, to check the interaction of these two variables.

10.2 Deindividuation and conformity

Deindividuation is an area first brought to experimental social psychology by Festinger, Pepitone and Newcomb (1952). These authors were concerned with examples of social behaviour where normally inhibited behaviours seemed to become uninhibited when a group of people got together. For example, aggression is seen to occur in demonstrations by large groups of people, sometimes by people who would not ordinarily aggress. Lynching, likewise, seems to need special conditions.

The phenomenon, then, is that disinhibited or counter-normative behaviours occur when people are in groups (Diener, 1980; Hogg and Abrams, 1988; Mann, Newton and Innes, 1982; Prentice-Dunn and Rogers, 1982; Reicher, 1982). This seems opposed to the social facilitation phenomenon that behaviour is *more* conforming when others are present (Chapter 5). There are special conditions to get a deindividuation setting, however, which are different to those of the typical social facilitation setting. Once again the social behaviour is continuous and it is the setting which changes.

The major conditions for deindividuation effects are the following. First, unlike social facilitation, the uninhibited behaviour is greater when in groups than when alone, but only in conjunction with the other conditions. Second, the deindividuation effects are stronger when the people in the group are made anonymous rather than identifiable. This condition is unlike social facilitation settings where the subject is less anonymous with the other person present, so the opposite result is understandable. Third, deindividuation settings usually change the responsibility of the subjects for their behaviour in some way (Guerin, 1991), whereas social facilitation subjects do not have this condition imposed. Fourth, deindividuation effects usually require an increase in arousal levels, whereas social facilitation effects increase arousal. Finally, deindividuation studies have often changed the subjects' level of self-awareness and found less conforming behaviour when either or both of private and public self-awareness have been reduced (Prentice-Dunn and Rogers, 1989).

A neat example of this research is the study by Diener, Fraser, Beaman and Kelem (1976), who looked at an anti-normative behaviour of children taking more candies or money than they were allowed during a Halloween trick-or-treat. They varied anonymity by asking half the children their names and where they lived; they measured whether the children were in a group or alone; and they lowered the responsibility of some groups by telling the children that the youngest one was to see that no extra candies were taken. The results showed that more candies were taken in the predicted deindividuation conditions: when the children were in groups, were anonymous, and were made less responsible. A further study along these lines also found that the presence of a mirror reduced stealing of extra candies, presumably by increasing (private) self-awareness (Beaman, Klentz, Diener and Svanum, 1979), although no independent measure of this was taken.

In terms of theory, the recent view of deindividuation is that in groups, especially when anonymous or with reduced responsibility, people become less self-aware and therefore stop monitoring and regulating their own behaviour (Diener, 1980; Prentice-Dunn and Rogers, 1982, 1989). This seems to be in opposition to the self-awareness hypothesis put forward in 5.2 and 5.3, where the presence of others was said to *increase* self-awareness. It was also mentioned there, however, that this might only refer to *public* self-awareness; *private* self-awareness is likely to decrease and it is this which is said to mediate self-regulation of behaviour rather than group-regulation of behaviour (Prentice-Dunn and Rogers, 1989). Group-regulation can also influence behaviour, but this is not now referred to as deindividuation: Prentice-Dunn and Rogers (1989), for example, explicitly separate it and call it accountability.

The view, then, which is common to many theories of social behaviour (Guerin, 1991; Hayes, Zettle and Rosenfarb, 1989; Nemeth, 1986; Prentice-Dunn and Rogers, 1989) is that behaviour can be controlled by both social and individual means. Under conditions such as increased private self-awareness (mirrors, self-attention, attention to goals and plans, non-salient group membership), control over behaviour can be taken away from the situation and based instead on previous personal experience (or verbal rules of 'tracking', Hayes, Zettle and Rosenfarb, 1989). This process leads to greater social conformity only when private and public standards match (Carver and Scheier, 1981b) and less conformity when deindividuation conditions are in place so that private self-awareness is reduced (Prentice-Dunn and Rogers, 1989).

The second process is that under certain other conditions (such as an evaluating person present, increased public self-awareness, an audience, a majority giving their view, salient group membership), control over behaviour can be taken away from the situation and replaced by verbal social standards (or verbal rules of 'pliance', Hayes, Zettle and Rosenfarb, 1989). These are usually social standards relevant to the persons present or the behaviours being evaluated, and can result in socially conforming behaviours and less uninhibited behaviour such as occur in deindividuation studies (Carver and Scheier, 1981b, public self-awareness; Hogg and Abrams, 1988; Hogg and Turner, 1987, social identity; Nemeth, 1986; Prentice-Dunn and

Rogers, 1989, accountability; Turner and Oakes, 1989, personal and social identity).

Behaviour analysis can also provide a viewpoint here. One factor which determines deindividuation is the lack of responsibility in a group for each member. While this has been taken as evidence for self-awareness in the social psychological literature, in behaviour analytic terms it means that there are less or weaker consequences for the behaviour of individuals when they are in a group (Guerin, 1991). The extreme case of this, when there is total anonymity and therefore total lack of social consequences, is also the extreme condition for deindividuation.

The point of all these different analyses is that the events occurring in social facilitation settings are not different from these other events – they just occur in a slightly different situation and therefore have different results. The social facilitation situation usually encompasses only a few other people, lack of anonymity, full responsibility for behaviour, evaluation, arousal, high private and public self-awareness, and salient norms of doing what the experimenter requests and doing well at a performance task. Varying any of these conditions will produce results which are found in other areas of social psychology. The question is whether it is worth having a separate label for this particular mix of conditions.

10.3 Social loafing

Social loafing refers to the phenomenon that people put in less effort when in groups, as compared with working alone. In the report which gave the name to social loafing, Latané, Williams and Harkins (1979) found that people would shout less if in a larger group, but only if the output was measured over the whole group. When individual outputs were recorded in the group, social loafing disappeared, and this has been found over a wide range of behaviours (see Williams, Nida, Baca and Latané, 1989). So one of the conditions of social loafing seems to be that the individual outputs are not identifiable. This makes the social loafing setting different to that of social facilitation. Again, it is argued that social loafing is not really a different set of responses, there is simply a different mix of conditions which produces different behaviour: the motivation of behaviour (facilitation or inhibition) is continuous and not a set of discrete phenomena.

Several authors have already related the social loafing phenomena to the social facilitation phenomena (Geen, 1991; Guerin, 1991; Harkins, 1987; Harkins and Szymanski, 1987; Mullen and Baumeister, 1987; Paulus, 1983; see also Griffith, Fichman and Moreland, 1989). These have been presented in different ways but the basic point seems to reflect that given in the last section, 10.2: that subjects conform less when they are not identifiable, and that they are usually less identifiable in a group. That is, the social consequences for individuals are usually less in groups.

The changes in consequences for subjects in social loafing studies have been manipulated in different ways. Originally the variable was called *identifiability* (Latané, Williams and Harkins, 1979), but is has more recently been referred to as both *accountability* and *evaluation*. A necessary condition for social loafing seems to be a lack of evaluation of the output or a lack of evaluation standards (Bartis, Szymanski and Harkins, 1988; Goethals and Darley, 1987; Harkins, 1987; Harkins and Szymanski, 1988, 1989; Williams, Harkins and Latané, 1981). We have already seen that the evaluation variable which affects social loafing also occurs in social facilitation research (5.1). In social loafing experiments groups work harder if their individual outputs are evaluated than if only the group total is evaluated; in co-working social facilitation experiments, individuals are typically evaluated individually and performance on simple tasks is increased.

What was suggested by Harkins (1987) was that social facilitation and social loafing have studied different cells of a virtual 2 × 2 design. Social facilitation has studied conditions of Co-action/Individual Evaluation versus Alone/Individual Evaluation, whereas social loafing has studied Co-action/No Individual Evaluation versus Alone/Individual Evaluation. The fourth cell of the design, the Alone/No Individual evaluation was claimed not to have been tested. What are still left out of this formulation, however, are the many audience studies where the other person present is not co-acting at all but passively present. This, in terms of the argument to be given in this section, is all that distinguishes social facilitation from social loafing.

Harkins (1987) went on to provide some evidence that this formulation holds. He had subjects do a brainstorming task either Alone or in Co-action, and either Evaluated or Not Evaluated. This forms the basic 2 × 2 design incorporating social loafing and co-performing social facilitation (but not audience effects as was pointed out above). Harkins (1987) also included another Co-action who had pooled results, which enhances the reduced identification of group membership. He found support that the social loafing and co-performing social facilitation variables were comparable: not having evaluation was similar to pooling of group results, both evaluation and co-acting (with evaluation held constant) increased motivation. Thus the variables seem merely to be manipulating the same responses in slightly different ways.

What is happening, then, is that social loafing is just like a setting of deindividuation or accountability (Prentice-Dunn and Rogers, 1989) but with three special conditions: first, that the people are in a co-acting group; second, that identifiability is reduced; and third, that the relevant social standard is doing well at the task provided, so that loafing becomes the measure of anti-normative behaviour rather than stealing or aggression. If it is recognized that reduced identifiability is inherent in most groups (Guerin, 1991), then social loafing also deals with a setting just like social facilitation but with two special conditions: the consequences for individuals are reduced through pooling the group performance results, and that only co-acting settings are used.

These links can all be put into behaviour analytic terms by saying that manipulating evaluation, identifiability, or accountability is manipulating the consequences for the individual (see Guerin, 1991). If a person's results are lost in the group then any unpleasant consequences are avoided or shared between the group members. It would be predicted from this viewpoint that if only *positive* consequences were to come from the task evaluation, then subjects would perform harder in groups and in fact try and 'individuate' themselves (Maslach, 1974). The only thing which makes social loafing a separate phenomenon is that it deals with the inherent changes in consequences (less identifiable) from being a group member. To be consistent with other motivational approaches, we should say that the phenomenon is one of increasing effort (loafing) by increasing consequences. This is because the basic task is not one which subjects would ordinarily carry out, but requires an experimenter induced standard. This point has been made independently by two authors (Geen, 1991; Guerin, 1991).

This returns to a point made in Chapters 7 and 9, and to some discussion points made by Harkins (1987): that until we have better theories and models of the underlying mechanisms, (in this case evaluation and other social consequences) we can only intuitively manipulate our variables. There is no clear understanding at present of what evaluation exactly is, how it functions, and how it can be manipulated. Until there is, we will always be guessing about the rôle of evaluation in social facilitation and social loafing effects. Behaviour analysis at least provides some foundation to this by looking at a wider category of social consequences.

10.4 Social comparison theory

Another area of social psychology to compare with social facilitation is social comparison theory (Festinger, 1954; Goethals and Darley, 1987; Suls and Wills, 1991). This area looks at how people compare what they are doing, and their views of themselves, to others. Clearly, if other people are present then an opportunity arises for social comparison which is not possible when alone. There are a few links which can therefore be made to the social facilitation phenomena.

First, some of the original emphasis in social comparison studies had to do with fear reduction when in groups. As we saw in Chapter 7, there is strong evidence that nonhuman animals reduce their fear in groups, although this might apply only to certain social species (Cottrell and Epley, 1977). It was originally suggested that with increased evaluation apprehension or fear there was a 'need' to find out the state of others (Festinger, 1954; Liebling and Shaver, 1973b; Schachter, 1959). Like nonhuman animals, the reduced fear from being with others might lead to an increase in other behaviours, however hard it might be to exactly predict *which* other behaviours. This fits with control systems theory (5.3), in that people need to compare their own behaviours with others when there is uncertainty about how to behave. When private self-awareness is low or gives no clear standards, an increase in public self-awareness might be necessary. In terms of the position developed in the last two sections of this paper, we can say that when there is evaluation apprehension but no clear standard of behaviour then people try to find a standard by watching what others are doing.

Another link between social comparison and social facilitation arose in Section 6.3. Sanders, Baron and Moore (1978) suggested that a need for social comparison information might lead to greater distraction during social facilitation tasks. If there was a time-constraint on the task, then this distraction could produce the social facilitation effects by increasing arousal levels.

A further link between social facilitation and social comparison is that during co-action studies, any social comparison information can affect performance levels, perhaps through expectancy levels of standards of behaviour (Seta, 1982), and also through possible competition (Conolley, Gerard and Kline, 1978; also 10.5 below). It is very difficult to get two people working on the same task without them trying to compare performance levels, as the early social facilitation literature found (Chapter 2). Since this cannot occur when working alone, the difference will usually be confounded in co-action studies. A method of testing for this would be to run two co-action groups with different false feedback, in order to check how much social comparison is playing a rôle.

These three connections between social comparison effects and social facilitation effects are probably just a first step (Hake and Vukelich, 1980; Hake, Vukelich and Kaplan, 1973). It seems fairly clear that a large difference between being alone and being with another person is that you can find out about their behaviour, whether or not this should be used as a comparison or behaviour standard, and whether or not fear and anxiety are present. People are a rich source of information and this will affect the behaviour of two people together in many and varied ways. This suggests that the social comparison research needs to find out what exactly people can learn from others, whatever the effect of this on their subsequent behaviour. When we know this we have a better chance of predicting the effects likely to arise from social comparisons, observational learning, and cueing within social facilitation settings. The same conclusion was made for the animal literature in Chapter 7: that until we know more about the animal we will not be able to predict what it will do when fear is reduced in a group nor what it can learn from other animals.

10.5 Competition

The early social facilitation experiments repeatedly noted that competition was difficult to reduce in co-action studies (Allport, 1924b; Dashiell, 1935). This was such a problem that, as we saw in Chapter 2, LaPiere and Farnsworth (1936) suggested: 'In fact, it is possible that social facilitation is nothing more than mild rivalry' (p. 377). In Chapter 8 we have also seen that a large number of social facilitation studies have confounded competition effects in their design (Geen and Gange, 1977).

Competition in social facilitation settings can be of two sorts. First, in co-action situations, there might be limited resources so the better of the two performers would come out on top. This classifies as a traditional competition effect and is usually analysed in terms of competition for scarce resources (Buskist and Morgan, 1987, 1988; Carron, 1980; Colman, 1982; Deutsch, 1949; Gergen, 1969; Hake and Olvera, 1978; Hake, Olvera and Bell, 1975; Kanak and Davenport, 1967; Rosenbaum, 1980; Rosenbaum, Moore, Cotton, Cook, Hieser, Shovar and Gray, 1980; Schmitt, 1984, 1986; Turner, 1981;). In such cases the social comparison opportunities and feedback available will determine the performance levels (e.g., Beck and Seta, 1980).

The second type of competition occurs when there is a standard of behaviour (personal or social) that two people *should* compete, whether or not the outcomes are scarce: in fact the ostensible outcomes might be irrelevant. In this case the performers are carrying out a standard of behaviour which is maintained by social reinforcement of a general kind rather than by the instrumental value of the particular outcomes (Guerin, 1992; Reykowski, 1982). With this form of competition there should clearly be cross-cultural differences, and indeed some evidence for this has been reported (e.g., Carment and Hodkin, 1973).

Buskist, Barry, Morgan and Rossi (1984) explored these two different paths to competition. Their subjects performed in a situation with competing outcomes such that only one of them could win. Some subjects were given orienting instructions that the situation would be a competitive one (verbally governed) while others learned to perform purely through the competitive outcomes (contingency governed). While subjects without the instructions still became competitive, they took longer. So in this case the social, verbal instructions set the occasion for competition, producing competition more quickly by setting a standard for competitive behaviour.

A more indirect link with the social facilitation research comes from the report that competition can produce drivelike effects (Steigleder, Weiss, Balling, Wenninger and Lombardo, 1980). This means that studies which have appeared to induce arousal from social facilitation conditions might have produced competition instead, especially when there was a co-action setting. Some of these same authors also found that the removal of competition can act as a reinforcer (Steigleder, Weiss, Cramer and Feinberg, 1978), thus suggesting that competition is like an aversive drive state. The subjects in Buskist et al. (1984), however, reported that they enjoyed the competitive situation. Clearly there are different types of competition, which further strengthens the point of this chapter that we need to know more about phenomena such as competition independently of social facilitation settings before we can comment more on their rôle in the social facilitation setting.

10.6 Implicit audiences

It has often been pointed out in the social facilitation literature that in one sense, we *always* carry an audience around with us (Chapter 8; Harkins, 1987; Markus, 1978), so we cannot have a true alone condition. While very little empirical work has been done on this phenomenon, we can review here some related work and make some suggestions about what might be going on.

Fridlund (1991) carried out an interesting study by having subjects view a 'pleasant video' under four different social conditions and measuring their facial expressions. Subjects viewed the video either alone, with a friend doing another task down a hall, with a friend viewing the same video down a hall, or with the two friends viewing together in the same room.

It was found that there was more smiling when a friend was watching the video than when alone or with a friend doing another task elsewhere. This result was the same whether or not the friend viewing the same video was present, so it was concluded that there was something social about smiling even if the other person was not present. Fridlund (1991) called this 'solitary smiling'. It might be recalled from Chapter 2 that Dashiell (1930) had found that merely synchronizing subjects in different rooms produced competition effects. Here subjects were primed with a different standard to that of competition and mere synchrony was sufficient for this.

Another relevant study by Baldwin and Holmes (1987) had female subjects visualize the faces of either two older members of their family or else two peers. In a supposedly unrelated task, they then had to rate the enjoyableness of some passages of writing, which included one passage about a sexual encounter. As predicted, the subjects rated the passage as less enjoyable when they had first visualized the older family members. Baldwin and Holmes (1987) interpreted this in cognitive terms, that the subjects had been primed with a private audience which influenced their standards of behaviour used to rate what they enjoyed or not. Similar results were found in Baldwin, Carrell and Lopez (1990).

The final example concerns the reports gathered by Suedfeld and Mocellin (1987) of people sensing the presence of another person or spirit. The Antarctic explorer Shackleton, for example, had 'a curious feeling on the march that there was another person with us' (Suedfeld and Mocellin, 1987, p. 39). These authors reviewed such reports and concluded that while stress is not a necessary antecedent, the phenomenon usually occurred in unusual or extreme circumstances, including great stress or arousal.

From a cognitive point of view, it seems that the situation (rather than the physical environment) is one in which another person has usually been present so that the image and cognitive schemata of a generalized person becomes primed. While this is likely to occur in stressful situations, when other people usually appear and are helpful, other conditions could also prime the imagery and thoughts.

From a behaviour analytic point of view, the behaviours of imagery and perception are maintained by reinforcement, however unobvious (Vaughan and Michael, 1982), so if the situation is discriminative of previous strong consequences then it will appear as if something is perceived (see Guerin, 1990). This is a natural phenomenon which occurs in many ways in ordinary life. For example, if we are given low level noise to listen to, it will seem as if we can 'hear' voices talking (Skinner, 1936). The conditions under which such 'presences' are felt or seen are all similar to ones which have been strongly reinforced in the past, such as receiving help from another person when in trouble.

These three areas of research suggest, then, that we 'carry other people around with us' either as our past history of reinforcement (behaviour analysis) or as stored schemata which are primed. In these ways we can always have an audience with us, but this is saying little more than that we have social standards of behaviour which we can follow alone as well as in the presence of another person who primes them. So social facilitation of social standards of behaviour really looks at the increase from the amount of social standards followed when alone to the amount followed when in the presence of another person. We will never have a condition of no standards of behaviour.

While this point has been implicit in Chapters 5 and 9, it is now clear that we do follow *some* social standards of behaviour even when alone. We can say that in the social facilitation setting we are primed to increase the conformity with social standards (in cognitive terms) or we can say that social facilitation settings have been discriminative of reinforcement when following such standards in the past (behaviour analytic terms).

10.7 Computer communication

In 8.4 we looked at the effects of computers in the social facilitation setting (e.g., Aiello and Svec, in press). It was mentioned there that some interesting work was being done on computer communication and how this affects social communication. While such studies are not about the social facilitation setting, they do suggest other interesting phenomena which occur when the presence of others is in a minimal form.

The earliest work of this type was done following the availability of telephone conferencing and television conferencing equipment (Rutter, 1987; Short, Williams and Christie, 1976; Stricklund, Guild, Barefoot and Paterson, 1978; Williams, 1977). It was found, for example, that gestural cues are not as important as might be expected, as long as the spoken or written communication is changed so as to provide equivalent cues for the listener (Rimé, 1982; Williams, 1977). In behaviour analytic terms we can say that the autoclitic functions of gestures (which are verbal behaviours) can be replaced effectively through spoken or written means. Group processes were also found to be changed in computer communication, since many traditional rôles, such as that of leader, become redundant or modified (Stricklund, Guild, Barefoot and Paterson, 1978).

Spears, Lea and Lee (1990) conducted an interesting experiment with a computer-mediated communication system to test the hypothesis that deindividuation would be greater when communicating by computer in separate rooms than when communicating by computer in the same room. While the procedure and measure of deindividuation was unfortunately very indirect, the evidence seemed to support their ideas.

In behaviour analytic terms it would be argued that the social consequences change dramatically when communication is not face-to-face. All of the normal consequences which maintain social behaviour must be put into direct spoken or written forms. This also supports the idea that changing the media of communication would change the deindividuating conditions (also see Siegel, Dubrovsky, Kiesler and McGuire, 1986). Verbal behaviour is inherently about changing the behaviour of a listener (Skinner, 1957), and this needs to be different if the listener is not physically present.

Perhaps the most extensive and interesting studies are those by Kiesler and her colleagues (Kiesler, Siegel and McGuire, 1984; McGuire, Kiesler and Siegel, 1987; Siegel, Dubrovsky, Kiesler and McGuire, 1986; Sproull and

Kiesler, 1986, 1991). They have researched computer-mediated communications and how they affect social behaviour, with a particular interest in electronic mail systems. They have done this both through looking at already existing electronic mail channels (Sproull and Kiesler, 1986) and through laboratory experiments (Siegel, Dubrovsky, Kiesler and McGuire, 1986).

Their results have shown that when electronically networked groups try to make decisions, the participation rates are more equal, they come up with more ideas for action, and speak more frankly with more self-expression. While the greater democracy is useful in getting ideas, it also has the disadvantage of taking longer and making it less likely that anything will be done. Some evidence also shows that less arguments were pursued in electronic discussions (McGuire, Kiesler and Siegel, 1987), and that people can try and dominate the network by making it impossible for others to interrupt. Like Spears et al. (1990), there was some evidence for more uninhibited behaviours during electronic discussions (Siegel, Dubrovsky, Kiesler and McGuire, 1986), which can be both a positive event, if people say things they would not normally say, or negative, if people start making anti-social comments or inappropriate jokes. Finally, the effects of status also decrease during electronic networking, since the cues for status are not so obvious when the other people cannot be seen.

It must be noted that many of these results are from laboratory settings where the participants have little experience with electronic mail. With increased experience it is likely that rules or standards for discussion would emerge so the decision time would decrease, but that the many benefits, such as equal participation, would also decrease.

The results of the telephone, video and computer communication studies help us to understand some of the background events going on in social facilitation studies, other than an increase or decrease in performance levels. As repeatedly pointed out, this needs to be known before we can say much more about what is happening in the social facilitation setting. Many fruitful studies can be arranged by considering the phenomena of social facilitation in relation to these media channels. For example, electronic communication would decrease arousal from physical threat but keep arousal from evaluation if consequences are still present from the listener to the sender. It is hoped that more cross-studies will be carried out in the future.

11 Conclusions and future social facilitation research

The major conclusion of this book must be that social facilitation consists of many phenomena which are common to other social psychological areas of interest (see Geen, 1989, 1991; Paulus, 1983). What defines social facilitation is the particular mix of conditions which is usually present in the social facilitation setting, rather than any defining phenomena such as an increase or decrease in responding.

The animal studies suggested that the changes in the presence of other animals are primarily due to disinhibition of fear responses. When in groups most animals spend less time with fear responses and this facilitates the performance of other behaviours. These other behaviours might be an increase in eating (for chicks), an increase in vigilance (e.g., Lazarus, 1979), or increased social interaction concomitant with decreases in other behaviours such as eating (for rats).

With humans there was some evidence for mere presence effects (Chapter 8). A model based on monitoring was presented as a possible explanation for such effects. While this is obviously not the last word, it at least provides a way of defining mere presence which goes beyond just defining it as the absence of any other effects.

Besides mere presence effects, there were many other phenomena evident in the presence of another person: apprehension about evaluation; changes in self-awareness; increases in self-presentation strategies; increases in behaviours for which other people have become discriminative stimuli; increases in verbal behaviours; behaviour inhibition (at least for rehearsal strategies); physical distraction; cognitive distraction; narrowing of attention; and increases in social comparisons. It has been suggested that we study the conditions in the various settings rather than the patterns of responding themselves. The responding increase in social facilitation settings is the same as the responding increase when social loafing is reduced. It is perhaps not fruitful to treat them as separate areas of discussion based on the responses. Instead, the particular mix of conditions which is present in social loafing and social facilitation settings needs to be studied.

11.1 The social facilitation phenomena

To summarize the events which are occurring in the typical social facilitation setting, this section outlines the probable series of events. As far as possible this will be neutral with regards to theory, or at least consistent with all the major theoretical frameworks. The section following outlines the conclusions with regard to theories of social facilitation.

Social facilitation has traditionally been a situation where there is a standard of behaviour to perform as well as possible. When working alone, the standards of behaviour are followed and a reasonable level of performance is achieved with automatic processing or contingency governed behaviour. When a person is present, there is first a monitoring process to assess possible social interaction or threats, since the presence of others has been correlated with these in the past. The monitoring involves an increased alertness compared to being alone, and this can affect the task performance by itself. The presence of another person has also been correlated in the past with social reinforcement for following the social standards of behaviour more closely (through evaluation), so behaviour becomes more closely controlled by the standards, especially if the person is the experimenter who has defined the most salient standard of behaviour – doing well at the task.

Concomitant with these changes there will be increased cognitive (verbal) and physical distraction from all the above going on, which can have both direct or indirect effects on task performance, especially if there is a time-pressure in doing the task. Also, any other relevant social standards of behaviour besides doing well at the task will be primed when the other person is present, although these have not usually been measured in the past. Such other standards might include polite behaviour, not talking to oneself, trying to act friendly, or any other self-presentations which have helped social interaction in the past.

In a *co-action* situation the other person is doing the same task. In this case their presence has been correlated, in the past, with comparison information which helps both the task performance and other socially conforming behaviours. In one sense, the function of the social comparison process is to get current information on what the social standards of behaviour might be. This can lead to competition if there are limited resources (outcomes) or if there is another social standard that people should generally try and compete in tasks.

Finally, in social facilitation situations where *evaluation* is emphasized, there will be stronger attempts to match the proper standards of behaviour, which will affect task performance in different ways for simple and complex tasks, will increase social comparison processes, will increase alertness and apprehension (since negative outcomes have been common in such situations before), and will increase self-presentation strategies. Increased evaluation and larger audiences seem to enhance the alertness to a point where it becomes dysfunctional in many cases, leading to stage-fright or test-anxiety.

Deindividuation situations are similar to social facilitation situations but the consequences which are normally inherent in having other people present are greatly reduced. This can occur through having large number of others in a cohesive group, through anonymity, through reducing responsibility verbally, through distraction from matching to social standards, or through decreasing matching to private and public standards in other ways (lowering self-awareness or very high arousal). Situations have usually been called deindividuation when the measures were of socially acceptable and unacceptable behaviours rather than of task performance. There are usually no task performance standards required as there are for social facilitation and social loafing.

Social loafing situations are ones similar to deindividuation but in which the people are performing similar tasks (not essential to deindividuation), the measurements (and standards) are of task performance rather than socially acceptable behaviours, and the consequences of individual task performance are reduced (rather than the consequences of socially acceptable behaviour as in deindividuation studies). The task consequences are usually reduced by changing the identifiability, evaluation, or accountability of individual scores, rather than through the methods used by deindividuation studies.

These, then, are the behavioural events associated with the social facilitation setting, some of which are shared by deindividuation and social loafing. What needs to be done experimentally in the future is to be able to produce these separately and find the conditions for doing so. Once one gets away from the idea of a single fixed social facilitation effect, mixtures of these three different research areas become possible.

11.2 Theories of social facilitation

It should be clear that most of the phenomena mentioned above need separate explanations, and separate descriptions of the conditions in their settings. There can no longer be one 'social facilitation' theory which covers all of these phenomena.

The problem which remains from Chapters 7, 8 and 9 is that a good many of the theories cannot be distinguished empirically from one another. They are either using different words to refer to the same event, or else they are dealing with different aspects of the same event. The criteria by which we decide between them are no longer whether the experimental evidence supports them or not, but rather, parsimony and usefulness. It is ironic that

Zajonc's (1965) theory was highly regarded, partly because of its parsimony, and that we still have to decide between theories on these grounds. The final section will suggest a reason for this state of affairs.

What was shown in Chapter 9, then, was that there were three major frameworks for dealing with all the phenomena present in social facilitation, social loafing, and deindividuation settings, and that no one of these could be shown to fit the empirical data (Chapters 7 and 8) better than another. Control systems theory can cover everything covered by a behaviour analytic approach and vice versa; control systems theory can cover everything covered by a cognitive approach and vice versa; a cognitive approach can cover everything covered by a behaviour analytic approach and vice versa; and self-presentation theory explains one particular aspect of the other three views. The only ways to decide between these frameworks are by judgements of parsimony, by examining the most basic philosophical assumptions (behaviour analysis, for example, does not require representations of the world in the head), or by pragmatic judgements of usefulness and ready applicability.

There could be an empirical way out of this dilemma, if an independent grounding for some of the effects could become available: that is, an explanation which could get evidence beyond the social facilitation effects themselves. A reliable and valid physiological measure which co-varied with the effects would help enormously, and this might yet be possible (Berntson, Cacioppo and Quigley, 1991). The same applies to better measures of attention and distraction; and there are indications that both of these could also occur (Moore and Baron, 1983; Moore et al., 1988).

I have emphasized the modern *behaviour analysis* approach in this book because it is much misunderstood (confused with Hullian behaviourism) and offers much in the way of a strong experimental and applied foundation. Whereas self-awareness theories, for example, might explain the same findings in different words, behaviour analysis has solid evidence for most of its concepts. Many of the self-awareness concepts cannot be operationalized, and sometimes cannot even be measured. So a behaviour analytic approach is probably worth pursuing. It also has the advantage that (unbeknownst to most psychologists) verbal behaviour is defined as an essentially social process, so the verbally-governed behaviours encompass all the properties of social knowledge and cannot be reduced to mere individual functioning (e.g., Guerin, in press).

The *control systems* theory might become unstuck because of its heavy reliance on standards of performance as a guiding construct. Whereas behaviour analysis has a division between contingency governed and rule or verbally-governed behaviours, and cognitive theory has the distinction between automatic and controlled performance, control systems do not deal as well with this aspect. The nearest to it is that between personal standards of behaviour and social standards of behaviour. This heavily taxes the construct of personal standards of behaviour, if it comes to mean any way of behaving which a person has learned through personal experience. There are ways of getting systems theories to work without processes of matching standards, however, and these might be worth pursuing, as would refining the concept of behaviour standards.

While the *cognitive* framework has been popular in social psychology for many years (Markus and Zajonc, 1985), there are signs that it is losing influence (Gergen, 1989; Gergen and Semin, 1990; Jones, 1985). One problem seems to be that having representations of the world in the head allows for almost any hypothetical processes, which makes cognitive theories some of the most underdetermined of all psychological theories. Another problem seems to be that social processes are not handled as well by cognitive theories, in that they need intervening representations of people in the head and so the social is reduced to individual cognitive processes.

Another well founded theory which might be useful in this arena is that of *social identity* (Hogg and Abrams, 1988; Hogg and Turner, 1987). This assumes a social basis to behaviour and begins to develop some links between social and non-social behaviours, although individual functioning is still reduced to cognitive processes. While its application to the social facilitation relevant phenomena has not yet been fully worked out (see Hogg and Abrams, 1988), nor tested, it has a strong potential for representing social facilitation results at a more sociological level.

11.3 Experimentation and truth

With regards to experimentation in social facilitation research, there needs to be a cleaner approach. With so many phenomena now known to occur even in such a simple setting, care must be taken to control all these. This may mean waiting for developments to occur in related areas before attempting to control them.

For example, in 7.13 and 10.5 it was pointed out that if we want to control for competition effects, as happened in the animal studies, we actually need to have a well developed theory about competition and the ways of manipulating it. If there is no theory of competition to follow, then experiments end up following their own 'lay' theories or intuitions about competition instead.

It is for this reason that I claim that some social facilitation effects might have to be left alone until another area develops further. An example of this might be the attention-conflict model. Until we have a developed theory of why people look at others and why they are distracted by them, we cannot properly proceed in a social facilitation setting. Gaining social comparison information is one guess, and a very good one (Sanders, Baron and Moore, 1978), but other reasons for distraction probably exist. The theory of allocating attention to other people needs to be developed first. This was one point of the monitoring model, given in 4.4: that the conditions for looking at other people were spelt out, albeit ones to do with threat and fear rather than social conformity.

It is also for this reason that I claim that experimenting with social facilitation mini-theories (such as outlined in Chapters 4, 5, and 6) might be a bad strategy for social facilitation research. While it looks as if a new mini-theory can be tested against another, there will always be implications and assumptions for many other social facilitation phenomena, and hence theories, which remain hidden. For example, as was related in 9.1, producing more self-references with someone else present looked, in 1975, as if it uniquely supported a self-awareness theory, because of the way it was verbally expressed as a theory, but even the original Drive theory can reasonably predict that self-references are dominant and therefore will increase in the presence of others.

The conclusion from these arguments is that it might be more worthwhile to look at the whole motivational and learning basis to social behaviour, rather than develop mini-theories which are designed to cover a few isolated phenomena. The major contenders for this are control systems theory, behaviour analysis, and social cognition. At present we cannot decide between these broad perspectives through experimentation, but the results of social facilitation experiments make more sense within one of these than expressed as a mini-theory unto itself.

This conclusion is really an argument for *coherence* theories of truth over *correspondence* theories of truth (see Quine, 1960). Correspondence theories claim that truth will occur if an hypothesis correctly corresponds to an event in the world. This assumption underlies the whole approach of experimental social psychology, outlined in Chapter 2, which has been developing since Allport (1920). *Coherence* theories, on the other hand, argue that truth comes from a whole system of hypotheses, not from any individual members of this system. This means that observations and experiments on phenomena and events still need to be carried out, but the results found do not support only one set of hypotheses. A whole system of hypotheses can always be changed in order to accommodate any failed hypothesis.

The effect of this is to suggest that social facilitation researchers pursue their interest within a few larger frameworks of group and social processes. It has been considered worthwhile, therefore, in this book, to separate the phenomena of events taking place in certain settings from the theories or words used to describe those events. Thus researchers should concentrate on learning what conditions produce or reduce these events, rather than testing mini-theories which try to explain them. Because our theories are under-determined, we need to go back to the basic events and observations of those events.

This change also has the effect of forcing researchers to make broader observations than just the minimum which will supposedly decide between two mini-theories. It will no longer suffice to debate miniscule differences in performance measures, since it has been argued that these will never actually decide between two theories. Instead, more thorough and detailed recording of all the changes occurring in the presence of another person need to be collated (as far as this is possible, of course). Obviously we cannot measure too much at any one time, but it is claimed that the experimental method which has been used in social psychology since Allport (1924) has led to a too restricted observational data base. The experimental method of Bernard (1865/1957; also Sidman, 1960; Thompson, 1984), for example, might be more suitable. This emphasizes the control over events, so that researchers can induce and remove the events by controlling the situational variables.

As stressed in Chapter 7 for animals, collecting more detailed data should include the innate responses and the learning history of the organism as much as this is possible. For humans this might include a behavioural assessment or a personality assessment (see Geen, 1980, for some personality variables). The many phenomena which are encountered need to be dealt with in one of the larger frameworks.

In the longer term, this broader type of study should turn into a behavioural ecology, where other people are included as important features of the environment. This means that the motivational organization of behaviour and its relation to the presence of other people will be mapped out. The motivational organization will also, hopefully, be linked into a more solid biological basis and also into a sociological and ecological framework.

Despite losing its name, social facilitation will then stand as the best exemplar of research which links the individually motivated behaviours and their biological bases to the socially motivated behaviours with their sociological-ecological basis. It will be a setting in which the major phenomena can be seen to occur when one person is with another person, whether these phenomena are biologically innate, are learned through individual experience with other people (contingency governed), or are learned through experience as social rules and standards (verbally govern-ed).

References

Abel, T. M. (1938) The influences of social facilitation on motor performance at different levels of intelligence, *American Journal of Psychology*, 51, 379–389.

Abrams, D., and Manstead, A. S. R. (1981) A test of theories of social facilitation using a musical task, *British Journal of Social Psychology*, 20, 271–278.

Ader, R., and Tatum, R. (1963) Free-operant avoidance conditioning in individual and paired human subjects, *Journal of the Experimental Analysis of Behavior*, 6, 357–359.

Aiello, J. R., and Svec, C. M. (in press) Computer monitoring of work performance: Extending the social facilitation framework to electronic presence, *Journal of Applied Social Psychology*.

Allee, W. C., Greenberg, B., Rosenthal, G. M., and Frank, P. (1948) Some effects of social organization on growth in the green sunfish, *Lepomis cyanellus*. *Journal of Experimental Zoology*, 108, 1–19.

Allee, W. C., and Masure, R. H. (1936) A comparison of maze behavior in paired and isolated shell-parrakeets (*Melopsittacus undulatus* Shaw) in a two-alley problem box, *Journal of Comparative Psychology*, 22, 131–156.

Allport, F. H. (1920) The influence of the group upon association and thought, *Journal of Experimental Psychology*, 3, 159–182.

(1924a) *Social psychology*. New York: Houghton Mifflin Company.

(1924b) Editorial comment upon the effect of an audience, *Journal of Abnormal and Social Psychology*, 18, 342–344.

Altman, I. (1975) *The environment and social behavior*. Monterey, California: Brooks Cole.

Amoroso, D. M., Brown, M., Pruesse, M., Ware, E. E., and Pilkey, D. W. (1972) The effects of physiological measurement and presence of others on ratings of erotic stimuli, *Canadian Journal of Behavioural Science*, 4, 191–203.

Amoroso, D. M. and Walters, R. H. (1969) Effects of anxiety and socially mediated anxiety reduction on paired-associated learning, *Journal of Personality and Social Psychology*, 11, 388–396.

Anderson, C. A. (1929) An experimental study of 'Social Facilitation' as affected by 'intelligence'. *American Journal of Sociology*, 34, 874–881.

Anderson, E. E. (1939) The effect of the presence of a second animal upon emotional behavior in the male albino rat, *Journal of Social Psychology*, 10, 265–268.

Anderson, K. J. (1990) Arousal and the inverted-U. hypothesis: A critique of Neiss's 'Reconceptualizing arousal', *Psychological Bulletin*, 107, 96–100.

Anderson, K. J. and Revelle, W. (1982) Impulsivity, caffeine and proofreading: A test of the Easterbrook hypothesis, *Journal of Experimental Psychology: Human Perception and Performance*, 8, 614–624.

Andersson, H., and Brehmer, B. (1977) Social facilitation and inhibition in the social judgement theory paradigm, *Umea Psychological Reports*, No. 132.

Andrew, R. J. (1974) Arousal and the causation of behaviour, *Behaviour*, 51, 135–165.

Angermeier, W. F., Schaul, L. T., and James, W. T. (1959) Social conditioning in rats, *Journal of Comparative and Physiological Psychology*, 52, 370–372.

Archer, J. (1969) Contrasting effects of group housing and isolation on subsequent open field exploration in laboratory rats, *Psychonomic Science*, 14, 234–235.

(1976) The organization of aggression and fear in vertebrates. In P. G. Bateson and P. H. Klopfer, *Perspectives in Ethology* (Vol. 2, pp. 231–298) New York: Plenum Press.

Argyle, M. and Graham, J. A. (1976) The Central Europe experiment: Looking at persons and looking at objects, *Environmental Psychology and Nonverbal Behaviour*, 1, 6–16.

Armstrong, E. A. (1951) The nature and function of mimesis, *Bulletin of Animal Behaviour*, 9, 46–58.

Asch, S. (1952) Effects of group pressure upon the modification and distortion of judgments. In E. E. Maccoby, T. M. Newcomb and E. L. Hartley, *Readings in social psychology* (pp. 174–183) London: Methuen.

Athey, T. R. and McIntyre, R. M. (1987) Effect of rater training on rater accuracy: Levels-of-processing theory and social facilitation theory perspectives, *Journal of Applied Psychology*, 72, 567–572.

Bacon, S. J. (1974) Arousal and the range of cue utilization, *Journal of Experimental Psychology*, 102, 81–87.

Baldwin, A. L. and Levin, H. (1958) Effects of public or private success or failure on children's repetitive motor behavior, *Child Development*, 29, 363–372.

Baldwin, M. W., Carrell, S. E., and Lopez, D. F. (1990) Priming relationship schemas: My advisor and the pope are watching me from the back of my mind, *Journal of Experimental Social Psychology*, 26, 435–545.

Baldwin, M. W. and Holmes, J. G. (1987) Salient private audiences and awareness of the self, *Journal of Personality and Social Psychology*, 53, 1087–1098.

Bales, R. F., Strodtbeck, F. L., Mills, T. M., and Roseborough, M. E. (1951) Channels of communication in small groups, *American Sociological Review*, 16, 461–468.

Bandura, A. (1977) *Social learning theory*, Englewood Cliffs, New Jersey: Prentice Hall.

Bankart, C. P., Bankart, B. M., and Burkett, M. (1974) Social factors in acquisition of bar pressing by rats, *Psychological Reports*, 34, 1051–1054.

Barash, D. P. (1972) Human ethology: The snack-bar security syndrome, *Psychological Reports*, 31, 577–578.

Barefoot, J. C., and Kleck, R. E. (No date) *The effects of race and physical proximity of a co-actor on the social facilitation of dominant responses*, Unpublished manuscript, Dartmouth College.

Bargh, J. A., Cohen, J. L. (1978) Mediating factors in the arousal-performance relationship, *Motivation and Emotion*, 2, 243–257.

Barnett, S. A., and Cowan, P. E. (1976) Activity, exploration, curiosity and fear: An ethological study. *Interdisciplinary Science Reviews*, 1, 43–62.

Baron, R. A. (1971) Aggression as a function of audience presence and prior anger arousal, *Journal of Experimental Social Psychology*, 7, 515–523.

Baron, R. S. (1986) Distraction-conflict theory: Progress and problems, In L. Berkowitz, *Advances in experimental social psychology* (Vol. 19, pp. 1–40), New York: Academic Press.

Baron, R. S., Moore, D., and Sanders, G. S. (1978) Distraction as a source of drive in social facilitation research, *Journal of Personality and Social Psychology*, 36, 816–824.

Barrett, J. E. (1977) Behavioral history as a determinant of the effects of *d*-amphetamine on punished behavior, *Science*, 198, 67–69.

Bartis, S., Szymanski, K., and Harkins, S. G. (1988) Evaluation and performance: A two-edged knife. *Personality and Social Psychology Bulletin*, 14, 242–251.

Bartlett, F. C. (1932) *Remembering*, London: Cambridge University Press.

Bauer, R. H., and Turner, J. H. (1974) Effects of social conditions and time of testing on activity and striking of goldfish (*Carassius auratus*), *Bulletin of the Psychonomic Society*, 4, 12–14.

Baum, M. (1969) Extinction of an avoidance response motivated by intense fear: Social facilitation of the action of response prevention (flooding) in rats, *Behavior Research and Therapy*, 7, 57–62.

Baumeister, A. A., and Forehand, R. (1970) Social facilitation of body rocking in severely retarded patients, *Journal of Clinical Psychology*, 26, 303–305.

Baumeister, R. F. (1982) A self-presentational view of social phenomena, *Psychological Bulletin*, 91, 3–26.

Beaman, A. L., Klentz, B., Diener, E., and Svanum, S. (1979) Self-awareness and transgression in children: Two field experiments, *Journal of Personality and Social Psychology*, 37, 1835–1846.

Beasley, J. (1958) Comparison of the performance of individuals and three-member groups in a maze learning situation, *Perceptual and Motor Skills*, 8, 291–294.

Beatty, M. J. (1980) Social facilitation and listening comprehension, *Perceptual and Motor Skills*, 51, 1222.

Beck, H. P., and Seta, J. J. (1980) The effects of frequency of feedback on a simple coaction task, *Journal of Personality and Social Psychology*, 38, 75–80.

Becker, W. M., and Franks, W. (1975) Social facilitation in the albino rat, *Journal of General Psychology*, 92, 31–41.

Bell, P. A., Loomis, R. J. and Cervone, J. C. (1982) Effects of heat, social facilitation, sex differences and task difficulty on reaction time, *Human Factors*, 24, 19–24.

Bell, P. A., and Yee, L. A. (1989) Skill level and audience effects on performance of a karate drill, *Journal of Social Psychology*, 129, 191–200.

Benedict, J. O., Cofer, J. L., and Cole, M. W. (1980) A study of Zajonc's theory of social facilitation using a wheel-turn Sidman avoidance response in rats, *Bulletin of the Psychonomic Society*, 15, 236–238.

Bennett, M. B. (1946) Factors influencing performance on group and individual tests of intelligence: II. Social facilitation, *Journal of Educational Psychology*, 37, 347–358.

Berger, S. M. (1966) Observer practice and learning during exposure to a model, *Journal of Personality and Social Psychology*, 3, 696–701.

Berger, S. M., Bailey, H. C., Fleming, K. B., Thomas, T. S., and Nicoliello, M. J. (1983) *Some effects of an audience on information processing*, Unpublished paper, University of Massachusetts.

Berger, S. M., Carli, L. L., Garcia, R., and Brady, J. J. (1982) Audience effects in anticipatory learning: A comparison of drive and practice-inhibition analyses, *Journal of Personality and Social Psychology*, 42, 478–486.

Berger, S. M., Carli, L. L., Hammersla, K. S., Karshmer, J. F., and Sanchez, M. E. (1979) Motoric and symbolic mediation in observational learning, *Journal of Personality and Social Psychology*, 37, 735–746.

Berger, S. M., Hampton, K. L., Carli, L. L., Grandmaison, P. S., Sadow, J. S., Donath, C. H., and Herschlag, L. R. (1981) Audience-induced inhibition of overt practice during learning, *Journal of Personality and Social Psychology*, 40, 479–491.

Berger, S. M., and Hecken, M. H. (1980) *Observer mediation and learning in the presence of a stranger*, Unpublished paper, University of Massachusetts.

Bergum, B. O., and Lehr, D. J. (1962) Vigilance performance as a function of paired monitoring, *Journal of Applied Psychology*, 46, 341–343.

(1963) Effects of authoritarianism on vigilance behavior, *Journal of Applied Psychology*, 47, 75–77.

Berkey, A. S., and Hoppe, R. A. (1972) The combined effect of audience and anxiety on paired-associates learning, *Psychonomic Science*, 29, 351–353.

Berlyne, D. E. (1960) *Conflict arousal and curiosity*, New York: McGraw Hill.

Bernard, C. (1865/1957) *An introduction to the study of experimental medicine*, New York: Dover Publications.

Berntson, G. G., Cacioppo, J. T., and Quigley, K. S. (1991) Autonomic determinism: The modes of autonomic control, the doctrine of autonomic space, and the laws of autonomic constraint, *Psychological Review*, 98, 459–487.

Bertram, B. C. R. (1978) Living in groups: Predators and prey. In J. R. Krebs and N. B. Davies, *Behavioural ecology: An evolutionary approach* (pp. 64–96) Oxford: Blackwell.

Bertram, B. C. R. (1980) Vigilance and group size in ostriches, *Animal Behaviour*, 28, 278–286.

Bird, A. M. (1973) Effects of social facilitation upon females' performance of two psychomotor tasks, *Research Quarterly*, 44, 322–330.

Birke, L. I. A. (1974) Social facilitation in the Bengalese Finch, *Behaviour*, 48, 111–122.

Blank, T. O. (1979) *Eighty years of social facilitation: Arousal, attention and filtering*, Unpublished paper, University of Missouri.

Blank, T. O. (1980) Observer and incentive effects on word association responding, *Personality and Social Psychology Bulletin*, 6, 267–272.

Blank, T. O., Staff, I., and Shaver, P. (1976) Social facilitation of word associations: Further questions, *Journal of Personality and Social Psychology*, 34, 725–733.

Bode, D. L., and Brutton, E. J. (1963) A palmar sweat investigation of the effect of an audience upon stage fright. *Speech Monographs*, 30, 92–96.

Boice, R., and Adams, N. (1983) Degrees of captivity and aggressive behavior in domestic Norway rats, *Bulletin of the Psychonomic Society*, 21, 149–152.

Boice, R., Quanty, C. B., and Williams, R. C. (1974) Competition and possible dominance in turtles, toads, and frogs, *Journal of Comparative and Physiological Psychology*, 86, 1116–1131.

Bolles, R. C. (1975) *Theory of motivation* (2nd Edition), New York: Harper & Row.

Bond, C. F. (1982) Social facilitation: A self-presentational view, *Journal of Personality and Social Psychology*, 42, 1042–1050.

Bond, C. F., and Titus, L. J. (1983) Social facilitation: A meta-analysis of 241 studies, *Psychological Bulletin*, 94, 265–292.

Borchelt, P. L., and Overmann, S. R. (1974) Development of dustbathing in Bobwhite quail; I: Effects of age, experience, texture of dust, strain, and social facilitation, *Developmental Psychobiology*, 7, 305–313.

Borden, R. J. (1980) Audience influence, In P. B. Paulus, *Psychology of group influence* (pp. 99–131), Hillsdale, NJ: Erlbaum.

Borden, R. J., Hendrick, C., and Walker, J. W. (1976) Affective, physiological and attitudinal consequences of audience presence, *Bulletin of the Psychonomic Society*, 7, 33–36.

Borden, R. J., and Walker, J. W. (1978) Influence of self-observation *versus* other-observation on immediate and delayed recall, *Journal of General Psychology*, 99, 293–298.

Bowman, R. A., and Dunn, J. M. (1978) Effects of peer presence on psychomotor measures with EMR. children, *Exceptional Children*, 48, 449–451.

Bray, R. M., and Sugarman, R. (1980) Social facilitation among interacting groups, *Personality and Social Psychology Bulletin*, 6, 137–142.

Breckler, S. J., and Greenwald, A. G. (1986) Motivational facets of the self, In R. M. Sorrentino and E. T. Higgins, *Handbook of motivation and cognition: Foundations of social behavior* (pp. 145–164), New York: Guilford Press.

Broadbent, D. E. (1971) *Decision and stress*, New York: Academic Press.

Broadbent, D. E., FitzGerald, P., and Broadbent, M. H. P. (1986) Implicit and explicit knowledge in the control of complex systems, *British Journal of Psychology*, 77, 33–50.

Broadhurst, P. L. (1957) Emotionality and the Yerkes-Dodson law, *Journal of Experimental Psychology*, 54, 345–352.

Brockner, J., and Hutton, A. J. B. (1978) How to reverse the vicious cycle of low self-esteem: The Importance of attentional focus, *Journal of Experimental Social Psychology*, 14, 564–578.

Brockway, B. F. (1964) Social influences on reproductive physiology and ethology of Budgerigars (*Melopsittacus undulatus*), *Animal Behavior*, 12, 493–501.

Broen, W. E., and Storms, L. H. (1961) A reaction potential ceiling and response decrements in complex situations, *Psychological Review*, 68, 405–415.

Bronson, G. W. (1968a) The fear of novelty. *Psychological Bulletin*, 69, 350–358.
(1968b) The development of fear in man and other animals, *Child Development*, 39, 409–430.

Brown, C. P. (1978) Social facilitation of pecking following differential rearing. *Animal Learning and Behavior*, 6, 94–97.

Brown, C. P., and Kiely, P. C. (1974) The role of early experience and emotionality in social facilitation of pecking in chickens, *Animal Behaviour*, 22, 100–109.

Brown, J. S., and Farber, I. E. (1968) Secondary motivational systems, *Annual Review of Psychology*, 19, 99–134.

Brown, M., Amoroso, D. M., Ware, E. E., Pruesse, M., and Pilkey, D. W. (1973) Factors affecting viewing time of pornography, *Journal of Social Psychology*, 90, 125–135.

Brown, W. P. (1965) The Yerkes-Dodson law repealed, *Psychological Reports*, 17, 663–666.

Bruce, R. H. (1937) An experimental analysis of social factors affecting performance of white rats motivated by the thirst drive in a field situation, *Psychological Bulletin*, 34, 738.

(1941) An experimental analysis of social factors affecting the performance of white rats. *Journal of Comparative Psychology*, 31, 363–377.

Bruder, R. H., and Lehrman, D. S. (1967) Role of the mate in the elicitation of hormone-induced incubation behavior in the ring dove, *Journal of Comparative and Physiological Psychology*, 63, 382–384.

Bruen, K., and Dunham, D. W. (1973) Effects of social stimuli on nest building in the zebra finch (*Poephila guttata*), *Animal Behavior*, 21, 183–190.

Bruning, J. L., Capage, J. E., Kozuh, G. F., Young, P. F., and Young, W. E. (1968) Socially induced drive and the range of cue utilization, *Journal of Personality and Social Psychology*, 9, 242–244.

Bruning, J. L., and Mettee, D. R. (1966) The effects of various social factors on motivation in a competitive situation. *Journal of Social Psychology*, 70, 295–297.

Buck, R. W., and Parke, R. D. (1972) Behavioral and physiological responses to the presence of a friendly or neutral person in two types of stressful conditions, *Journal of Personality and Social Psychology*, 24, 143–153.

Burger, J. M. (1987) Increased performance with increased personal control: A self-presentational interpretation, *Journal of Experimental Social Psychology*, 23, 350–360.

Burnham, W. H. (1905) The hygiene of home study, *Pedagogical Seminary*, 12, 213–230.

(1910) The group as a stimulus to mental activity, *Science*, 31, 761–676.

Burri, C. (1931) The influence of an audience upon recall, *Journal of Education Psychology*, 22, 683–690.

Burtt, H. E. (1921) The inspiration-expiration ratio during truth and falsehood, *Journal of Experimental Psychology*, 4, 1–21.

Burwitz, L., and Newell, K. M. (1972) The effects of mere presence and coactors on learning a motor skill, *Journal of Motor Behavior*, 4, 99–102.

Buskist, W. F., Barry, A., Morgan, D., and Rossi, M. (1984) Competitive fixed interval performance in humans: Role of 'orienting' instructions, *The Psychological Record*, 34, 241–257.

Buskist, W., and Morgan, D. (1987) Competitive fixed-interval performance in humans, *Journal of the Experimental Analysis of Behavior*, 47, 145–158.

(1988) Method and theory in the study of human competition, in G. Davey and C. Cullen, *Human operant conditioning and behavior modification*, (pp. 167–195), New York: John Wiley.

Cacioppo, J. T., and Petty, R. E. (1983) *Social psychophysiology*, New York: Guilford Press.

Cacioppo, J. T., Rourke, P. A., Marshall-Goodell, B. S., Tassinary, L. G., and Baron, R. S. (1990) Rudimentary physiological effects of mere observation, *Psychophysiology*, 27, 177–186.

Caine, N. G. (1990) Unrecognized anti-predator behaviour can bias observational data, *Animal Behaviour*, 39, 195–197.

Carlin, A. S., Bakker, C. B., Halpern, L., and Dee Post, R. (1972) Social facilitation of marijuana intoxication: Impact of social set and pharmacological activity, *Journal of Abnormal Psychology*, 80, 132–140.

Carment, D. W. (1970a) Rate of simple motor responding as a function of differential outcomes and the actual or implied presence of a coactor, *Psychonomic Science*, 20, 115–116.

(1970b) Rate of simple motor responding as a function of coaction, competition and sex of participants, *Psychonomic Science*, 19, 342–343.

Carment, D. W., and Hodkin, B. (1973) Coaction and competition in India and Canada, *Journal of Cross-Cultural Psychology*, 4, 459–469.

Carment, D. W., and Latchford, M. (1970) Rate of simple motor responding as a function of presence or absence of coaction, sex of participants, and the presence of the experimenter, *Psychonomic Science*, 20, 253–254.

Carr, A., and Hirth, H. (1961) Social facilitation in green turtle siblings, *Animal Behaviour*, 9, 68–70.

Carron, A. V. (1971) Reactions to 'Anxiety and motor behavior', *Journal of Motor Behavior*, 3, 181–188.

(1980) *Social psychology of sport*, Ithaca, NY: Mouvement Publications.

Carron, A. V., and Bennett, B. (1976) The effects of initial habit strength differences upon performance in a coaction situation, *Journal of Motor Behavior*, 8, 297–304.

Carver, C. S. (1979) A cybernetic model of self-attention processes, *Journal of Personality and Social Psychology*, 37, 1251–1281.

Carver, C. S., and Scheier, M. F. (1978) Self-focusing effects of dispositional self-consciousness, mirror presence, and audience presence, *Journal of Personality and Social Psychology*, 36, 324–332.

(1980) *A control systems analysis of social facilitation*, Unpublished paper, University of Miami.

(1981a) *Attention and self-regulation: A control-theory approach to human behavior*, New York: Springer Verlag.

(1981b) The self-attention-induced feedback loop and social facilitation, *Journal of Experimental Social Psychology*, 17, 545–568.

(1982) Control theory: A useful conceptual framework for personality-social, clinical, and health psychology, *Psychological Bulletin*, 92, 111–135.

Catania, A. C. (1984) *Learning* (2nd Ed.), Englewood Cliffs, NJ: Prentice Hall.

Chapman, A. J. (1973a) Social facilitation of laughter in children, *Journal of Experimental Social Psychology*, 9, 528–541.

(1973b) An electromyographic study of apprehension about evaluation, *Psychological Reports*, 33, 811–814.

(1974) An electromyographic study of social facilitation: A test of the 'mere presence' hypothesis, *British Journal of Psychology*, 65, 123–128.

(1975) Humorous laughter in children, *Journal of Personality and Social Psychology*, 31, 42–49.

Chapman, A. J., and Wright, D. S. (1976) Social enhancement of laughter: An experimental analysis of some companion variables, *Journal of Experimental Child Psychology*, 21, 201–218.

Chase, P. N. (1988) A problem of history: Assessing and controlling the learning history of sophisticated subjects, *Experimental Analysis of Human Behavior Bulletin*, 6, 3–8.

Chatillon, J. F. (1970) Analyse expérimentale des réactions à la présence d'autrui, *Psychologie Francaise*, 15, 69–84.

Chen, S. C. (1937) Social modification of the activity of ants in nest-building, *Physiological Zoology*, 10, 420–436.

Chevrette, J. M. (1968) The effect of peer observation on selected tests of physical performance, *Journal of Psychology*, 70, 113–119.

Church, R. M. (1962) The effects of competition on reaction time and palmar skin conductance, *Journal of Abnormal and Social Psychology*, 65, 32–40.

Claridge, G. (1981) Arousal, In G. Underwood and R. Stevens, *Aspects of consciousness* (Vol. 2, pp. 119–147), London: Academic Press.

Clark, N. J., and Fouts, G. T. (1973) Effects of positive, neutral, and negative experiences with an audience on social facilitation, *Perceptual and Motor Skills*, 37, 1008–1010.

Clayton, D. (1976a) The effects of pre-test conditions on social facilitation of drinking in ducks, *Animal Behaviour*, 24, 125–134.

(1976b) Social facilitation of drinking of a partially satiated duckling, *Animal Learning and Behavior*, 4, 391–395.

(1978) Socially facilitated behaviour, *Quarterly Review of Biology*, 53, 373–392.

Clower, B. J., and Dabbs, J. M. (1974) Effects of sex and physical distance on arousal and task performance, *Catalog of Selected Documents in Psychology*, 4, 71.

Cofer, C. N., and Appley, M. H. (1964) *Motivation: Theory and research*, New York: Wiley.

Cohen, J. L. (1979) Social facilitation: Increased evaluation apprehension through permanency of record, *Motivation and Emotion*, 3, 19–33.

(1980) Social facilitation: Audience versus evaluation apprehension effects, *Motivation and Emotion*, 4, 21–34.

Cohen, J. L., and Davis, J. H. (1973) Effects of audience status, evaluation, and time of action on performance with hidden-word problems. *Journal of Personality and Social Psychology*, 27, 74–85.

Cohen, S., and Lezak, A. (1977) Noise and inattentiveness to social cues, *Environment and Behavior*, 9, 559–572.

Collias, N. E., Brandman, M., Victoria, J. K., Kiff, L. F., and Rischer, C. E. (1971) Social facilitation in weaverbirds: Effects of varying the sex ratio, *Ecology*, 52, 829–836.

Collias, N. E., Victoria, J. K., and Shallenberger, R. J. (1971) Social facilitation in weaverbirds: Importance of colony size, *Ecology*, 52, 823–828.

Collins, B. E. (1986) Towing a fragment of abnormal behavior into the mainstream of social psychology: Hyperactivity, *Journal of Social and Clinical Psychology*, 4, 488–496.

Colman, A. (1982) *Game theory and experimental games*, New York: Pergamon.

Colquhoun, W. P., and Corcoran, D. W. J. (1964) The effects of time of day and social isolation on the relationship between temperament and performance, *British Journal of Social and Clinical Psychology*, 3, 226–231.

Connolly, K. (1968) The social facilitation of preening behaviour in *Drosophila melanogaster*, *Animal Behaviour*, 16, 385–391.

Conolley, E. S., Gerard, H. B., and Kline, T. (1978) Competitive behavior: A manifestation of motivation for ability comparison, *Journal of Experimental Social Psychology*, 14, 123–131.

Cook, T. D., and Leviton, L. C. (1980) Reviewing the literature: A comparison of traditional methods with meta-analysis, *Journal of Personality*, 48, 449–472.

Cooper, H. M. (1982) Scientific guidelines for conducting integrative research reviews, *Review of Educational Research*, 52, 291–302.

Cooper, J. J., and Levine, R. L. (1973) Effects of social interaction on eating and drinking in two subspecies of deermice, *Peromyscus maniculatus bairdii* and *Peromyscus maniculatus gracilis*, *Animal Behaviour*, 21, 421–428.

Corriveau, D. P., Contildes, K., and Smith, N. F. (1978) Social facilitation following response prevention in the rat, *Psychological Reports*, 43, 127–133.

Cottrell, N. B. (1968) Performance in the presence of other human beings: Mere presence and affiliation effects, In E. C. Simmel, R. A. Hoppe, and G. A. Milton, *Social facilitation and imitative behavior* (pp. 91–110) Boston: Allyn and Bacon.

(1972) Social facilitation, In C. G. McClintock, *Experimental social psychology* (pp. 185–236), New York: Holt.

Cottrell, N. B., and Epley, S. W. (1977) Affiliation social comparison, and socially mediated stress reduction, In J. M. Sulls and R. L. Miller, *Social comparison processes: Theoretical and empirical perspectives* (pp. 43–68), Washington, DC: Hemisphere.

Cottrell, N. B., Rittle, R. H., Wack, D. L. (1967) The presence of an audience and list type (competitional or noncompetitional) as joint determinants of performance in paired-associates learning, *Journal of Personality*, 35, 425–434.

Cottrell, N. B., Wack, D. L., Sekerak, G. J., and Rittle, R. H. (1968) Social facilitation of dominant responses by the presence of an audience and the mere presence of others, *Journal of Personality and Social Psychology*, 9, 245–250.

Cowan, P. E. (1977) Neophobia and neophilia: New-object and new-place reactions of three *Rattus* species, *Journal of Comparative and Physiological Psychology*, 91, 63–71.

Cox, F. N. (1966) Some effects of test anxiety and presence or absence of other persons on boys' performance on a repetitive motor task, *Journal of Experimental Child Psychology*, 3, 100–112.

(1968) Some relationships between test anxiety, presence or absence of male persons, and boy's performance on a repetitive motor task, *Journal of Experimental Child Psychology*, 6, 1–12.

Craig, K. D., Best, H., and Reith, G. (1974) Social determinants of reports of pain in the absence of painful stimulation, *Canadian Journal of Behavioural Science*, 6, 169–177.

Crandell, R. (1974) Social facilitation: Theories and research, In A. A. Harrison, *Explorations in psychology* (pp. 94–106), Monterey, California: Brooks/Cole.

Crawford, M. P. (1939) The social psychology of the vertebrates, *Psychological Bulletin*, 36, 407–446.

Criddle, W. D. (1971) The physical presence of other individuals as a factor in social facilitation, *Psychonomic Science*, 22, 229–230.

Cunningham, W. L., and Roberts, A. E. (1973) Acquisition and maintenance of Sidman avoidance with paired rat subjects. *Animal Learning and Behavior*, 1, 44–48.

Dabbs, J. M., and Clower, B. J. (1973) An ultrasonic motion detector, with data on stare, restriction of movement and startle, *Behavioral Research Methods and Instrumentation*, 5, 475–476.

Dashiell, J. F. (1930) An experimental analysis of some group effects, *Journal of Abnormal and Social Psychology*, 25, 190–199.

(1935) Experimental studies of the influence of social situations on the behavior of individual human adults, In C. Murchison, *A handbook of social psychology* (pp. 1097–1158), Worcester, MA: Clark University Press.

Davidson, P. O., and Kelly, W. R. (1973) Social facilitation and coping with stress, *British Journal of Social and Clinical Psychology*, 12, 130–136.

Davis, J. H., Carey, M. H., Foxman, P. N., and Tarr, D. B. (1968) Verbalization, experimenter presence, and problem solving, *Journal of Personality and Social Psychology*, 8, 299–302.

Davitz, J. R., and Mason, D. J. (1955) Socially facilitated reduction of a fear response in rats, *Journal of Comparative and Physiological Psychology*, 48, 149–151.

Deci, E. L., and Ryan, R. M. (1980) The empirical exploration of intrinsic motivational processes, In L. Berkowitz, *Advances in experimental social psychology* (Vol. 13, pp. 39–80), New York: Academic Press.

Deffenbacher, K. A., Platt, G. J., and Williams, M. A. (1974) Differential recall as a function of socially induced arousal and retention interval, *Journal of Experimental Psychology*, 103, 809–811.

DeGrandpre, R. J., Buskist, W., and Cush, D. (1990) Effects of orienting instructions on sensitivity to scheduled contingencies, *Bulletin of the Psychonomic Society*, 28, 331–334.

Deguchi, H. (1984) Observational learning from a radical-behavioristic viewpoint, *The Behavior Analyst*, 7, 83–95.

Delfini, L. F., and Fouts, G. T. (1974) Acquisition of social facilitation in rats: A methodological study, *Perceptual and Motor Skills*, 39, 807–814.

Deni, R. (1977a) Inhibition of operant responding in Japanese quail during brief visual exposure to a companion, *Perceptual and Motor Skills*, 44, 251–257.

(1977b) Duration of exposures to a conspecific and social inhibition of operant behavior in Japanese quail, *Psychological Reports*, 41, 63–70.

Deni, R., and Jorgensen, B. W. (1976a) Inhibition of fixed interval bar-pressing in rats during exposure to a trained companion. *Psychological Reports*, 39, 243–246.

(1976b) Social inhibition of barpressing in undeprived rats, *Bulletin of the Psychonomic Society*, 7, 487–488.

Desportes, J-P. (1969) Les effets de la coprésence passive, *L'Année Psychologue*, 69, 615–634.

Desportes, J-P., and Dequeker, A. (1971) Effet de la présence de l'expérimentateur sur la performance de sujets anxieux et non anxieux, *Bulletin du C.E.R.P.*, 20, 93–98.

(1973/74) Les effets de la présence de l'expérimentateur: Facilitation et inhibition sociales de la performance, *Bulletin du C.E.R.P.*, 23, 241–245.

Desportes, J-P., and Lemaine, G. (1969) L'Effet de la présence d'un spectateur: Elévation du niveau de tension generale ou implication? *Psychologie Francaise*, 14, 173–183.

Dethier, V. G. (1966) Insects and the concept of motivation, In D. Levine, *Nebraska symposium on motivation* (pp. 105–136), Lincoln University of Nebraska Press.

Deutsch, M. (1949) A theory of cooperation and competition, *Human Relations*, 2, 129–152.

Dey, M. K. (1949) An attempt to analyse the effect of non-competitive co-acting groups, *Indian Journal of Psychology*, 24, 86–95.

Diener, E. (1980) Deindividuation: The absence of self-awareness and self-regulation in group members, In P. B. Paulus, *Psychology of group influence* (pp. 209–242), Hillsdale, NJ: Erlbaum.

Diener, E., Fraser, S. C., Beaman, A. L., and Kelem, R. T. (1976) Effects of deindividuation variables on stealing among halloween trick-or-treaters, *Journal of Personality and Social Psychology,* 33, 178–183.

Diener, E., and Srull, T. K. (1979) Self-awareness, psychological perspective, and self-reinforcement in relation to personal and social standards, *Journal of Personality and Social Psychology,* 37, 413–423.

Dimond, S., and Lazarus, J. (1974) The problem of vigilance in animal life, *Brain, Behavior and Evolution,* 9, 60–79.

Donoghue, E. E., McCarrey, M. W., and Clement, R. (1983) Humour appreciation as a function of canned laughter, a mirthful companion, and field dependence: Facilitation and inhibitory effects, *Canadian Journal of Behavioural Science,* 15, 150–162.

Drew, G. C. (1937) The recurrence of eating in rats after apparent satiation, *Proceedings of the Zoological Society of London,* 107, 95–106.

Dua, J. K. (1977) Effect of audience on acquisition and extinction of avoidance, *British Journal of Social and Clinical Psychology,* 16, 207–212.

Duflos, A. (1967) Le travail en groupe favorise-t-il les réponses dominantes aux dépens des réponses rares. *Bulletin du C.E.R.P.,* 16, 323–336.

Duflos, A., Zalenska, M., and Desportes, J-P. (1969) La facilitation sociale: Un vieux problème toujours sans solution, *Bulletin du C.E.R.P.,* 18, 27–42.

Duval, S., Duval, V. H., and Neely, R. (1979) Self-focus, felt responsibility, and helping behavior, *Journal of Personality and Social Psychology,* 37, 1769–1778.

Duval, S., and Wicklund, R. A. (1972) *A theory of objective self-awareness,* New York: Academic Press.

(1973) Effects of objective self-awareness on attribution of causality, *Journal of Experimental Social Psychology,* 9, 17–31.

Easterbrook, J. A. (1959) The effect of emotion on cue utilization and the organization of behavior, *Psychological Review,* 66, 183–201.

Eibl-Eibesfeldt, I. (1974) *Love and hate,* New York: Schocken Books.

(1978), Phylogenetic adaptations as determinants of aggressive behavior in man, In W. W. Hartup and J. De Wit, *Origins of aggression* (pp. 27–55), New York: Mouton.

Ekdahl, A. G. (1929) The effect of attitude on free word association-time, *Genetic Psychology Monographs,* 5, 253–338.

Elliot, E. S., and Cohen, J. L. (1981) Social facilitation effects via interpersonal distance, *Journal of Social Psychology,* 114, 237–249.

Ellsworth, P. C., Carlsmith, J. M., and Henson, A. (1972) The stare as a stimulus to flight in human subjects: A series of field experiments, *Journal of Personality and Social Psychology,* 21, 302–311.

Ellsworth, P. C., Friedman, H. S., Perlick, D., and Hoyt, M. E. (1978) Some effects of gaze on subjects motivated to seek or avoid social comparison, *Journal of Experimental Social Psychology,* 14, 69–87.

Ellsworth, P. C. and Langer, E. J. (1976) Staring and approach: An interpretation of the stare as a nonspecific activator, *Journal of Personality and Social Psychology,* 33, 117–122.

Epley, S. W., and Cottrell, N. B. (1977) Effect of presence of a companion on speed of escape from electric shock, *Psychological Reports*, 40, 1299–1308.

Evans, J. F. (1971) Social facilitation in a competitive situation, *Canadian Journal of Behavioural Science*, 3, 276–281.

Evans, S. M. (1970) Some factors affecting the flock behaviour of red avadavats (*Amandava amandava*) with particular reference to clumping, *Animal Behaviour*, 18, 762–767.

Farnsworth, P. R. (1928) Concerning so-called group effects, *Journal of Genetic Psychology*, 35, 587–594.

Farnsworth, P. R., and Behner, A. (1931) A note on the attitude of social conformity, *Journal of Social Psychology*, 2, 126–128.

Farnsworth, P. R., and Williams, M. F. (1937) The accuracy of the median and mean of a group of judgements, *Journal of Social Psychology*, 7, 237–239.

Farr, R. M. and Moscovici, S. (1984) *Social representations*, London: Cambridge University Press.

Féré, C. (1887) *Sensation et mouvement*, Paris: Alcan.

Ferris, G. R., Beehr, T. A., and Gilmore, D. C. (1978) Social facilitation: A review and alternative conceptual model, *Academy of Management Review*, 3, 338–347.

Ferris, G. R., and Rowland, K. M. (1980) Effects of audience, task familiarity, and subject sex on performance quantity and quality: Social facilitation implications for work behavior, *Academy of Management Proceedings*, 40, 146–150.

Festinger, L. (1954) A theory of social comparison processes, *Human Relations*, 7, 114–140.

(1964) Motivations leading to social behavior, In R. C. Teevan and R. C. Birney, *Theories of motivation in personality and social psychology* (pp. 138–161), Princeton: NJ: Van Nostrand.

Festinger, L., Pepitone, A., and Newcomb, T. (1952) Some consequences of deindividuation in a group, *Journal of Abnormal and Social Psychology*, 47, 382–389.

Fisher, R. A. (1925) *Statistical methods for research workers*, Edinburgh: Oliver and Boyd.

(1935) *The design of experiments*, Edinburgh: Oliver & Boyd.

Foot, H. C. (1973) Group learning and performance: A reclassification, *British Journal of Social and Clinical Psychology*, 12, 7–17.

Forgas, J. P., Brennan, G., Howe, S., Kane, J. F., and Sweet, S. (1980) Audience effects on squash players' performance, *Journal of Social Psychology*, 111, 41–47.

Fouts, G. T. (1972) Charity in children: The influence of 'charity' stimuli and an audience, *Journal of Experimental Child Psychology*, 13, 303–309.

(1979) Social anxiety and social facilitation, *Psychological Reports*, 44, 1065–1066.

(1980) Effect of sex of audience on speed of performance of preadolescents, *Perceptual and Motor Skills*, 51, 565–566.

Fouts, G. T., and Jordan, L. (1973) The effect of an audience on free associations to emotional words, *Journal of Community Psychology*, 1, 45–47.

Fouts, G. T., and Parton, D. A. (1974) Imitation by children in primary grades: Effects of vicarious habit and social drives, *Perceptual and Motor Skills*, 38, 155–160.

Franchina, J. J., Dyer, A. B., Zaccaro, S. J., and Schulman, A. H. (1986) Socially facilitated drinking behavior in chicks (*Gallus domesticus*): Relative effects of drive and stimulus mechanisms, *Animal Learning and Behavior*, 14, 218–222.

Frank, L. H., and Meyer, M. E. (1970) Food imprinting in domestic chicks as a function of social contact and number of companions, *Psychonomic Science*, 19, 393–395.

(1974) Social facilitation in the chick: Evidence for facilitation of learning, *Bulletin of the Psychonomic Society*, 3, 196–198.

Fraser, D. C. (1953) The relation of an environmental variable to performance in a prolonged visual task, *Quarterly Journal of Experimental Psychology*, 5, 31–32.

Freedman, J. L. (1979) Reconciling apparent differences between the responses of humans and other animals to crowding, *Psychological Review*, 86, 80–85.

Fridlund, A. J. (1991) Sociality of solitary smiling: Potentiation by an implicit audience, *Journal of Personality and Social Psychology*, 60, 229–240.

Froming, W. J., Walker, G. R., and Lopyan, K. J. (1982) Private and public self-awareness: When personal attitudes conflict with societal expectations, *Journal of Experimental Social Psychology*, 18, 476–487.

Fuller, R. G. C., and Sheehy-Skeffington, A. (1974) Effects of group laughter on responses to humorous material, a replication and extension, *Psychological Reports*, 35, 531–534.

Fushimi, T. (1990) A functional analysis of another individual's behavior as discriminative stimulus for a monkey, *Journal of the Experimental Analysis of Behavior*, 53, 285–291.

Gabrenya, W. K., and Arkin, R. M. (1979) Motivation, heuristics, and the psychology of prediction, *Motivation and Emotion*, 3, 1–17.

Gaioni, S. J., and Ross, L. E. (1982) Distress calling induced by reductions in group size in ducklings reared with conspecifics or imprinting stimuli, *Animal Learning and Behavior*, 10, 521–529.

Gale, A. and Baker, S. (1981) In vivo or in vitro? Some effects of laboratory environments, with particular reference to the psychophysiology experiment, In M. J. Christie and P. G. Mellet, *Foundations of psychosomatics* (pp. 363–384), New York: John Wiley.

Gale, A., Lucas, B., Nissim, R., and Harpham, B. (1972) Some EEG. correlates with face-to-face contact, *British Journal of Social and Clinical Psychology*, 11, 326–332.

Gallup, G. G., Montevecchi, W. A., and Swanson, E. T. (1972) Motivational properties of mirror-image stimulation in the domestic chicken, *Psychological Record*, 22, 193–199.

Ganzer, V. J. (1968) Effects of audience presence and test anxiety on learning and retention in a serial learning situation, *Journal of Personality and Social Psychology*, 8, 194–199.

Gardner, E. L. and Engel, D. R. (1971) Imitational and social facilitatory aspects of observational learning in the laboratory rat, *Psychonomic Science*, 25, 5–6.

Gastorf, J. W., Suls, J., and Sanders, G. S. (1980) Type A coronary-prone behavior pattern and social facilitation, *Journal of Personality and Social Psychology*, 38, 773–780.

Gates, G. S. (1924) The effects of an audience upon performance, *Journal of Abnormal and Social Psychology*, 18, 334–342.

Gates, G. S., and Rissland, L. Q. (1923) The effect of encouragement and discouragement upon performance, *Journal of Educational Psychology*, 14, 21–26.

Gates, M. F., and Allee, W. C. (1933) Conditioned behavior of isolated and grouped cockroaches on a simple maze, *Journal of Comparative Psychology*, 15, 331–358.

Geen, R. G. (1971) Social facilitation and long-term recall, *Psychonomic Science*, 24, 89–90.

(1973) Effects of being observed on short- and long-term recall, *Journal of Experimental Psychology*, 100, 395–398.

(1974) Effects of evaluation apprehension on memory over intervals of varying length, *Journal of Experimental Psychology*, 102, 908–910.

(1976a) Test anxiety, observation, and range of cue utilization, *British Journal of Social and Clinical Psychology*, 15, 253–259.

(1976b) The role of the social environment in the induction and reduction of anxiety, In C. D. Spielberger and I. G. Sarason, *Stress and anxiety* (Vol. 3, pp. 105–126), Washington D.C.: Hemisphere.

(1977) Effects of anticipation of positive and negative outcomes on audience anxiety, *Journal of Consulting and Clinical Psychology*, 45, 715–716. Extended report, available from the author, was also consulted.

(1979) Effects of being observed on learning following success and failure experience, *Motivation and Emotion*, 3, 355–371.

(1980) The effects of being observed on performance, In P. B. Paulus, *Psychology of group influence* (pp. 61–97), Hillsdale, New Jersey: Erlbaum.

(1981a) Effects of being observed on persistence at an insoluble task, *British Journal of Social Psychology*, 20, 211–216.

(1981b) Evaluation apprehension and social facilitation: A reply to Sanders, *Journal of Experimental Social Psychology*, 17, 252–256.

(1983) Evaluation apprehension and social facilitation/inhibition, *Motivation and Emotion*, 7, 203–212.

(1985) Evaluation apprehension and response withholding in solution of anagram, *Personality and Individual Differences*, 6, 293–298.

(1989) Alternative conceptions of social facilitation, In P. B. Paulus, *Psychology of group influence* (2nd Ed., pp. 15–51), Hillsdale, New Jersey: Erlbaum.

(1991) Social motivation, *Annual Review of Psychology*, 42, 377–399.

Geen, R. G., and Bushman, B. J. (1987) Drive theory: Effects of socially engendered arousal, In B. Mullen and G. R. Goethals, *Theories of group behavior* (pp. 89–109), New York: Springer.

Geen, R. G., and Gange, J. J. (1977) Drive theory of social facilitation: Twelve years of theory and research, *Psychological Bulletin*, 84, 1267–1288.

Gergen, K. J. (1969) *The psychology of behavior exchange*, Reading, MA: Addison-Wesley.

(1989) Social psychology and the wrong revolution, *European Journal of Social Psychology*, 19, 463–484.

Gergen, K. J., and Semin, G. R. (1990) Everyday understanding in science and daily life, In G. R. Semin and K. J. Gergen (Eds), *Everyday understanding* (pp. 1–18), London: Sage.

Gibson, J. J., and Pick, A. D. (1963) Perception of another person's looking behavior, *American Journal of Psychology*, 76, 368–394.

Glaser, A. N. (1982) Drive theory of social facilitation: A critical reappraisal, *British Journal of Social Psychology*, 21, 265–282.

Glass, D. C., Gordon, A., and Henchy, T. (1970) The effects of social stimuli on psychophysiological reactivity to an aversive film, *Psychonomic Science*, 20, 255–256.

Gleason, P. E., Weber, P. G., and Weber, S. P. (1977) Effect of group size on avoidance learning in zebra fish, *Brachydanio rerio* (Pisces: Cyprinidae), *Animal Learning and Behavior*, 5, 213–216.

Goethals, G., and Darley, J. (1987) Social comparison theory: Self-evaluation and group life, In B. Mullin and G. Goethals, *Theories of group behavior* (pp. 21–47), New York: Springer-Verlag.

Goffman, E. (1959) *The presentation of self in everyday life*, New York: Doubleday-Anchor.

(1963) *Interaction ritual*, New York: Anchor.

Good, K. J. (1973) Social facilitation: Effects of performance anticipation, evaluation, and response competition on free associations, *Journal of Personality and Social Psychology*, 28, 270–275.

Gore, W. V., and Taylor, D. A. (1973) The nature of an audience as it affects social inhibition, *Representative Research in Social Psychology*, 4, 18–27.

Gottlieb, B. W. (1982) Social facilitation influences on the oral reading performance of academically handicapped children, *American Journal of Mental Deficiency*, 87, 153–158.

Green, B. F., and Hall, J. A. (1984) Quantitative methods for literature reviews, *Annual Review of Psychology*, 35, 37–53.

Greenberg, C. I., and Firestone, I. J. (1977) Compensatory responses to crowding: Effects of personal space intrusion and privacy reduction, *Journal of Personality and Social Psychology*, 35, 637–644.

Greer, D. L. (1983) Spectator booing and the home advantage: A study of social influence in the basketball arena, *Social Psychology Quarterly*, 46, 252–261.

Griffith, T. L., Fichman, M., and Moreland, R. L. (1989) Social loafing and social facilitation: An empirical test of the cognitive-motivational model of performance, *Basic and Applied Social Psychology*, 10, 253–271.

Groff, B. D., Baron, R. S., and Moore, D. L. (1983) Distraction, attentional conflict, and drivelike behavior, *Journal of Experimental Social Psychology*, 19, 359–380.

Grush, J. E. (1978) Audiences can inhibit or facilitate competitive behavior, *Personality and Social Psychology Bulletin*, 4, 119–122.

Guerin, B. (1983) Social facilitation and social monitoring: A test of three models, *British Journal of Social Psychology*, 22, 203–214.

(1986a) The effects of mere presence on a motor task, *Journal of Social Psychology*, 126, 399–401.

(1986b) Mere presence effects in humans: A review, *Journal of Experimental Social Psychology*, 22, 38–77.

(1989a) Reducing evaluation effects in mere presence, *Journal of Social Psychology*, 129, 183–190.

(1989b) Social inhibition of behavior, *Journal of Social Psychology*, 129, 225–233.

(1990) Gibson, Skinner, and perceptual responses, *Behavior and Philosophy*, 18, 43–54.

(1991) Anticipating the consequences of social behavior, *Current Psychology: Research and Reviews*, 10, 131–162.

(1992) Social behavior as discriminative stimulus and consequence in social anthropology, *The Behavior Analyst*, 15.

(in press) Behavior analysis and the social construction of knowledge, *American Psychologist*.

(in press) Behavior analysis and social psychology, *Journal of the Experimental Analysis of Behavior*.

Guerin, B., and Innes, J. M. (1981) Awareness of cognitive processes: Replications and revisions, *Journal of General Psychology*, 104, 173–189.

(1982) Social facilitation and social monitoring: A new look at Zajonc's mere presence hypothesis, *British Journal of Social Psychology*, 21, 7–18.

(1984) Explanations of social facilitation: A review, *Current Psychological Research and Reviews*, 3, 32–52.

(1990) Varieties of attitude change: Cognitive responding and maintenance of cognitive responding, *Australian Journal of Psychology*, 42, 139–155.

Gunnar, M. R., Gonzalez, C. A., and Levine, S. (1980) The role of peers in modifying behavioral distress and pituitary-adrenal response to a novel environment in year-old rhesus monkeys, *Physiology and Behavior*, 25, 795–798.

Gurnee, H. (1937) Maze learning in the collective situation, *Journal of Personality*, 3, 437–443.

(1939) Effect of collective learning upon the individual participants, *Journal of Abnormal and Social Psychology*, 34, 529–532.

(1962) Group learning, *Psychological Monographs*, 76, n. 13, 1–30.

Haas, J., and Roberts, G. C. (1975) Effect of evaluative others upon learning and performance of a complex motor task, *Journal of Motor Behavior*, 7, 81–90.

Haines, H., and Vaughan, G. M. (1979) Was 1898 a 'great date' in the history of experimental social psychology? *Journal of the History of the Behavioral Sciences*, 15, 323–332.

Hake, D. F., Donaldson, T., and Hyten, C. (1983) Analysis of discriminative control by social behavioral stimuli, *Journal of the Experimental Analysis of Behavior*, 39, 7–23.

Hake, D. F., and Laws, D. R. (1967) Social facilitation of responses during a stimulus paired with electric shock, *Journal of the Experimental Analysis of Behavior*, 10, 387–392.

Hake, D. F., and Olvera, D. (1978) Cooperation, competition, and related social phenomena, In A. C. Catania and T. A. Brigham, *Handbook of applied behavior analysis: Social and instructional processes* (pp. 208–245), New York: Irvington.

Hake, D. F., Olvera, D., and Bell, J. C. (1975) Switching from competition to sharing or cooperation at large response requirements: Competition requires more responding, *Journal of the Experimental Analysis of Behavior*, 24, 343–354.

Hake, D. F., Powell, J., and Olsen, R. (1969) Conditioned suppression as a sensitive baseline for social facilitation, *Journal of the Experimental Analysis of Behavior*, 12, 807–816.

Hake, D. F., and Vukelich, R. (1980) Rate of auditing self and coactor performance scores as a supplementary monitor of reinforcer effectiveness, *Behavior Modification*, 4, 265–280.

Hake, D. F., Vukelich, R., and Kaplan, S. J. (1973) Audit responses: Responses maintained by access to existing self or coactor scores during non-social parallel work, and cooperation procedures, *Journal of the Experimental Analysis of*

Behavior, 19, 409–423.

Hale, E. B. (1956) Social facilitation and forebrain function in maze performance of green sunfish, *Lepomis cyanellus*, *Physiological Zoology*, 29, 93–107.

Hall, E. G., and Bunker, L. K. (1979) Locus of control as a mediator of social facilitation effects during motor skill learning, *Journal of Sport Psychology*, 1, 332–335.

Hall, E. T. (1966) *The hidden dimension*, Garden City, New York: Doubleday.

Hamberger, L. K., and Lohr, J. M. (1981) Effect of trainer's presence and response-contingent feedback on biofeedback-relaxation training, *Perceptual and Motor Skills*, 53, 15–24.

Hamrick, C., Cogan, D., and Woolam, D. (1971) Social facilitation effects on runway and maze behavior in mice, *Psychonomic Science*, 25, 171–173.

Hanawalt, N. G., and Ruttiger, K. F. (1944) The effect of an audience on remembering, *Journal of Social Psychology*, 19, 259–272.

Harackiewicz, J. M., Sansone, C., and Manderlink, G. (1985) Competence, achievement orientation, and intrinsic motivation: A process analysis, *Journal of Personality and Social Psychology*, 48, 493–508.

Harkins, S. G. (1987) Social loafing and social facilitation, *Journal of Experimental Social Psychology*, 23, 1–18.

Harkins, S. G., Latané, B., and Williams, K. (1980) Social loafing: Allocating effort or taking it easy, *Journal of Experimental Social Psychology*, 16, 457–465.

Harkins, S. G., and Szymanski, K. (1987) Social loafing and social facilitation: New wine in old bottles, In C. Hendrick, *Group processes and intergroup relations* (pp. 167–188), London: Sage.

(1988) Social loafing and self-evaluation with an objective standard, *Journal of Experimental Social Psychology*, 24, 354–365.

(1989) Social loafing and group evaluation, *Journal of Personality and Social Psychology*, 56, 934–941.

Harlow, H. F. (1932) Social facilitation of feeding in the albino rat, *Journal of Genetic Psychology*, 41, 211–221.

Harlow, H. F., and Yudin, H. C. (1933) Social behavior of primates: 1. Social facilitation of feeding in the monkey and its relation to attitudes of ascendence and submission, *Journal of Comparative Psychology*, 16, 171–185.

Harper, L. V., and Sanders, K. M. (1975) The effects of adult's eating on young children's acceptance of unfamiliar foods, *Journal of Experimental Child Psychology*, 20, 206–214.

Harrell, W. A., and Schmitt, D. R. (1973) Effects of a minimal audience on physical aggression, *Psychological Reports*, 32, 651–657.

Hartnett, J. J., Gottlieb, J., and Hayes, R. L. (1976) Social facilitation theory and experimenter attentiveness, *Journal of Social Psychology*, 99, 293–294.

Hatfield, F. C. (1972) Effect of prior experience, access to information and level of performance on individual and group performance ratings, *Perceptual and Motor Skills*, 35, 19–26

Hayduk, L. A. (1983) Personal space: Where we now stand, *Psychological Bulletin*, 94, 293–335.

Hayes, S. C. (1986) The case of the silent dog – Verbal reports and the analysis of rules, *Journal of the Experimental Analysis of Behavior*, 45, 351–363.

(1989) *Rule-governed behavior: Cognition, contingencies, and instructional control*, Reno, Nevada: Context Press.

Hayes, S. C., Brownstein, A. J., Haas, J. R., and Greenway, D. E. (1986) Instructions, multiple schedules, and extinction: Distinguishing rule-governed from schedule-controlled behavior, *Journal of the Experimental Analysis of Behavior*, 46, 137–147.

Hayes, S. C., Rosenfarb, I., Wulfert, E., Munt, E. D., Korn, Z., and Zettle, R. D. (1985) Self-reinforcement effects: An artifact of social standard setting? *Journal of Applied Behavior Analysis*, 18, 201–214.

Hayes, S. C., Zettle, R. D. and Rosenfarb, I. (1989) Rule-following. In S. C. Hayes and *Rule-governed behavior: Cognition, contingencies, and instructional control* (pp. 191–220), Reno, Nevada: Context Press.

Hebb, D. O. (1949) *The organization of behavior*, New York: Wiley.

(1955) Drives and the CNS. (conceptual nervous system), *Psychological Review*, 62, 243–254.

Henchy, T., and Glass, D. C. (1968) Evaluation apprehension and the social facilitation of dominant and subordinate responses, *Journal of Personality and Social Psychology*, 10, 446–454.

Henning, J. M., and Zentall, T. R. (1981) Imitation, social facilitation, and the effects of ACTH. 4–10 on rats' bar-pressing behavior, *American Journal of Psychology*, 94, 125–134.

Hess, E. (1973) *Imprinting*, New York: Van Nostrand.

Heylen, A. G. (1978) *Social facilitation*, Unpublished Honours thesis, University of Adelaide.

Hicks, D. J. (1968) Effects of co-observer's sanctions and adult presence on imitative aggression, *Child Development*, 39, 303–309.

Higgs, W. J., and Joseph, K. B. (1971) Effect of real and anticipated audiences on verbal learning and reproduction, *Journal of Social Psychology*, 85, 41–49.

Hill, W. F. (1957) Comments on Taylor's 'Drive theory and manifest anxiety', *Psychological Bulletin*, 54, 490–493.

Hillery, J. M., and Fugita, S. S. (1975) Group size in employment testing, *Educational and Psychological Measurement*, 35, 745–750.

Hinde, R. A. (1953) The term 'Mimesis', *British Journal of Animal Behaviour*, 1, 7–9.

(1960) Energy models of motivation, *Symposia of the Society for Experimental Biology*, 14, 199–213.

(1970) *Animal Behavior*, New York: McGraw Hill.

Hogan, J. A., and Abel, E. L. (1971) Effects of social factors on response to unfamiliar environments in *Gallus gallus spadiceus*, *Animal Behaviour*, 19, 687–694.

Hogg, M. A., and Abrams, D. (1988) *Social identifications*, London: Routledge.

Hogg, M. A., and Turner, J. C. (1987) Social identity and conformity: A theory of referent informational influence, In W. Doise and S. Moscovici, *Current issues in European social psychology*, (pp. 139–182), Cambridge: Cambridge University Press.

Holder, E. E. (1958) Learning factors in social facilitation and social inhibition in rats, *Journal of Comparative and Physiological Psychology*, 51, 60–64.

Hollingworth, H. L. (1935) *The psychology of the audience*, New York: American Book Company.

Hoogland, J. L. (1979) The effect of colony size on individual alertness of prairie dogs (Scuiridae: *Cynomys* spp.), *Animal Behaviour*, 27, 394–407.

Hormuth, S. E. (1982) Self-awareness and drive theory: Comparing internal standards and dominant responses, *European Journal of Social Psychology*, 12, 31–45.

Hosey, G. R., Wood, M. Thompson, R. J., and Druck, P. L. (1985) Social facilitation in a 'non-social' animal, the centipede *Lithobius forficatus*, *Behavioral Processes*, 10, 123–130.

Houston, J. P. (1970) Effects of audiences upon learning and retention, *Journal of Experimental Psychology*, 86, 449–453.

Hoyenga, K. T., and Aeschleman, S. (1969) Social facilitation of eating in the rat, *Psychonomic Science*, 14, 239–241.

Hrycaiko, D. W., and Hrycaiko, R. (1980) Palmar sweating in an evaluative audience situation, *Journal of Social Psychology*, 111, 269–280.

Hughes, R. N. (1969) Social facilitation of locomotion and exploration in rats, *British Journal of Psychology*, 60, 385–388.

Hull, C. L. (1943) *Principles of behavior: An introduction to behavior theory*, New York: Appleton-Century-Crofts.

Hunt, P. J., and Hillery, J. M. (1973) Social facilitation in a coaction setting: An examination of the effects over learning trials, *Journal of Experimental Social Psychology*, 9, 563–571.

Huntermark, J. M., and Witte, K. L. (1978) Vigilance performance as related to task instructions, coaction, and knowledge of results, *Bulletin of the Psychonomic Society*, 12, 325–328.

Husband, R. W. (1940) Cooperative versus solitary problem solution, *Journal of Social Psychology*, 11, 405–409.

Hutchinson, V. Q., and Cotten, D. J. (1973) Effects of audience and anxiety level on learning and performance of a complex gross motor skill by college women, *Perceptual and Motor Skills*, 36, 1103–1108.

Ichheiser, G. (1930) Über die Veränderung der Leistungsbereitschaft durch das Bewusstsein einen Zuschauer zu haben, *Psychotechnologie Zeitschrift*, 5, 52–53.

Inglis, I. R., and Lazarus, J. (1981) Vigilance and flock size in brent geese: The edge effect, *Zeitschrift für Tierpsychologie*, 57, 193–200.

Innes, J. M. (1972) The effect of presence of co-workers and evaluative feedback on performance of a simple reaction time task, *European Journal of Social Psychology*, 2, 466–470.

(1980) Fashions in social psychology. In R. Gilmour and S. Duck, *The development of social psychology* (pp. 137–162), London: Academic Press.

Innes, J. M., and Gordon, M. I. (1985) The effects of mere presence and mirror upon performance of a motor task, *Journal of Social Psychology*, 125, 479–484.

Innes, J. M., and Sambrooks, J. E. (1969) Paired-associate learning as influenced by birth order and the presence of others. *Psychonomic Science*, 16, 109–110.

Innes, J. M., and Young, R. F. (1975) The effect of presence of an audience, evaluation apprehension and objective self-awareness on learning, *Journal of Experimental Social Psychology*, 11, 35–42.

Isozaki, M. (1979) An experimental study of the determinants of social facilitation, *Japanese Journal of Experimental Social Psychology*, 19, 49–60.

Jackson, J. M. and Latané, B. (1981) All alone in front of all those people: Stage fright as a function of number and type of co-performers and audience, *Journal of Personality and Social Psychology*, 40, 73–85.

James, W. (1910) *Psychology: The briefer course*, New York: Holt.

James, W. T. (1953) Social facilitation of eating behavior in puppies after satiation, *Journal of Comparative and Physiological Psychology*, 46, 427–428.

   (1954) Secondary reinforced behavior in an operant situation among dogs, *Journal of Genetic Psychology*, 85, 129–133.

   (1960) The development of social facilitation of eating in puppies, *Journal of Genetic Psychology*, 96, 123–127.

   (1961) Relationship between dominance and food intake in individual and social eating in puppies, *Psychological Reports*, 8, 478.

James, W. T., and Cannon, D. J. (1955) Variation in social facilitation of eating behavior in puppies, *Journal of Genetic Psychology*, 87, 225–228.

James, W. T., and Gilbert, T. F. (1955) The effect of social facilitation on food intake of puppies fed separately and together for the first 90 days of life, *British Journal of Animal Behaviour*, 3, 131–133.

Janssens, L., and Nuttin, J. R. (1976) Frequency perception of individual and group successes as a function of competition, coaction and isolation, *Journal of Personality and Social Psychology*, 34, 830–836.

Jennings, T., and Evans, S. M. (1980) Influences of position in the flock and flock size on vigilance in the starling, *Sturnus vulgaris, Animal Behaviour*, 28, 634–635.

Jessor, R., and Hammond, K. R. (1957) Construct validity and the Taylor Anxiety Scale, *Psychological Bulletin*, 54, 161–170.

Johnson, C. D., and Davis, J. H. (1972) An equiprobability model of risk-taking, *Organizational Behavior and Human Performance*, 8, 159–175.

Johnson, E. S., and Baker, R. F. (19073) The computer as experimenter: New results, *Behavioural Science*, 18, 377–385.

Jones, E. E. (1985) Major developments in social psychology during the past five decades, In G. Lindzey and E. Aronson, *Handbook of social psychology* (3rd Ed., Vol. I, pp. 47–107) New York: Random House.

Jones, E. E., and Gerard, H. B. (1967) *Foundations of social psychology*, New York: Wiley.

Jones, E. E., Pittman, T. S. (1982) Toward a general theory of strategic self-presentation, In J. Suls, *Psychological perspectives on the self* (Vol. I, pp. 231–262), Hillsdale, NJ: Erlbaum.

Jones, R. B. (1987) Open-field behaviour in domestic chicks (*Gallus domesticus*): The influence of the experimenter, *Biology of Behaviour*, 12, 100–115.

Jones, R. B., and Harvey, S. (1987) Behavioural and adrenocortical responses of domestic chicks to systematic reductions in group size and to sequential disturbance of companions by the experimenter, *Behavioural Processes*, 14, 291–303.

Kanak, N. J., and Davenport, D. G. (1967) Between-subject competition: A rat race, *Psychonomic Science*, 7, 87–88.

Karakashian, S. J., Gyger, M., and Marler, P. (1988) Audience effects on alarm calling in chickens (*Gallus gallus*), *Journal of Comparative Psychology*, 102, 129–135.

Karst, T. O., and Most, R. (1973) A comparison of stress measures in an experimental analogue of public speaking, *Journal of Consulting and Clinical Psychology*, 41, 342–348.

Katahn, M. (1966) Interaction of anxiety and ability in complex learning situations, *Journal of Personality and Social Psychology*, 3, 475–479.

Kawamura-Reynolds, M. (1977) Motivational effects of an audience in the content of imaginative thought, *Journal of Personality and social Psychology*, 35, 912–919.

Keating, J. P., and Latané, B. (1976) Politicians on TV: The image is the message, *Journal of Social issues*, 32, 116–132.

Kelley, H. H., and Thibaut, J. W. (1954) Experimental studies in group problem solving and process, In G. Lindzey and E. Aronson, *Handbook of social psychology* (pp. 735–785). Cambridge, MA: Addison Wesley.

Khalique, N. (1979) Effects of the presence of similar and dissimilar individuals on the speed of verbal learning, *Psychologia*, 22, 95–98.

——— (1980) Effect of increasing number of passive spectators on the speed of verbal learning. *Psychologia*, 23, 47–49.

Kieffer, L. F. (1977) Relationship of trait anxiety, peer presence, task difficulty, and skill acquisition of sixth-grade boys, *Research Quarterly*, 48, 550–561.

Kiesler, S. B. (1966) Stress, affiliation and performance, *Journal of Experimental Research in Personality*, 1, 227–235.

Kiesler, S., Siegel, J., and McGuire, T. W. (1984) Social psychological aspects of computer-mediated communication, *American Psychologist*, 39, 1123–1134.

Kissel, S. (1965) Stress-reducing properties of social stimuli, *Journal of Personality and Social Psychology*, 2, 378–384.

Kleck, R. E., Vaughan, R. C., Cartwright-Smith, J., Vaughan, K. B., Colby, C. Z., and Lanzetta, J. T. (1976) Effects of being observed on expressive, subjective, and physiological responses to painful stimuli, *Journal of Personality and Social Psychology*, 34, 1211–1218.

Kleinke, C. L., and Pohlen, P. D. (1971) Affective and emotional responses as a function of other person's gaze and cooperativeness in a two-person game, *Journal of Personality and Social Psychology*, 17, 308–313.

Klinger, E. (1969) Feedback effects and social facilitation of vigilance performance: Mere coaction versus potential evaluation, *Psychonomic Science*, 14, 161–162.

Kljaic, S. (1974) [Social facilitation of free association] In *Psiholske razpnave: IV. Kongress psihologov SERFJ*. Ljubljana, Yugoslavia: University of Ljubljana Press, 1972. (From *Psychological Abstracts*, 1974, 57, No. 2330.)

Knowles, E. S. (1980) An affiliative conflict theory of personal and group spatial behavior, In P. B. Paulus, *Psychology of group influence* (pp. 133–188), Hillsdale, New Jersey: Erlbaum.

——— (1983) Social physics and the effects of others: Test of the effects of audience size and distance on social judgment and behavior, *Journal of Personality and Social Psychology*, 45, 1263–1279.

Knowles, E. S., Kreuser, B., Haas, S., Hyde, M., and Schuchart, G. E. (1976) Group size and the extension of social space boundaries, *Journal of Personality and Social Psychology*, 33, 667–654.

Kobasigawa, A. (1968) Inhibitory and disinhibitory effects of models on sex-inappropriate behavior in children, *Psychologia*, 11, 86–96.

Kohfeld, D. L., and Wietzel, W. (1969) Some relations between personality factors and social facilitation, *Journal of Experimental Research in Personality*, 3, 287–292.

Kozar, B. (1973) The effects of a supportive and nonsupportive audience upon learning a gross motor skill, *International Journal of Sport Psychology*, 4, 27–38.

Krueger, W. C. F. (1936) Note concerning group influence upon Otis S-A. Test scores, *Journal of Educational Psychology*, 27, 554–555.

Krupski, A., and Boyle, P. R. (1978) An observational analysis of children's behavior during a simple reaction-time task: The role of attention, *Child Development*, 49, 340–347.

Kuhl, J. (1985) Volitional mediators of cognition-behavior consistency: Self-regulatory processes and action versus state orientation, In J. Kuhl and J. Beckmann, *Action control: From cognition to behavior* (pp. 101–128), New York: Springer.

Kumar, P. and Bhandari, R. (1974) A study of group effect on individual performance, *Behaviorometric*, 4, 15–17.

Kumar, P., and Kriplani, N. D. (1972) A study of differential effects of social situations on individual behavior, *Indian Journal of Experimental Psychology*, 6, 78–80.

Kushnir, T. (1978) The importance of familiarization with the history of experimental social psychology: A tribute to J. F. Dashiell, *European Journal of Social Psychology*, 8, 407–411.

(1981) The status of arousal in recent social facilitation literature, *Social Behaviour and Personality*, 9, 185–190.

Kushnir, T., and Duncan, K. D. (1978) An analysis of social facilitation effects in terms of signal detection theory, *Psychological Record*, 28, 535–541.

Lacey, J. I. (1967) Somatic response patterning and stress: Some revisions of activation theory, In M. H. Appley and R. Trumbull, *Psychological Stress: Issues in Research* (pp. 14–37), New York: Appleton-Century-Crofts.

Laird, D. A. (1923) Changes in motor control and individual variations under the influence of 'razzing', *Journal of Experimental Psychology*, 6, 236–246.

Lambert, W. E., and Lowy, F. H. (1957) Effects of the presence and discussion of others on expressed attitude, *Canadian Journal of Psychology*, 11, 151–156.

Landers, Daniel M. (1980) The arousal-performance relationship revisited, *Research Quarterly for Exercise and Sport*, 51, 77–90.

Landers, Daniel M., Bauer, R. S., and Feltz, D. L. (1978) Social facilitation during the initial stages of motor learning: A re-examination of Marten's audience study, *Journal of Motor Behavior*, 10, 325–337.

Landers, Daniel M., and McCullagh, P. D. (1976) Social facilitation of motor performance, *Exercise and Sport Science Reviews*, 4, 125–162.

Landers, Donna M. (1975) Observational learning of a motor skill: temporal spacing of demonstrations and audience presence, *Journal of Motor Behavior*, 7, 281–287.

Landers, Donna M., and Landers, Daniel M. (1973) Teacher versus peer models: Effects of model's presence and performance level on motor behavior, *Journal of Motor Behavior*, 5, 129–139.

Langenes, D. J., and White, G. M. (1975) Some effects of social stimulation on maze running in rats, *Psychological Reports*, 36, 639–644.

Langer, E. J., Fiske, S., Taylor, S. E. & Chanowitz, B. (1976) Stigma, staring and discomfort: A novel-stimulus hypothesis, *Journal of Experimental Social Psychology*, 12, 451–463.

LaPiere, R. T., and Farnsworth, P. R. (1936) *Social psychology*, New York: McGraw HJill.

Larsson, K. (1956) *Conditioning and sexual behavior in the male albino rat*, Stockholm: Almqvist and Wiksell.

Latané, B. (1969) Gregariousness and fear in laboratory rats, *Journal of Experimental Social Psychology*, 5, 61–69.

(1981) The psychology of social impact, *American Psychologist*, 36, 343–356.

Latané, B., and Glass, D. C. (1968) Social and nonsocial attraction in rats, *Journal of Personality and Social Psychology*, 9, 142–146.

Latané, B., Poor, D., and Sloan, L. (1972) Familiarity and attraction to social and nonsocial objects by rats, *Psychonomic Science*, 26, 171–172.

Latané, B., Schneider, E., Waring, P. & Zweigenhaft, R. (1971) The specificity of social attraction in rats, *Psychonomic Science*, 23, 28–29.

Latané, B., Williams, K., and Harkins, S. (1979) Many hands make light the work: The causes and consequences of social loafing, *Journal of Personality and Social Psychology*, 37, 823–832.

Laughlin, P. R., Chenoweth, R. E., Farrell, B. B., and McGrath, J. E. (1972) Concept attainment as a function of motivational and task complexity, *Journal of Experimental Psychology*, 96, 54–59.

Laughlin, P. R., and Jaccard, J. J. (1975) Social facilitation and observational learning of individuals and cooperative pairs, *Journal of Personality and Social Psychology*, 32, 873–879.

Laughlin, P. R., and Wong-McCarthy, W. J. (1975) Social inhibition as a function of observation and recording of performance, *Journal of Experimental Social Psychology*, 11, 560–571.

Lazarus, J. (1979) Flock size and behaviour in captive red-billed weaverbirds (*Quelea quelea*): Implications for social facilitation and the functions of flocking, *Behaviour*, 71, 127–145.

Lee, V. L. (1984) Some notes on the subject matter of Skinner's *Verbal Behavior*, *Behaviorism*, 12, 29–40.

Lee, V. L. (1988) *Beyond behaviorism*, Hillsdale, New Jersey: Erlbaum.

LeFrancois, J. R., Chase, P. N., and Joyce, J. H. (1988) The effects of a variety of instructions on human fixed-interval performance, *Journal of the Experimental Analysis of Behavior*, 49, 383–393.

Lepley, W. M. (1937) Competitive behavior in the albino rat, *Journal of Experimental Psychology*, 21, 194–201.

Lepley, W. M. (1939) The social facilitation of locomotor behavior in the albino rat, *Journal of Experimental Psychology*, 24, 106–109.

Lepoivre, H., and Pallaud, B. (1985) Social facilitation in a troop of guinea baboons (*Papio papio*) living in an enclosure, *Behavioural Processes*, 11, 405–418.

Levin, H., Baldwin, A. L., Gallwey, M., and Paivio, A. (1960) Audience stress, personality, and speech, *Journal of Abnormal and Social Psychology*, 61, 469–473.

Levine, J. M., and Zentall, T. R. (1974). Effect of a conspecific's presence on deprived rats' performance: Social facilitation vs distraction/imitation, *Animal Learning and Behavior*, 2, 119–122.

Levy, S. G., and Fenley, N. F. (1979) Audience size and likelihood and intensity of response during a humorous movie, *Bulletin of the Psychonomic Society*, 13, 409–412.

Leyhausen, P. (1979) Aggression, fear and attachment: Complexities and interdependencies, In M. von Cranach, K. Foppa, W. Lepenies and D. Ploog, *Human Ethology* (pp. 253–264), London: Cambridge University Press.

Liebling, B. A., and Shaver, P. (1973a) Evaluation, self-awareness, and task performance, *Journal of Experimental Social Psychology*, 9, 297–306.

(1973b) Social facilitation and social comparison processes, *Proceedings, 81st Annual Convention, American Psychological Association*, 327–328.

Lindsay, D. R., Dunsmore, D. G., Williams, J. D. and Syme, G. J. (1976) Audience effects on the mating behavior of rams, *Animal Behaviour*, 24, 818–821.

Livingston, M. V., Landers, D. M., and Dorrance, P. B. (1974) Comparison of coacting individuals' motor performance for varying combinations of initial ability, *Research Quarterly*, 45, 310–317.

Loftus, G. R., and Mackworth, N. H. (1978) Cognitive determinants of fixation location during picture viewing, *Journal of Experimental Psychology: Human Perception and Performance*, 4, 565–572.

Lombardi, C. M., and Curio, E. (1985) Social facilitation of mobbing in the zebra finch *Taeniopygia guttata*, *Bird Behaviour*, 6, 34–40.

Lombardo, J. P., and Catalano, J. F. (1975) The effect of failure and the nature of the audience on performance of a complex motor task, *Journal of Motor Behavior*, 7, 29–35.

(1978) Failure and its relationship to the social facilitation effect: Evidence for a learned drive interpretation of the social facilitation effect, *Perceptual and Motor Skills*, 46, 823–829.

Lord, C., and Haith, M. M. (1974) The perception of eye contact, *Perception and Psychophysics*, 16, 413–416.

Lorge, I. D., Fox, J., Davitz, J. and Brenner, M. (1958) A survey of studies contrasting the quality of group performance and individual performance, *Psychological Bulletin*, 55, 337–372.

Lynn, R. (1966) *Attention, arousal, and the orientation reaction*, London: Pergamon.

MacRoberts, B. R., and MacRoberts, M. H. (1972) Social stimulation of reproduction in herring and lesser black-backed gulls, *Ibis*, 114, 495–506.

Mallenby, T. W. (1976) Facilitating the disappearance of perceptual error to the Poggendorff illusion, *Language and Speech*, 19, 193–199.

Malott, R. W., and Garcia, M. E. (1991) Role of private events in rule-governed behavior, In L. J. Hayes and P. N. Chase, *Dialogues on verbal behavior* (pp. 237–254), Reno, Nevada: Context Press.

Malpass, L. F., and Fitzpatrick, E. D. (1959) Social facilitation as a factor in reaction to humor, *Journal of Social Psychology*, 50, 295–303.

Mann, L., Newton, J. W., and Innes, J. M. (1982) A test of deindividuation and emergent norm theories of crowd aggression, *Journal of Personality and Social Psychology*, 42, 260–272.

Manstead, A. S. R., and Semin, G. R. (1980) Social facilitation effects: Mere enhancement of dominant responses? *British Journal of Social and Clinical Psychology*, 19, 119–136.

Marchand, P., and Vachon, L. (1976) La coprésence passive et la performance motrice, *Mouvement*, 11, 39–47.

Marina, J. F., and Bauermeister, J. J. (1974) Socially facilitated extinction of a conditioned avoidance response, *Bulletin of the Psychonomic Society*, 3, 161–163.

Markus, H. (1978) The effect of mere presence on social facilitation: An unobtrusive test, *Journal of Experimental Social Psychology*, 14, 389–397.

(1981) The drive for integration: Some comment, *Journal of Experimental Social Psychology*, 17, 257–261.

Markus, H., and Zajonc, R. B. (1985) The cognitive perspective in social psychology. In G. Lindzey and E. Aronson, *Handbook of social psychology* (3rd Ed., Vol. 1, pp. 137–230), New York: Random House.

Marler, P. (1976) On animal aggression: The role of strangeness and familiarity, *American Psychologist*, 31, 239–246.

Marr, M. J. (1985) 'Tis the gift to be simple: A retrospective appreciation of Mach's *The science of mechanics*, *Journal of the Experimental Analysis of Behavior*, 44, 129–138.

Martens, R. (1969a) Effect of an audience on learning and performance of a complex motor skill, *Journal of Personality and Social Psychology*, 12, 252–260.

(1969b) Effect on performance of learning a complex motor task in the presence of spectators, *Research Quarterly*, 40, 317–323.

(1969c) Palmar sweating and the presence of an audience, *Journal of Experimental Social Psychology*, 5, 371–374.

(1971) Anxiety and motor behavior: A review, *Journal of Motor Behavior*, 3, 151–179.

(1974) Arousal and motor performance, *Exercise and Sport Sciences Review*, 2, 155–188.

Martens, R., and Landers, D. M. (1969) Coaction effects on a muscular endurance task, *Research Quarterly*, 40, 733–737.

(1972) Evaluation potential as a determinant of coaction effects, *Journal of Experimental Social Psychology*, 8, 347–359.

Martin, B. (1961) The assessment of anxiety by physiological and behavioral measures, *Psychological Bulletin*, 58, 234–255.

Martin, S. A. and Knight, J. M. (1985) Social facilitation effects resulting from locus of control using human and computer experiments, *Computers in Human Behavior*, 1, 123–130.

Martin, W. W., and Rovira, M. L. (1981) An experimental analysis of discriminability and bias in eye-gaze, *Journal of Nonverbal Behavior*, 5, 155–163.

Marx, M. H., Witter, D. W., and Mueller, J. H. (1972) Interaction of sex and training method in human multiple-choice learning, *Journal of Social Psychology*, 88, 37–42.

Mash, E. J., and Hedley, J. (1975) Effect of observer as a function of prior history of social interaction, *Perceptual and Motor Skills*, 40, 659–669.

Maslach, C. (1974) Social and personal bases of individuation, *Journal of Personality and Social Psychology*, 29, 411–425.

Mason, J. R., and Reidinger, R. F. (1981) Effects of social facilitation and observational learning on feeding behavior of the red-winged blackbird (*Agelaius phoeniceus*), *The Auk*, 98, 778–784.

Mason, J. W., and Brady, J. V. (1964) The sensitivity of psychoendocrine systems to social and physical environment, In P. H. Leiderman and D. Shapiro, *Psychological approaches to social behavior* (pp. 4–23), Stanford, California: Stanford University Press.

Matlin, M. W., and Zajonc, R. B. (1968) Social facilitation of word associations, *Journal of Personality and Social Psychology*, 10, 455–460.

Matusewicz, C. (1974) Wplyw obecnosci innych na poziom wykonania czynnosci. *Przeglad Psychlogiczny*, 17, 11–29.

May, J. G., and Dorr, D. (1968) Imitative pecking in chicks as a function of early social experience, *Psychonomic Science*, 11, 175–176.

Mayer, A. (1904) Über, Einzel-und Gesamtleistung des Schulkindes, *Sammlung von Abhandlungen zur Psychologischen*, Pädagogik. I.Band,4. Heft. Leipzig.

Mayes, B. T. (1978) Some boundary considerations in the application of motivational models, *Academy of Management Review*, 3, 51–58.

McBride, G. (1971) On the evolution of human language, In J. Kristeva, J., Rey-Debore and D. J. Umiker, *Essays in semiotics* (pp. 560–566), Paris: Mouton.

McBride, G., King, M. G., and James, J. W. (1965) Social proximity effects of galvanic skin response in adult humans, *Journal of Psychology*, 61, 153–157.

McCullagh, P. D. and Landers, D. M. (1976) Size of audience and social facilitation, *Perceptual and Motor Skills*, 42, 1067–1070.

McDougall, W. (1923) *An outline of psychology*. London: Methuen.

McDowell, J. J., and Wixted, J. T. (1988) The linear systems theory's account of behavior maintained by variable-ratio schedules, *Journal of the Experimental Analysis of Behavior*, 49, 143–169.

McGhee, P. E. (1973) Birth order and social facilitation of humor, *Psychological Reports*, 33, 105–105.

McGuire, T. W., Kiesler, S., and Siegel, J. (1987) Group and computer-mediated discussion effects in risk decision making, *Journal of Personality and Social Psychology*, 52, 917–930.

Mead, G. H. (1934) *Mind, self, and society from the standpoint of a social behaviorist*, Chicago: University of Chicago Press.

Meddock, T. D., Parsons, J. A., and Hill, K. T. (1971) Effects of an adult's presence and praise on young children's performance, *Journal of Experimental Child Psychology*, 12, 197–211.

Meglino, B. M. (1976). The effect of evaluation on dominance characteristics: An extension of social facilitation theory, *Journal of Psychology*, 92, 167–172.

Meumann, E. (1904) Haus- und Schularbeit: Experimente an kindern der Volkschule, *Die Deutsche Schule*, 8, 278–303, 337–359, 416–431.

Meyer, M. E., and Frank, L. H. (1970) Food imprinting in the domestic chick: A reconsideration. *Psychonomic Science*, 19, 43–44.

Michael, J. (1980) The discriminative stimulus or SD., *The Behavior Analyst*, 3, 47–49.
(1982) Distinguishing between discriminative and motivational functions of stimuli, *Journal of Experimental Analysis of Behaviour*, 37, 149–155.
(1988) Establishing operations and the mand. *The Analysis of Verbal Behavior*, 6, 3–9.

Michaels, J. W., Blommel, J. M., Brocato, R. M., Linkous, R. A., and Rowe, J. S. (1982) Social facilitation and inhibition in a natural setting, *Replications in Social Psychology*, 2, 21–24.

Millard, W. J. (1979) Stimulus properties of conspecific behavior, *Journal of the Experimental Analysis of Behavior*, 32, 283–296.

Miller, F. G., Hurkman, M. F., Feinberg, R. A., and Robinson, J. B. (1979) Status and evaluation potential in the social facilitation and impairment of task performance, *Personality and Social Psychology Bulletin*, 5, 381–385.

Miller, G. A., Galanter, E., and Pribram, K. H. (1960) *Plans and the structure of behavior*, New York: Holt, Rinehart and Winston.

Mintz, L. I., and Collins, B. E. (1985) Qualitative influences on the perception of movement: An experimental study, *Journal of Abnormal Child Psychology*, 13, 143–153.

Miyamoto, M. (1979) Social facilitation on finger maze learning, *Japanese Psychological Research*, 21, 94–98.

Moede, W. (1914) Der wetteifer, seine struktur und sein ausmass, *Zeitschrift für Paedagogische Psychologie*, 15, 353–368.

Moore, D. L., and Baron, R. S. (1983) Social facilitation: A psycho-physiological analysis, In J. T. Cacioppo and R. E. Petty, *Social psychophysiology* (pp. 435–466), New York: Guilford.

Moore, D. L., Baron, R. S., Logel, M. L., Sanders, G. S., and Weert, T. C. (1988) Methodological note: Assessment of attentional processing using a parallel phenomenon strategy, *Personality and Social Psychology Bulletin*, 14, 565–572.

Moore, D. L., Byers, D. A., and Baron, R. S. (1981) Socially mediated fear reduction in rodents: Distraction, communication, or mere presence? *Journal of Experimental Social Psychology*, 17, 485–505.

Moore, H. T. (1917) Laboratory tests of anger, fear, and sex interest, *American Journal of Psychology*, 28, 390–395.

Morris, D. (1954) The reproductive behaviour of the zebra finch (*Peophila guttata*), with special reference to pseudofemale behaviour and displacement activities, *Behaviour*, 6, 271–322.

Morris, E. K. (1988) Contextualism: The world view of behavior analysis, *Journal of Experimental Child Psychology*, 46, 289–323.

Morrison, B. J., and Hill, W. F. (1967) Socially facilitated reduction of the fear response in rats raised in groups or in isolation, *Journal of Comparative and Physiological Psychology*, 63, 71–76.

Morrissette, J. O., Hornseth, J. P., and Sheller, K. (1975) Team organization and monitoring performance, *Human Factors*, 17, 296–300.

Moruzzi, G. (1969) Sleep and instinctive behaviour, *Archives of Italian Biology*, 107, 175–216.

Mukerji, N. P. (1940) An investigation of ability in work in groups and in isolation, *British Journal of Psychology*, 30, 352–356.

Mullen, B., and Baumeister, R. F. (1987) Group effects on self-attention and performance: Social loafing, social facilitation, and social impairment, In C. Hendrick, *Group processes and intergroup relations* (pp. 189–206), London: Sage.

Murphy, G., and Murphy, L. B. (1931) *Experimental social psychology*, New York: Harper and Brothers.

Musante, G., and Anker, J. M. (1972) E's presence: Effect on S's performance, *Psychological Reports*, 30, 903–904.

Musick, S. A., Beehr, T., and Gilmore, D. C. (1981) Effects of perception of presence of audience and achievement instructions on performance of a simple task, *Psychological Reports*, 49, 535–538.

Neiss, R. (1988) Reconceptualizing arousal: Psychobiological states in motor performance, *Psychological Bulletin*, 103, 345–366.

Nemeth, C. (1986) Differential contributions of majority and minority influence, *Psychological Review*, 93, 23–32.

Newman, A., Dickstein, R., and Gargan, M. (1978) Developmental effects in social facilitation and in being a model, *Journal of Psychology*, 99, 143–150.

Nichols, K. A., and Champness, B. G. (1971) Eye gaze and the GSR., *Journal of Experimental Social Psychology*, 7, 623–626.

Nisbett, R. E., and Bellows, N. (1977) Verbal reports about casual influences on social judgments: Private access versus public theories, *Journal of Personality and Social Psychology*, 35, 613–624.

Nisbett, R. E., and Wilson, T. D. (1977) Telling more than we can know: Verbal reports on mental processes, *Psychological Review*, 84, 231–259.

Noble, C. E., Fuchs, J. E., Robel, D. P., and Chambers, R. W. (1958) Individual vs. social performance on two perceptual-motor tasks, *Perceptual and Motor Skills*, 8, 131–134.

Norman, D. A. (1980) Twelve issues of cognitive science, *Cognitive Science*, 4, 1–32.

Norman, D. A., and Shallice, T. (1980) *Attention to action: Willed and automatic control of behavior*, (Technical Report No. 99), San Diego: University of California, Center for Human Information Processing.

Olla, B. L., and Samet, C. (1974) Fish-to-fish attraction and the facilitation of feeding behavior as mediated by visual stimuli in striped mullet, *Mugil cephalus*, *Journal of the Fisheries Research Board of Canada*, 31, 1621–1630.

Orcutt, J. D., and Anderson, R. E. (1974) Human-computer relationships: Interactions and attitudes, *Behavior Research Methods & Instrumentations*, 6, 219–222.

Paivio, A. (1965) Personality and audience influence, In B. Maher, *Progress in experimental personality research*. New York: Academic Press.

Palermo, D. S., and Jenkins, J. J. (1964) *Word association norms: Grade school through college*, Minneapolis: University of Minnesota Press.

Paloutzian, R. F. (1975) Effects of deindividuation, removal of responsibility, and coaction on impulsive cyclical aggression, *Journal of Psychology*, 90, 163–169.

Passman, R. H. (1977) Providing attachment objects to facilitate learning and reduce distress: Effects of mothers and security blankets, *Developmental Psychology*, 13, 25–28.

Paterson, C. E., Philips, C. W., and Pettijohn, T. F. (1980) Environmental influences on a pegboard task, *Perceptual and Motor Skills*, 51, 533–534.

Patterson, M. L. (1976) An arousal model of interpersonal intimacy, *Psychological Review*, 83, 235–245.

Pattinson, M. D., and Pasewark, R. A. (1980) Effects of modelling and audience on an aversive task, *Psychological Reports*, 47, 879–882.

Paul, L., Miley, W. M., and Mazzagatti, N. (1973) Social facilitation and inhibition of hunger-induced killing by rats, *Journal of Comparative and Physiological Psychology*, 84, 162–168.

Paulus, P. B. (1980) Crowding, In P. B. Paulus, *Psychology of group processes* (pp. 245–289), Hillsdale, New Jersey: Erlbaum.

(1983) Group influences on individual task performance, In P. B. Paulus, *Basic group processes* (pp. 97–120), New York: Springer.

Paulus, P. B., Annis, A. B., and Risner, H. T. (1978) An analysis of the mirror-induced objective self-awareness effect, *Bulletin of the Psychonomic Society*, 12, 8–10.

Paulus, P. B., and Cornelius, W. L. (1974) An analysis of gymnastic performance under conditions of practice and spectator observation, *Research Quarterly*, 45, 56–63.

Paulus, P. B., and Murdoch, P. (1971) Anticipated evaluation and audience presence in the enhancement of dominant responses, *Journal of Experimental Social Psychology*, 7, 280–291.

Paulus, P. B., and Nagar, D. (1989) Environmental influences on groups, In P. B. Paulus, *Psychology of group processes* (2nd Ed., pp. 111–140), Hillsdale, New Jersey: Erlbaum.

Paulus, P. B., Shannon, J. C., Wilson, D. L., and Boone, T. D. (1972) The effect of spectator presence on gymnastic performance in a field situation, *Psychonomic Science*, 29, 88–90.

Pederson, A. M. (1970) Effects of test anxiety and coacting groups on learning and performance, *Perceptual and Motor Skills*, 30, 55–62.

Pennebaker, J. W., (1980) Perceptual and environmental determinants of coughing, *Basic and Applied Social Psychology*, 1, 83–91.

Perl, R. E. (1933) The influence of a social factor upon the appreciation of humor, *American Journal of Psychology*, 45, 308–312.

Perlmutter, H. V., and Montmollin, G. D. (1952) Group learning of nonsense syllables, *Journal of Abnormal and Social Psychology*, 47, 762–769.

Pessin, J. (1933) The comparative effects of social and mechanical stimulation on memorizing, *American Journal of Psychology*, 45, 263–270.

Pessin, J., and Husband, R. W. (1933) Effect of social stimulation on human maze learning, *Journal of Abnormal and Social Psychology*, 28, 148–154.

Peterson, N. (1982) Feedback is not a new principle of behavior, *The Behavior Analyst*, 5, 101–102.

Petri, H. L. (1981) *Motivation: Theory and research*, Belmont, California: Wadsworth.

Petty, R. E., and Cacioppo, J. T. (1986) *Communication and persuasion: Central and peripheral routes to attitude change*, New York: Springer-Verlag.

Pfiffner, L. J., and O'Leary, S. G. (1987) The efficacy of all-positive management as a function of the prior use of negative consequences, *Journal of Applied Behavior Analysis*, 20, 265–271.

Pines, H. A. (1973) An attributional analysis of locus of control orientation and source of informational dependence, *Journal of Personality and Social Psychology*, 26, 262–272.

Pishkin, V., and Shurley, J. T. (1966) Social facilitation and sensory deprivation in operant behavior of rats, *Psychonomic Science*, 6, 335–336.

Platt, J. J., and James, W. T. (1966) Social facilitation of eating behavior in young opossums: I., Group vs. solitary feeding, *Psychonomic Science*, 6, 421–422.

Platt, J. J., Sutker, L. W., and James, W. T. (1968) Social facilitation of eating behavior in young opossums: II. The effects of isolation. *Psychonomic Science*, 10, 267–268.

Platt, J. J., Yaksh, T., and Darby, C. L. (1967) Social facilitation of eating behavior in armadillos, *Psychological Reports*, 20, 1136.

Porter, H. V. K. (1939) Studies in the psychology of stuttering, XIV. Stuttering phenomena in relation to size and personnel of audience, *Journal of Speech and Hearing Disorders*, 4, 323–333.

Poteet, D., and Weinberg, R. (1980) Competition trait anxiety, state anxiety and performance, *Perceptual and Motor Skills*, 50, 651–654.

Poulson, E. C. (1970) *Environment and human efficiency*, Illinois: Charles C. Thomas Publishers.

Premack, D., and Premack, A. J. (1963) Increased eating in rats deprived of running, *Journal of the Experimental Analysis of Behavior*, 6, 209–212.

Prentice-Dunn, S., and Rogers, R. W. (1982) Effects of public and private self-awareness on deindividuation and aggression, *Journal of Personality and Social Psychology*, 43, 503–513.

Prentice-Dunn, S., and Rogers, R. W. (1989) Deindividuation and the self-regulation of behavior, In P. B. Paulus, *Psychology of group influence* (2nd Ed., pp. 87–109), Hillsdale, New Jersey: Erlbaum.

Putz, V. R. (1975) The effects of different mode of supervision on vigilance behaviour, *British Journal of Psychology*, 66, 157–160.

Quarter, J., and Marcus, A. (1971) Drive level and the audience effect: A test of Zajonc's theory, *Journal of Social Psychology*, 83, 99–105.

Query, W. T., Moore, K. B. and Lerner, M. J. (1966) Social factors and chronic schizophrenia, *Psychiatric Quarterly*, 40, 504–514.

Quine, W. V. O. (1960) *Word and object*, Cambridge, Massachusetts: MIT. Press.

Rachlin, H., Logue, A. W., Gibbon, J., and Frankel, M. (1986) Cognition and behavior in studies of choice, *Psychological Review*, 93, 33–45.

Rajecki, D. W., Ickes, W., Corcoran, C., and Lenerz, K. (1977) Social facilitation of human performance: Mere presence effects, *Journal of Social Psychology*, 102, 297–310.

Rajecki, D. W., Kidd, R. F., and Ivins, B. (1976) Social facilitation in chickens: A different level of analysis, *Journal of Experimental Social Psychology*, 12, 233–246.

Rajecki, D. W., Kidd, R. F., Wilder, D. A., and Jaeger, J. (1975) Social factors in the facilitation of feeding in chickens: Effects of imitation, arousal or disinhibition? *Journal of Personality and Social Psychology*, 32, 510–518.

Rajecki, D. W., Wilder, D. A., Kidd, R. F., and Jaeger, J. (1976) Social facilitation of pecking and drinking in 'satiated' chickens, *Animal Learning and Behavior*, 4, 30–32.

Rasmussen, E. W. (1939) Social facilitation: An experimental investigation with albino rats, *Acta Psychologica*, 4, 275–294.

Ray, R. D., and Brown, D. A. (1975) A systems approach to behavior, *The Psychological Record*, 25, 459–478.

Redican, W. K. (1975) Facial expressions in nonhuman primates, In L. A. Rosenblum, *Primate behavior* (Vol. 4, pp. 103–194), New York: Academic Press.

Reicher, S. D. (1982) The determination of collective behaviour, In H. Tajfel, *Social identity and intergroup relations* (pp. 41–83), Cambridge: Cambridge University Press.

Reykowski, J. (1982) Social motivation, *Annual Review of Psychology*, 33, 123–154.

Rimé, B. (1982) The elimination of visible behaviour from social interactions: Effects on verbal, nonverbal and interpersonal variables, *European Journal of Social Psychology*, 12, 113–129.

Rittle, R. H., and Bernard, N. (1977) Enhancement of response rate by the mere physical presence of the experimenter, *Personality and Social Psychology Bulletin*, 3, 127–130.

Rivero, W. T. (1971) Survival stamina as a function of social interaction, *Psychonomic Science*, 23, 20.

Robert, M. (1990) Observational learning in fish, birds, and mammals: A classified bibliography spanning over 100 years of research, *The Psychological Record*, 40, 289–311.

Rosenbaum, M. E. (1980) Cooperation and competition, In P. B. Paulus, *Psychology of group influence* (pp. 291–331), Hillsdale, New Jersey: Erlbaum.

Rosenbaum, M. E., Moore, D. L., Cotton, J. L., Cook, M. S., Hieser, R. A., Shovar, M. N., and Gray, M. J. (1980) Group productivity and process: Pure and mixed reward structures and task interdependence, *Journal of Personality and Social Psychology*, 39, 626–642.

Rosenquist, H. S., and Shoberg, J. D. (1968) Social determinants in reversed alphabet printing, *Perceptual and Motor Skills*, 27, 200.

Ross, S., and Ross, J. G. (1949a) Social facilitation of feeding behavior in dogs: I. Group and solitary feeding, *Journal of Genetic Psychology*, 74, 97–108.

(1949b) Social facilitation of feeding behavior in dogs: II. Feeding after satiation, *Journal of Genetic Psychology*, 74, 293–304.

Ruger, H. A. (1910) The psychology of efficiency, *Archives of Psychology*, No. 15.

Rule, B. G., and Evans, J. F. (1971) Familiarization, the presence of others and group discussion effects on risk-taking, *Representative Research in Social Psychology*, 2, 28–32.

Rutter, D. (1987) *Communicating by telephone*, Oxford: Pergamon.

Rutter, D. R., and Stephenson, G. M. (1979) The functions of looking: Effects of friendship on gaze, *British Journal of Social and Clinical Psychology*, 18, 203–205.

Sakagami, S. F., and Hayashida, K. (1962) Work efficiency in heterospecific ant groups composed of hosts and their labour parasites, *Animal Behaviour*, 10, 96–104.

Sanchez, H., and Clark, N. T. (1981). Test of Weiss and Miller's social facilitation hypothesis: Are audiences aversive? *Perceptual and Motor Skills*, 53, 767–772.

Sanders, G. S. (1981) Driven by distraction: An integrative review of social facilitation theory and research, *Journal of Experimental Social Psychology*, 17, 227–251.

(1984) Self-presentation and drive in social facilitation, *Journal of Experimental Social Psychology*, 20, 312–322.

Sanders, G. S., and Baron, R. S. (1975) The motivating effects of distraction on task performance, *Journal of Personality and Social Psychology*, 32, 956–963.

Sanders, G. S., Baron, R. S., and Moore, D. L. (1978) Distraction and social comparison as mediators of social facilitation effects, *Journal of Experimental Social Psychology*, 14, 291–303.

Sanna, L. J., and Shotland, R. L. (1990) Valence of anticipated evaluation and social facilitation, *Journal of Experimental Social Psychology*, 26, 82–92.

Sapolsky, B. S., and Zillman, D. (1978) Enjoyment of a televised sport contest under different social conditions of viewing, *Perceptual and Motor Skills*, 46, 29–30.

Sasfy, J., and Okun, M. (1974) Form of evaluation and audience expertness as joint determinants of audience effects, *Journal of Experimental Social Psychology*, 10, 461–467.

Schachter, S. (1959) *The psychology of affiliation*, Stanford: Stanford University Press.

Schank, R. C., and Abelson, R. P. (1977) *Scripts, plans, goals, and understanding*, Hillsdale, NJ: Erlbaum.

Schauer, A. H., Seymour, W. R., and Geen, R. G. (1985) Effects of observation and evaluation on anxiety in beginning counselors: A social facilitation analysis, *Journal of Counseling and Development*, 63, 279–285.

Scheier, M. F., and Carver, C. S. (1983) Self-directed attention and the comparison of self with standards, *Journal of Experimental Social Psychology*, 19, 205–222.

Scheier, M. F., Fenigstein, A., and Buss, A. H. (1974) Self-awareness and physical aggression, *Journal of Experimental Social Psychology*, 10, 264–273.

Schlenker, B. (1980) *Impression management: The self-concept, social identity, and interpersonal relations*, Belmont, CA: Brooks/Cole.

Schmidt, F. (1904) Experimentelle untersuchungen über die Hausaufgaben des Schulkindes, *Sammlung von Abhandlungen zur Psychologischen*, Pädagogik I. Band, 3. Heft. Leipzig.

Schmitt, B. H., Gilovich, T., Goore, N., and Joseph, L. (1986) Mere presence and social facilitation: One more time, *Journal of Experimental Social Psychology*, 22, 242–248.

Schmitt, D. R. (1984) Interpersonal relations: Cooperation and competition, *Journal of the Experimental Analysis of Behavior*, 42, 377–383.

(1986) Competition: Some behavioural issues, *The Behavior Analyst*, 9, 27–34.

Schneider, W., and Shiffren, R. M. (1977) Controlled and automatic human information processing: I. Detection, search and attention, *Psychological Review*, 84, 1–53.

Schramm, W., and Danielson, W. (1958) Anticipated audiences as determinants of recall, *Journal of Abnormal and Social Psychology*, 56, 282–283.

Scott, J. P. (1968) Social facilitation and allelomimetic behavior, In E. C. Simmel, R. A. Hoppe, and G. A. Milton, *Social facilitation and imitative behavior* (pp. 55–72), Boston: Allyn and Bacon.

Scott, J. P., and Marston, M-V. (1950) Social facilitation and allelomimetic behavior in dogs, II. The effects of unfamiliarity, *Behaviour*, 2, 135–143.

Scott, J. P., and McCray, C. (1967) Allelomimetic behavior in dogs: Negative effects of competition on social facilitation, *Journal of Comparative and Physiological Psychology*, 63, 316–319.

Scruton, D. M., and Herbert, J. (1972) The reaction of groups of captive talapoin monkeys to the introduction of male and female strangers of the same species, *Animal Behaviour*, 20, 463–473.

Seidman, D., Bensen, S. B., Miller, I., and Meeland, T. (1957) Influence of a partner on tolerance for a self-administered electric shock, *Journal of Abnormal and Social Psychology*, 54, 210–212.

Sengupta, N. N., and Sinha, CPN. (1926) Mental work in isolation and in group, *Indian Journal of Psychology*, 1, 106–110.

Seta, C. E., Seta, J. J., Donaldson, S., and Wang, M. A. (1988) The effects of evaluation on organizational processing, *Personality and Social Psychology Bulletin*, 14, 604–609.

Seta, J. J. (1982) The impact of comparison processes on coactors' task performance, *Journal of Personality and Social Psychology*, 42, 281–291.

Seta, J. J., and Hassan, R. K. (1980) Awareness of prior success or failure: A critical factor in task performance, *Journal of Personality and Social Psychology*, 39, 70–76.

Seta, J. J., Paulus, P. B., and Risner, H. T. (1977) The effects of group composition and evaluation on task performance, *Bulletin of the Psychonomic Society*, 9, 115–117.

Seta, J. J., Wang, M. A., Crisson, J. E., and Seta, C. E. (1989) Audience composition and felt anxiety: Impact averaging and summation, *Basic and Applied Social Psychology*, 10, 57–72.

Shaver, P., and Liebling, B. A. (1976) Explorations in the drive theory of social facilitation, *Journal of Social Psychology*, 99, 259–271.

Shaw, M. E. (1932) A comparison of individuals and small groups in the rational solution of complex problems, *American Journal of Psychology*, 44, 491–504.

Shelley, H. P. (1965) Eating behavior: Social facilitation or social inhibition, *Psychonomic Science*, 3, 521–522.

Sherif, M. (1935) A study of some social factors in perception, *Archives of psychology*, 187.

Sherrington, C. (1906) *The integrative activity of the nervous system*, New Haven: Yale University Press.

Shiffren, R. M., and Schneider, W. (1977) Controlled and automatic human information processing: II. Perceptual learning, automatic attending and a general theory, *Psychological Review*, 84, 127–187.

Short, J., Williams, E. and Christie, B. (1976) *The social psychology of telecommunications*, Chichester: Wiley.

Shrauger, J. S. (1972) Self-esteem and reactions to being observed by others, *Journal of Personality and Social Psychology*, 23, 192–200.

Sidman, M. (1960) *Tactics of scientific research*, New York: Basic Books.

(1986) Functional analysis of emergent verbal classes, In T. Thompson and M. D. Zeiler, *Analysis and integration of behavioral units* (pp. 213–245), Hillsdale, New Jersey: Erlbaum.

Siegel, G. M., and Haugen, D. (1964) Audience size and variations in stuttering behavior, *Journal of Speech and Hearing Research*, 7, 381–388.

Siegel, J., Dubrovsky, V., Kiesler, S., and McGuire, T. W. (1986) Group processes in computer-mediated communication, *Organizational Behavior and Human Decision Processes*, 37, 157–187.

Silver, B. D., Abramson, P. R., and Anderson, B. A. (1986) The presence of others and overreporting of voting in American National Elections, *Public Opinion Quarterly*, 50, 228–239.

Simmel, E. C. (1962) Social facilitation and exploratory behavior in rats, *Journal of Comparative and Physiological Psychology*, 55, 831–833.

Simmel, E. C., Baker, E., and Collier, S. M. (1969) Social facilitation of exploratory behavior in preschool children, *Psychological Record*, 19, 425–430.

Simmel, E. C., and McGee, D. P. (1966) Social facilitation of exploratory behavior in rats: Effects of increased exposure to novel stimuli, *Psychological Reports*, 18, 587–590.

Simpson, H. M., and Molloy, F. M. (1971) Effects of audience anxiety on pupil size, *Psychophysiology*, 8, 491–496.

Singer, R. N. (1965) Effect of spectators on athletes and non-athletes performing a gross motor task, *Research Quarterly*, 36, 473–482.

(1970) Effect of an audience on performance of a motor task, *Journal of Motor Behavior*, 11, 88–95.

Skinner, B. F. (1936) The verbal summator and a method for the study of latent speech, *Journal of Psychology*, 2, 71–107.

(1938) *The behavior of organisms*, New York: Appleton-Century.

(1950) Are theories of learning necessary? *Psychological Review*, 57, 193–216.

(1953) *Science and human behavior*, New York: MacMillan.

(1957) *Verbal behavior*, New York: Appleton-Century-Crofts.

(1969) *Contingencies of reinforcements: A theoretical analysis*, Englewood Cliffs: Prentice Hall.

(1974) *About behaviorism*, New York: Alfred Knopf.

(1981) Selection by consequences, *Science*, 213, 501–504.

(1985) Cognitive science and behaviourism, *British Journal of Psychology*, 76, 290–301.

Smith, K. (1984) "Drive": In defense of a concept, *Behaviorism*, 12, 71–114.

Smith, L. E., and Crabbe, J. (1976) Experimenter role relative to social facilitation and motor learning, *International Journal of Sport Psychology*, 7, 158–168.

Smith, P. C., and Evans, P. R. (1973) Studies of the shorebirds at Lindisfarne, Northumberland, I., Feeding ecology and behaviour of the Bar-tailed Godwit, *Wildfowl*, 24, 135–139.

Smith, W. (1957) Social 'learning' in domestic chicks, *Behaviour*, 11, 40–45.

Sommer, R., and Sommer, B. A. (1989) Social facilitation effects in coffeehouses, *Environment and Behavior*, 21, 651–6766.

Sorce, J., and Fouts, G. (1973) Level of motivation in social facilitation of a simple task, *Perceptual and Motor Skills*, 37, 567–572.

Sorrentino, R. M., and Sheppard, B. H. (1978) Effects of affiliation-related motives on swimmers in individual versus group competition: A field experiment, *Journal of Personality and Social Psychology*, 36, 704–714.

Soukup, M. A., and Somervill, J. W. (1979) Effects of sex role and an audience on approaching a snake by mildly-fearful subjects, *Perceptual and Motor Skills*, 49, 572.

Spears, R., Lea M., and Lee, S. (1990) De-individuation and group polarization in computer-mediated communication, *British Journal of Social Psychology*, 29, 121–134.

Spence, K. W. (1956) *Behavior theory and conditioning*, New Haven: Yale University Press.

(1960) Cognitive versus stimulus-response theories of learning. In K. W. Spence, *Behavior theory and learning: Selected papers* (pp. 245–265), Englewood Cliffs, NJ: Prentice-Hall.

Spence, K. W., Farber, I. E., and McFann, H. H. (1956) The relation of anxiety (drive) level to performance in competitional and non-competitional paired-associates learning, *Journal of Experimental Psychology*, 52, 296–305.

Spence, K. W., Taylor, J., and Ketchel, R. (1956) Anxiety (drive) level and degree of competition in paired-associates learning, *Journal of Experimental Psychology*, 52, 306–310.

Sproull, L. and Kiesler, S. (1986) Reducing social context cues: Electronic mail in organizational communication, *Management Science*, 32, 1492–1512.

(1991, September) Computer, networks and work, *Scientific American*, 265, 84–91.

Stamm, J. S. (1961) Social facilitation in monkeys, *Psychological Reports*, 8, 479–484.

Steigleder, M. K., Weiss, R. F., Balling, S. S., Wenninger, V. L., and Lombardo, J. P. (1980) Drivelike motivational properties of competitive behavior, *Journal of Personality and Social Psychology*, 38, 93–104.

Steigleder, M. K., Weiss, R. F., Cramer, R. E., and Feinberg, R. A. (1978) Motivating and reinforcing functions of competitive behavior, *Journal of Personality and Social Psychology*, 36, 1291–1301.

Stotland, E., and Zander, A. (1958) Effects of public and private failure on self-evaluation, *Journal of Abnormal and Social Psychology*, 56, 223–229.

Street, W. R. (1974) Brainstorming by individuals, coacting and interacting groups, *Journal of Applied Psychology*, 59, 433–436.

Stricklund, L. H., Guild, P. D., Barefoot, J. C., and Paterson, S. A. (1978) Teleconferencing and leadership emergence, *Human Relations*, 31, 583–596.

Strobel, M. G. (1972) Social facilitation of operant behavior in satiated rats, *Journal of Comparative and Physiological Psychology*, 80, 502–508.

Strobel, M. G., Freedman, S. L., and MacDonald, G. E. (1970) Social facilitation of feeding in newly hatched chickens as a function of imprinting, *Canadian Journal of Psychology*, 24, 207–215.

Strobel, M. G., and MacDonald, G. E. (1974) Induction of eating in newly hatched chicks, *Journal of Comparative and Physiological Psychology*, 86, 493–502.

Strube, M. J., Miles, M. E., and Finch, W. H. (1981) The social facilitation of a simple task: Field tests of alternative explanations, *Personality and Social Psychology Bulletin*, 7, 701–707.

Suarez, S. D., and Gallup, G. G. (1981) Predatory overtones of open-field testing in chickens, *Animal Learning and Behavior*, 9, 153–163.

(1982) Open-field behavior in chickens: The experimenter is a predator, *Journal of Comparative and Physiological Psychology*, 96, 432–439.

Sudd, J. H. (1971) The effect of tunnel depth and of working in pairs on the speed of excavation in ants (*Formica lemani* Bondriot), *Animal Behaviour*, 19, 677–686.

(1972) The absence of social enhancement of digging in pairs of ants (*Formica lemani* Bondriot), *Animal Behaviour*, 20, 813–819.

Suedfeld, P., and Mocellin, J. S. P. (1987) The 'sensed presence' in unusual environments, *Environment and Behavior*, 19, 33–52.

Suls, J. and Wills, T. A. (1991) *Social comparison: Contemporary theory and research*, Hillsdale, NJ: Erlbaum.

Swain, J., Stephenson, G. M., and Dewey, M. E. (1982), 'Seeing a stranger': Does eye-contact reflect intimacy? *Semiotica*, 42, 107–118.

Tachibana, T. (1974a) Social influence on eating behavior in an approach-withdrawal situation by albino rats: I. An unrestrained demonstrator rat in a single box, *The Annual of Animal Psychology*, 24, 25–29.

(1974b) Social influence on eating behavior in an approach-withdrawal situation by albino rats: II. Effect of the presence of an anaesthetized rat, *The Annual of Animal Psychology*, 24, 99–103.

Taylor, G. T. (1981) Fear and affiliation in domesticated male rats. *Journal of Comparative and Physiological Psychology*, 95, 685–693.

Taylor, J. A. (1953) A personality scale of manifest anxiety, *Journal of Abnormal and Social Psychology*, 48, 285–290.

Taylor, J. A., and Rechtschlaffen, A. (1959) Manifest anxiety and reversed alphabet printing, *Journal of Abnormal and Social Psychology*, 58, 221–224.

Taylor, J. A., and Spence, K. W. (1952) The relationship of anxiety level to performance in serial learning, *Journal of Experimental Psychology*, 44, 61–64.

Taylor, J. H., Thompson, C. E. and Spassoff, D. (1937) The effects of conditions of work and various suggested attitudes on production and reported feelings of tiredness and boredness, *Journal of Applied Psychology*, 21, 431–450.

Taylor, S. E., and Langer, E. J. (1977) Pregnancy: A social stigma? *Sex Roles*, 3, 27–35.

Tedeschi, J. T. (1981) *Impression management theory and social psychological research*, New York: Academic Press.

Terris, W., and Rahhal, D. K. (1969) Generalized resistance to the effects of psychological stressors, *Journal of Personality and Social Psychology*, 13, 93–97.

Thayer, R. E., and Moore, L. E. (1972) Reported activation and verbal learning as a function of group size (social facilitation) and anxiety-inducing instructions, *Journal of Social Psychology*, 88, 277–287.

Thelen, M. H., Rehagen, N. J., and Akamattsu, T. J. (1974) Model reward and imitation: The effect of the presence of the experimenter and the model rewarder, *Journal of Personality*, 87, 311–318.

Thompson, T. (1984) The examining magistrate for nature: A retrospective review of Claude Bernard's *An introduction to experimental medicine*, *Journal of the Experimental Analysis of Behavior*, 41, 211–216.

Tolman, C. W. (1964) Social facilitation of feeding behavior in the domestic chick, *Animal Behaviour*, 12, 245–251.

(1965a) Emotional behavior and social facilitation of feeding in domestic chicks, *Animal Behaviour*, 13, 493–496.

(1965b) Social dominance and feeding behavior in domestic cockerels, *Psychological Reports*, 17, 890.

(1967a) The effects of tapping sounds on feeding behavior of domestic chicks, *Animal Behaviour*, 15, 145–148.

(1967b) The feeding behaviour of domestic chicks as a function of rate of pecking by a surrogate companion, *Behaviour*, 29, 57–62.

(1968a) The varieties of social stimulation in the feeding behavior of domestic chicks, *Behaviour*, 30, 275–286.

(1968b) The role of the companion in social facilitation of animal behavior. In E. C. Simmel, R. A. Hoppe and G. A. Milton, *Social facilitation and imitative behavior* (pp. 33–54). Boston: Allyn & Bacon.

(1969) Social feeding in domestic chicks: Effects of food deprivation of nonfeeding companions, *Psychonomic Science*, 15, 234.

Tolman, C. W., and Wellman, A. W. (1968) Social feeding in domestic chicks: A test of the disinhibition hypothesis, *Psychonomic Science*, 11, 35–36.

Tolman, C. W., and Wilson, G. F. (1965) Social feeding in domestic chicks, *Animal Behaviour*, 13, 134–142.

Tolman, E. C. (1932) *Purposive behavior in animals and men*, New York: Century Co.

Travis, L. E. (1925) The effect of a small audience upon eye-hand coordination, *Journal of Abnormal and Social Psychology*, 20, 142–146.

Travis, L. E. (1928) The influence of the group upon the stutterer's speed in free association, *Journal of Abnormal and Social Psychology*, 23, 45–51.

Treichler, F. R., Graham, M. M., and Schweikert, G. E. (1971) Social facilitation of the rat's responding in extinction, *Psychonomic Science*, 22, 291–292.

Triplett, N. (1898) The dynamogenic factors in pacemaking and competition. *American Journal of Psychology*, 9, 507–533.

Turner, E. R. A. (1964) Social feeding in birds, *Behaviour*, 24, 1–47.

Turner, J. C. (1981) The experimental social psychology of intergroup behaviour, In J. C. Turner and H. Giles, *Intergroup behavior* (pp. 66–101), Oxford: Basil Blackwell.

Turner, J. C., and Oakes, P. J. (1989) Self-categorization theory and social influence, In P. B. Paulus, *Psychology of group influence* (2nd Ed. pp. 233–725), Hillsdale, New Jersey: Erlbaum.

Uematsu, T. (1970) Social facilitation of feeding behavior in fresh-water fish, I. *Rhodeus, Acheilognathus* and *Rhinogobius, The Annual of Animal Psychology,* 20, 87–95.

(1971a) Social facilitation in feeding behavior of the guppy. I. Preliminary experiment, *Japanese Journal of Ecology,* 21, 48–51.

(1971b) Social facilitation in feeding behavior of the guppy. II. Experimental analysis of mechanisms, *Japanese Journal of Ecology,* 21, 54–67.

Uematsu, T., and Ogawa, S. (1975) Social facilitation of feeding behavior in fresh-water fish. III. The Himedaka, *Oryzias latipes, The Annual of Animal Psychology,* 25, 57–64.

Uematsu, T., and Saito, K. (1973) Social facilitation of feeding behaviour in fresh-water fish. II. The Himedaka, *Oryzias latipes, The Annual of Animal Psychology,* 23, 43–47.

Van Heerden, J., and Hoogstraten, J. (1981) Through the one-way mirror, *Psychological Reports,* 49, 719–724.

Van Tuinen, M., and McNeel, S. P. (1975) A test of the social facilitation theories of Cottrell and Zajonc in a coaction situation, *Personality and Social Psychology Bulletin,* 1, 604–607.

Vargas, E. A. (1988) Verbally-governed behavior and event-governed behavior, *The Analysis of Verbal Behavior,* 6, 11–22.

Vaughan, G. M., and Guerin, B. (1992) *Norman Triplett: sports psychologist not social psychologist.* Unpublished paper, University of Auckland and University of Waikato, New Zealand.

Vaughan, M. E., and Michael, J. L. (1982) Automatic reinforcement: An important but ignored concept, *Behaviorism,* 10, 217–227.

Victoria, J. K., and Collias, N. E. (1973) Social facilitation of egg-laying in experimental colonies of a weaverbird, *Ecology,* 54, 399–405.

Vince, M. A. (1964) Social facilitation of hatching in the bobtail quail, *Animal Behaviour,* 12, 531–534.

Vogel, H. H., Scott, J. P., and Marston, M-V. (1950) Social facilitation and allelomimetic behavior in dogs, I. Social facilitation in a non-competitive situation, *Behaviour,* 2, 121–134.

Wachtel, P. L. (1967) Conceptions of broad and narrow attention, *Psychological Bulletin,* 68, 417–429.

Walk, R. D., and Walters, K. (1984) Ecological depth perception: Ducklings tested together and alone, *Bulletin of the Psychonomic Society,* 22, 368–371.

Wanchisen, B. A. (1990) Forgetting the lessons of history, *The Behavior Analyst,* 13, 31–37.

Wankel, L. M. (1972) Competition in motor performance: An experimental analysis of motivational components, *Journal of Experimental Social Psychology,* 8, 427–437.

(1975) The effects of social reinforcement and audience presence upon the motor performance of boys with different levels of initial ability, *Journal of Motor Behavior,* 7, 207–216.

(1977) Audience size and trait anxiety effects upon state anxiety and motor performance, *Research Quarterly,* 48, 181–186.

Wapner, S., and Alper, T. G. (1952) The effect of an audience on behavior in a choice situation, *Journal of Abnormal and Social Psychology,* 47, 222–229.

Warren, J. L., Bryant, R. C., Petty, F., and Byrne, W. L. (1975) Group training in goldfish (*Carassius auratus*): Effects on acquisition and retention, *Journal of Comparative and Physiological Psychology*, 89, 933–938.

Watson, G. B. (1928) Do groups think more efficiently than individuals? *Journal of Abnormal and Social Psychology*, 23, 328–336.

Wechkin, S. (1970) Social relationships and social facilitation of object manipulation in *Macaca mulatta*, *Journal of Comparative and Physiological Psychology*, 73, 456–460.

Wegner, D. M., and Giuliano, T. (1980) Arousal-induced attention to the self, *Journal of Personality and Social Psychology*, 38, 719–726.

Wegner, N., and Zeaman, D. (1956) Team and individual performance on a motor learning task, *Journal of General Psychology*, 55, 127–142.

Weiner, B. (1966) Role of success and failure in the learning of easy and complex tasks, *Journal of Personality and Social Psychology*, 3, 339–344.

Weiner, B., and Schneider, K. (1971) Drive versus cognitive theory: A reply to Boor and Harmon, *Journal of Personality and Social Psychology*, 18, 258–262.

Weiner, H. (1964) Conditioning history and human fixed-interval performance, *Journal of the Experimental Analysis of Behavior*, 7, 383–385.

Weiss, R. F., and Miller, F. G. (1971) The drive theory of social facilitation, *Psychological Review*, 78, 44–57.

Weiss, R. F., Miller, F. G., Langan, C. J., and Cecil, J. S. (1971) Social facilitation of attitude change, *Psychonomic Science*, 22, 113–114.

Welford, A. T. (1976) *Skilled performance*, Glenview, Illinois: Scott Foresman and Company.

Welty, J. C. (1934) Experiments in group behaviour of fish, *Physiological Zoology*, 7, 85–128.

Weston, S. B., and English, H. B. (1926) The influence of the group on psychological test scores, *American Journal of Psychology*, 37, 600–601.

Wheeler, L., and Davis, H. (1967) Social disruption of performance on a DRL. schedule, *Psychonomic Science*, 7, 249–250.

Wicklund, R. A. (1975) Objective self-awareness, In L. Berkowitz, *Advances in experimental social psychology* (Vol. 8, pp. 233–275), New York: Academic Press.

Wicklund, R. A., and Duval, S. (1971) Opinion change and performance facilitation as a result of objective self-awareness, *Journal of Experimental Social Psychology*, 7, 319–342.

Williams, E. (1977) Experimental comparisons of face-to-face and mediated communications: A review, *Psychological Bulletin*, 84, 963–976.

Williams, J. M. (1976) Effects of evaluative and nonevaluative coactors upon male and female performance of simple and complex motor tasks, In R. W. Christina and D. M. Landers, *Psychology of motor behavior and sport* (Vol. 2, pp. 24–32), Champaign, IL: Human Kinetics.

Williams, K., Harkins, S., and Latané, B. (1981) Identifiability as a deterrent to social loafing: Two cheering experiments, *Journal of Personality and Social Psychology*, 40, 303–311.

Williams, K. D., Nida, S. A., Baca, L. D., and Latané, B. (1989) Social loafing and swimming: Effects of identifiability on individual and relay performance of intercollegiate swimmers. *Basic and Applied Social Psychology*, 10, 73–81.

Williamson, E. G. (1926) Allport's experiments in 'Social Facilitation', *Psychological Monographs*, 35, 138–143.

Wilson, G. F. (1968) Early experience and facilitation of feeding in domestic chicks, *Journal of Comparative and Physiological Psychology*, 66, 800–802.

Winslow, C. N. (1944) The behavior of cats. I. Competitive and aggressive behavior in an experimental runway situation, *Journal of Comparative and Physiological Psychology*, 37, 297–313.

Wirtz, P., and Wawra, M. (1986) Vigilance and group size in *Homo sapiens*, *Ethology*, 71, 283–286.

Wittgenstein, L. (1953) *Philosophical investigations*, Oxford: Basil Blackwell.

Wolfgang, A. (1967) Effects of social cues and task complexity in concept identification, *Journal of Educational Psychology*, 58, 36–40.

Worringham, C. F., and Messick, D. M. (1983) Social facilitation of running: An unobtrusive study, *Journal of Social Psychology*, 121, 23–29.

Yarbus, A. L. (1967) *Eye movement and vision*, New York: Plenum Press.

Yarczower, M., and Daruns, L. (1982) Social inhibition of spontaneous facial expressions in children, *Journal of Personality and Social Psychology*, 43, 831–837.

Zajonc, R. B. (1965) Social facilitation, *Science*, 149, 269–274.

  (1966) *Social psychology: An experimental approach*, Belmont, California: Wadsworth.

  (1968a) Cognitive theories in social psychology, In G. Lindzey and E. Aronson, *Handbook of social psychology* (2nd Ed., Vol. 1, pp. 320–411), New York: Random House.

  (1968b) Social facilitation in cockroaches, In E. C. Simmel, R. A. Hoppe and G. A. Milton, *Social facilitation and imitative behavior* (pp. 73–87), Boston: Allyn & Bacon.

  (1972a) *Animal social behaviour*, Morristown, New Jersey: General Learning Press.

  (1972b) *Compresence*, Paper presented at the meeting of the Midwestern Psychological Society, Cleveland. Partly reprinted as Zajonc (1980).

  (1980) Compresence. In P. B. Paulus, *Psychology of group influence* (pp. 35–60), Hillsdale, New Jersey: Erlbaum.

Zajonc, R. B., and Crandell, R. (No date) Unpublished data, cited in Zajonc (1972b).

Zajonc, R. B., Heingartner, A., and Herman, E. M. (1969) Social enhancement and impairment of performance in the cockroach, *Journal of Personality and Social Psychology*, 13, 83–92.

Zajonc, R. B., and Sales, S. M. (1966) Social facilitation of dominant and subordinate responses, *Journal of Experimental Social Psychology*, 2, 160–168.

Zajonc, R. B., Wolosin, R. J., Wolosin, M. A., and Loh, W. D. (1970) Social facilitation and imitation in group risk-taking, *Journal of Experimental Social Psychology*, 6, 26–46.

Zentall, T. R., and Hogan, D. E. (1976) Imitation and social facilitation in the pigeon, *Animal Learning and Behavior*, 4, 427–430.

Zentall, T. R., and Levine, J. M. (1972) Observational learning and social facilitation in the rat, *Science*, 178, 1220–1221.

Zucker, S. H. (1978) Sensitivity of retarded children's classroom performance to social psychological influences, *Educational Training of the Mentally Retarded*, 13, 189–194.

Author index

Subject index